D0200402

COMMON INTEREST

COMMON GOOD

Creating Value through Business and Social Sector Partnerships

SHIRLEY SAGAWA
ELI SEGAL

HARVARD BUSINESS SCHOOL PRESS
BOSTON, MASSACHUSETTS

Library of Congress Cataloging-in-Publication Data

Sagawa, Shirley, 1961–
    Common interest, common good : creating value through business
and social sector partnerships / Shirley Sagawa and Eli Segal.
      p.   cm.
    Includes bibliographical references and index.
    ISBN 0-87584-848-6
    1. Social responsibility of business—United States.   2. Social
service—United States.   3. Charities—United States.
I. Segal, Eli, 1943–   . II. Title.
HD60.5.U5S24   1999
658.4'08—dc21   99-29533
                                                                CIP

*The paper used in this publication meets the requirements of the American
National Standard for Permanence of Paper for Publications and Documents
in Libraries and Archives Z39.48-1992.*

This book is dedicated to our most valued partners:

Gregory Baer and Phyllis Segal

CONTENTS

TO THE READER

Hillary Rodham Clinton

EVEN IN TIMES OF STRONG ECONOMIC GROWTH, the United States has struggled with challenges that neither individuals, government, business, nor volunteerism can tackle alone: How do we extend our prosperity to those who have not yet achieved it? How do we nurture and support strong families? How do we strengthen the bonds of community and instill an ethic of service in our children? Long ago I concluded that the solutions to such challenges lie not in big government, nor the free market, nor the voluntary sector alone. Rather, if we are to make further progress, we must find ways to foster greater responsibility and cooperation among all sectors of society.

That is why this book, with its insightful analysis of how cross-sector partnerships can work, is so important. Shirley Sagawa and Eli Segal bring to the discussion years of experience in business, government, and the social sector. They have created partnerships that resulted in new resources for nonprofits, goodwill and publicity for businesses, and a strengthened civil society.

My own experience confirms the value of these kinds of partnerships. In my travels around our country and the world, I have seen firsthand the changes that have begun to take place as governments and economic interests recognize the importance of a strong civil society. In an effort to nurture these relationships, I have spoken with business, government, and nonprofit leaders about why it is in their interests to work together.

For example, based on research about the importance of reading to the development of young brains, I launched the Prescription for Reading Partnership in 1997. Publishers, booksellers, pediatricians, librarians, health centers, and others worked together to make sure that every infant and toddler who went to a doctor returned home with a book. By the end of 1998, 5,000 doctors had been trained to prescribe reading, and "prescriptions" for books were being sent home by doctors approximately 200,000 times a year. Scholastic, a leading children's book publisher, and two nonprofits, First Book and Reach Out and Read, offered challenge grants amounting to 5,000 books for every $100,000 raised nationally.

In this country, we have a longstanding tradition of government working with the private sector to support the arts. As honorary chair of the President's Committee on the Arts and the Humanities, I was involved in the creation of the Coming Up Taller awards, which identify and reward programs that reach at-risk youth through the arts and humanities. In 1997, my office introduced the Samsonite Corporation to the program. The company, which had been looking for ways to help children, recruited celebrities to create works of art on suitcases and donated the proceeds from the sale of the suitcases to Coming Up Taller. Samsonite's enthusiasm led to the participation of 40 more companies.

I have seen some other wonderful examples of successful public-private partnerships as I worked with my husband to make sure that every citizen receives adequate medical care. The Children's Health Insurance Program (CHIP), created by the Balanced Budget Act, inspired a broad-based coalition of public and private groups to educate and assist parents in enrolling their children in Medicaid or state insurance plans. In order to fulfill its mission, however, this extraordinary effort needed a boost from the private sector in the form of a major public relations campaign to reach out to eligible families. Among the many corporate partners who stepped in to help are Bell Atlantic, Pfizer, K-Mart, General Motors, ABC, NBC, Univision, Turner Entertainment, and Viacom.

Another domestic initiative dependent on a healthy public-private partnership is the White House Millennium Council's Save America's Treasures program, designed to inspire all Americans to help preserve and protect our country's natural, historic, and cultural treasures. Our nonprofit partners, led by the National Trust for Historic Preservation, worked with dozens of corporate partners, including Warner Brothers, Polo Ralph Lauren, and General Electric to save some of our most endangered national symbols, such as the flag that inspired Francis Scott Key to write the Star-Spangled Banner and Thomas Edison's Invention Factory.

Cross-sector partnerships are also beginning to work abroad. The transition from communism over the last two decades left many countries economically unstable and facing problems such as antiquated and dysfunctional health care systems. I have visited scores of hospitals and clinics around the world that are in desperate need of access to new technology, training, and resources. After a visit to Latvia, I was able to connect three hospitals in Riga with four here in St. Louis through the American International Health Alliance, a U.S. Agency for International Development grantee. Their partnership established special programs and medical protocols in maternal/child health, cardiology, hospice, pediatric infectious disease, community health, and administration.

Vital Voices, an initiative of the State Department, involves international corporate partners, such as Ford and Marriott, supporting programs to ensure the full participation of women in the economic, social, and political progress of their countries. As I have met participants at Vital Voices conferences, I have been impressed at the important role that corporations, together with nonprofit partners, can play in helping women gain the tools they need to take their rightful places in society.

Although we can point to many successful cross-sector partnerships, they are often the result of trial and error. Lacking a clear direction, each new initiative must test the waters again and expend substantial resources as they once again look for the path to success. What is needed is some practical advice for those seeking to partner—analyses of what has worked, what has failed, and why. That is what this book provides.

The innovative and highly successful partnerships I've described here are just a few examples of the creative new paradigm defined in *Common Interest, Common Good*. No two people could be more qualified than Shirley Sagawa and Eli Segal to introduce us to the possibilities and the pitfalls of these kinds of partnerships. It was they who broke new ground in this area by bringing the president's proposed national service program to fruition. In the first four years after my husband signed the bill creating AmeriCorps, more than 100,000 young Americans answered the call to citizen service in their country. The success of AmeriCorps is due, in no small measure, to Eli and Shirley and to their prodigious talent, their untiring effort, and their ingenuity in bringing public and private sector leaders together as partners.

We have both an obligation and an opportunity to galvanize for-profit and nonprofit entities to work together to face the challenges of the next century. Shirley and Eli's experience and research will help to encourage them to take that first step and will offer them critical advice and guidance along the way.

Hillary Rodham Clinton

FOREWORD
Rosabeth Moss Kanter

LET'S START WITH THE PEOPLE. To know Shirley Sagawa and Eli Segal is to understand why they, of all people, are the perfect team to write a practical and inspiring book about new partnerships.

At first glance, this might not be obvious. After all, they are two lawyers trained in an adversarial tradition and seasoned in the partisan excesses of political campaigns—hardly the background to become experts on collaboration. But if stretching across boundaries and reaching out—far out—to create loyal friends were Olympic events, Shirley and Eli would win gold medals.

They proved it at AmeriCorps, the flagship of the Corporation for National Service, which President Clinton chose Eli to lead, and Eli chose Shirley to manage. There they combined Eli's entrepreneurial experience growing successful businesses (the toys, puzzles, and games he sold delighted millions) with Shirley's experience getting things done from inside government and nonprofit establishments. There they borrowed all the good pragmatic ideas they could find in the private sector and harnessed them to an idealistic public sector effort to mobilize people of all ages to serve their communities. There they built wide bipartisan support and financial sponsorship for community service programs across

America. There they discovered the common interests that businesses and nonprofits could share in improving their country.

The spirit of enterprise and the spirit of volunteerism have always been two of America's greatest distinguishing strengths. Today, as Sagawa and Segal show us, enterprising nonprofits and socially aware businesses are blending these two spirits into a potent new mix.

A big new idea is emerging in America: that business models and social values provide a powerful combination. The realization is dawning that new alliances between private and social sectors can get things done that were never done before to energize businesses and transform communities.

Everywhere I look, businesses are discovering social values, and social purpose organizations are discovering business principles. And both are finding that they can create new benefits for their stakeholders by reaching out to the other. The partnerships that result are pathbreaking and inspiring, as well as strategic and effective. This wonderful book tells the stories of these "close friendships" between organizations operating in totally different sectors. They are part of a movement to reinvent the way America mobilizes resources to solve problems.

It's about time we bridge the gap between businesses and nonprofits. For too long, they have lived in separate worlds. For too long, they have been viewed as opposites on so many dimensions. And for too long, American individualism, supported by a contract-oriented adversarial legal system, helped erect a series of walls that made every organization a fortress unto itself.

Until recently, too many corporations clothed their people in gray flannel straitjackets. Employees had to check their values at the door when they came to work. Except for check writing or arms-length payroll deductions for community causes, they generally contributed to their community on their own time. At the same time, nonprofits were the Cinderellas of endless charity balls, dressed up for a night to woo wealthy donors. Occasionally joined at the board level by executives who helped raise money, these two kinds of organizations were otherwise worlds apart. That fit the fortress mentality by which businesses were supposed to be managed.

Much of my own work as a Harvard Business School professor, corporate consultant, and boardroom adviser has centered around helping companies break out of their fortresses and liberate employees from their straitjackets, to tap the power of what I dubbed "collaborative advantage." Starting in the 1980s, and accelerating today, American businesses began to discover the value of partnerships. They reached out to work with their customers and suppliers in new ways, and they formed strategic alliances and joint ventures to get more done than they could do alone. Now community partnerships and alliances with nonprofits are the newest members of the business extended family.

For some not yet accustomed to thinking in this win-win way, these new partnerships invite skepticism and cynicism. Some people find it hard to believe that it is possible to make money *and* do good at the same time. So they look for flaws. There are concerns about nonprofits "going commercial" and concerns about businesses "going soft." Will nonprofits gear their activities to what will make money for their business sponsors, and will businesses neglect their core business if they get too wrapped up in contributing to their cause? Will nonprofits divert their attention from serving the community, and will businesses neglect the interests of shareholders or paying customers?

Shirley Sagawa and Eli Segal do not shy away from the problems of "New Value Partnerships," as they call them. They address the vulnerabilities both partners encounter when they make a public alliance that becomes a public stand. After all, each organization is staking its reputation on the performance of the other. When Save the Children partners with Denny's, which was accused of racial bias, they take a risk, just as Denny's does when Save the Children is attacked in the press for problems with the children its donors ostensibly sponsored. Boeing airplanes' safety record could appear to be at stake when it uses a sheltered workshop as a supplier. But the significance of these partnerships is that they blend capabilities without losing the distinctiveness of each. Calphalon knows how to make and market pots and pans; Share Our Strength (SOS) knows how to mobilize the enthusiasm of chefs and gourmets for drives against hunger.

The partnerships in this book represent new thinking about the benefits that accrue by reaching beyond an organization's familiar sphere. It's hard work to make decisions when there are so many differences between the organizations—for example, the difference between the dignified bankers of BankBoston paid well to minimize risk and the high-spirited risk-taking young volunteers of City Year working for a pittance to improve inner cities. But City Year's imagination and courage inspires and energizes more acts of imagination and courage from its banker friends. And a little of that banking discipline rubs off on City Year.

More than just an exchange of benefits, these new partnerships provoke change. The American Library Association got World Wide Web–savvy through a Microsoft alliance. Save the Children accelerated its plans to bring its developing country programs to America's own Third World (distressed inner cities) because of a Denny's partnership. New Value Partnerships also demand accountability from each partner, to be worthy of the partner's trust and reputation. Denny's can't backslide from its racial justice commitment once it makes promises to Save the Children, nor can SOS be irresponsible with the money Calphalon raises for its hunger programs.

Each partner needs to think about its assets and its values. "Individual excellence" is first on my list of ingredients for successful partnerships. To find the right nonprofit partners, businesses must know what they stand for. To attract business partners, nonprofits must think about their mission, their assets, and their impact in a sharper, more focused way. (One of Sagawa's and Segal's best gifts to nonprofits is the checklist of potential assets in chapter 10.)

Finding the common interests that businesses and nonprofits share is a path toward producing the common good—that is, benefits to society (and that means all of us). More is possible when organizations work collaboratively than when they operate alone. Arguably, many cities are better places today because businesses are joining forces with nonprofits at the local level to improve public schools, build playgrounds, bring libraries into the Information Age, and train people on welfare for good jobs.

Common Interest, Common Good takes us deeply inside seven partnerships. Each approach to business–nonprofit collaboration is brought to life through a vivid story of one illustrative partnership, with all the drama of getting together, working out the relationship, and loading it for success. There are also history lessons, brief visits to other partnerships, descriptions of what works and pitfalls to avoid. And when Sagawa and Segal draw lessons, you know they have been there, done that.

And you can do it, too—whether you are a business leader, a nonprofit executive, or a concerned citizen. If you care about America and want to know how to make a difference, you will find the stories in this book compelling, uplifting, and perhaps even life-changing.

The promise of the New Value Partnerships is multi-faceted:

- They can address human and community needs with powerful impact. They can find new ways to solve complex social problems that require resources from more than one organization and more than one sector.

- They can make acting on values a part of every workplace and every purchase decision. They can enhance civic culture and civil society. They can build a spirit of participation and collaboration across diverse groups in the community and across sectors.

- They can unleash creativity by finding powerful new ways to engage people—from the fun of building a playground with KaBOOM! to the enthusiasm of City Year's red-jacketed youth corps doing calisthenics in downtowns across America.

- And they can help make businesses more humane and human service organizations more businesslike.

What a powerful combination—collaborative advantage at its best. Thank you, Shirley and Eli, for finding these inspiring stories, examining them in a hard-headed way to extract the do's and don't's, and articulating a new model for working together across sectors. This is an excellent step toward making American communities better places and America a stronger nation.

Rosabeth Moss Kanter holds the Class of 1960 Chair as Professor of Business Administration at the Harvard Business School. She is also a consultant and advisor to leading organizations worldwide. She is the author of thirteen books, including the bestsellers *Men and Women of the Corporation*, *The Change Masters*, *When Giants Learn to Dance*, and *World Class*. Her latest book is *Rosabeth Moss Kanter on the Frontiers of Management*.

PREFACE

THIS BOOK GREW OUT OF A CHALLENGE: to design and later implement national service legislation on a large scale. This experience stimulated our thinking about a role for business in social sector programs and taught us some of the pitfalls and possibilities of cross-sector partnerships. Our respective backgrounds—Eli's as a successful businessman with interests in publishing and direct mail, and Shirley's as the crafter of social programs for children and families—gave us insights into both private enterprise and the social sector. Our experience inspired us to explore this topic more deeply and to find a way to help others develop fruitful cross-sector partnerships.

Our paths first crossed in the White House early in 1993. Eli was a long-term friend of President Clinton, serving in the 1992 campaign as chief of staff. Shortly before the inaugural, he had been given responsibility for making good a campaign promise to give young Americans the chance to earn money for college by performing a year of service. He invited Shirley, the First Lady's policy advisor, to a meeting to plot strategy for the bill because she had drafted and helped to pass legislation creating a national service pilot program several years before.

The legislation that we and our colleagues put together challenged much of the conventional wisdom applied to federal social policy. Many federal programs provide specific dollars to specific types of nonprofit—generally state or local government agencies to deliver specific services to a specific population in a specific way. The new national service program would specify the tool that would be provided—a person who would serve the community full-time for a year. But it would not specify the agency, the population to be served, or the specific service to be provided, all of which would be defined locally.

Although many people, including the President, referred to the new national service program as the "domestic Peace Corps," it differed in an important respect. In the 1960s, when the Peace Corps was created, there was a presumption that the federal government ought to have a major role in solving local problems. The Peace Corps is today, as it was when it was enacted in 1961, a federally run program. Federal employees select, train, and assign Peace Corps volunteers to postings overseas, then supervise them during their term of service.

The legislation we worked on would establish a domestic Peace Corps in spirit, but not in design. A service program for the 1990s might spend federal dollars, but it would do so with state and local organizations at the helm. The nonprofit organizations managing the program would recruit and select team members, organize them, and choose their service projects. They would receive a federal grant to pay team members a poverty-level stipend, and team members would receive a federally funded award they could use to pay college expenses or student loans. But the federal government would not pay the full tab. To ensure that there was local support for the program, any organization fielding teams would have to raise, in cash or through donations of goods and services, a portion of the funds it needed to operate the program.

In government jargon, these donations constitute "matching funds." Shirley's experience as a policymaker, working first as counsel for the Senate Labor and Human Resources Committee and later at the National Women's Law Center (a nonprofit women's legal policy organization) taught her that matching funds were a common feature of federal social programs. Federal policymakers like to make government dollars go further by requiring an organization to match a grant with additional sources of support.

But matching funds were often hard to come by, particularly in the mid-1990s, a time when state and local government dollars, like federal funds, were on the decline[1] and the number of nonprofit organizations seeking support was on the rise.[2] As a board member of several social sector organizations, Shirley knew leaders of many nonprofit organizations who spent at least a quarter of their time fundraising—cultivating contacts, drafting proposals, organizing events for donors. The idea of financially sustainable organizations that could solve seemingly intractable problems had great appeal. But where would these dollars come from?

Eli's experience in business gave him a different perspective. Eli had owned and run a series of profitable small- and medium-sized public and private companies since the middle of the 1970s. While he had served on the boards of a series of nonprofits, his business and pro bono lives were completely independent of each other until 1986, when a company he owned elected to sponsor a National Jigsaw Puzzle Championship. Conceived by the Dairy Barn, an entrepreneurial nonprofit in Athens, Ohio, as a way to fund its arts and crafts mission, the championship was born at the same time Eli was launching Bits & Pieces, a mail-order catalog featuring jigsaw puzzles. For Eli, sponsorship gave his fledgling catalog a cost-effective opportunity to achieve three objectives: develop a mailing list, create a "buzz" among puzzle aficionados, and begin to build a visible national brand through television and newspaper coverage.

The partnership between Bits & Pieces and the Dairy Barn was a success, strong enough for the parties to renew the relationship for a second year. Although Eli didn't dwell on it at the time, he was aware of the benefits of working with a nonprofit: the sponsorship gave his company the credibility and visibility he sought.

Reflecting on this experience, Eli believed it might be possible to attract private sector companies to support national service programs. A young program called City Year offered some evidence. City Year, based in Eli's hometown of Boston and founded by two of Shirley's law school classmates, had been created as an "action tank," designed to demonstrate that national service run by private organizations could be effective at teaching diverse teams of young people citizenship while meeting community needs. City Year's founders advocated a 50–50 public–private partnership, arguing that federal dollars should act as a "challenge grant," with every privately raised dollar matched by a federal one. We liked the idea. But when we briefed the President, he raised the concern that small grassroots organizations in low-income neighborhoods might have a hard time raising private funds. He asked us to establish a more modest matching requirement, and then to find ways to encourage greater private sector support.

AmeriCorps, the new national service program, was born September 23, 1993, just five months after the national service bill was introduced. That day would mark the beginning of a relentless effort to engage the business community in support for AmeriCorps. Consistent with the President's request, we had sought for the Corporation for National Service, the new federal corporation that would distribute the funding, the authority to solicit private funding. This capacity was unusual for agencies of the federal government, which could receive but not ask for donations unless specifically authorized to do so by legislation.

Eli was appointed to serve as the chief executive officer of the Corporation for National Service, and Shirley to serve as the managing director. We assembled a small team to help us reach out to businesses and foundations that could support local AmeriCorps programs.[3]

Our major goal was to interest private-sector funders in supporting local AmeriCorps programs. We were open to receiving assistance in all forms, including corporate volunteers, professional expertise, donated equipment and supplies, and job opportunities for AmeriCorps graduates. Our pitch was straightforward: AmeriCorps would tap the idealism and energy of a diverse group of Americans to benefit communities in tangible ways. They would tutor troubled students, restore natural habitats, organize neighborhood watch programs, and help the homeless. AmeriCorps members themselves would have the chance to obtain a GED if they didn't have a high school diploma; earn money for college or graduate school; learn job skills; and develop problemsolving, teamwork, and leadership skills. By connecting local groups and mobilizing other volunteers in pursuit of common goals, AmeriCorps would build community. And finally, investors in this program would know at the end of the year what their money bought—how many hours of service were provided, how many people helped, and what results could be attributed to AmeriCorps. Our hope was that the AmeriCorps logo, because of the program's built-in competition among sponsors and high program selection criteria, would become a "Good Housekeeping Seal of Approval" of sorts.

Because this program was known to be a top priority of the President, it was not difficult to gain the attention of corporate leaders. But convincing them to invest turned out to be more time consuming and frustrating than Eli first imagined. Although we had structured the Corporation for National Service to operate more like a private corporation than a traditional bureaucracy, it was still a federal agency, and funders were reluctant to donate directly to the government, even though their gifts were tax deductible. We had made it a policy not to pitch specific local AmeriCorps programs to potential donors, as doing so would have been unfair to the other programs. But funders wanted help channeling their donations to AmeriCorps sponsors in their own communities, or to those targeting specific issues. We wanted to explore whether we could license the AmeriCorps logo to companies for a fee. But the legal complexity inherent in doing so made this kind of arrangement impossible. Staff had many ideas about ways to engage the private sector and deluged us and the private sector outreach staff with requests for in-kind resources. But we found that it was just as time consuming to convince one company to donate 100 T-shirts as it was to raise $100,000 from another, and our resources were spread thin.

Despite these challenges, the Corporation for National Service was able to persuade major businesses and foundations to support Ameri-Corps. The General Electric Fund allocated $250,000 a year for Ameri-Corps grantees, to be selected by local GE and United Way leaders in communities where GE had a substantial presence. American Airlines donated tickets to fly AmeriCorps members to trainings and helped with recruitment by airing public service announcements on its flights. Nike, through its PLAY initiative (Participate in the Lives of America's Youth), supported AmeriCorps members in six cities. JP Morgan agreed to fund AmeriCorps Leaders, a cadre of national service graduates who would serve as team leaders in new AmeriCorps programs.

Others in the AmeriCorps network were even more successful at generating support for the program. Washington State convinced Micro-soft to wire all of the AmeriCorps programs in the state. City Year, already a leader in raising corporate support, was able to increase its size exponentially (from 100 young people serving each year to 1,000) by convincing private sector donors that their funds would be matched dollar for dollar. Between 1991 and 1998, City Year raised a total of $101 million, including $53.5 million from the private sector. Serve Houston, a new program modeled on City Year, convinced local companies— Enron, Tenneco Gas, Shell Oil, and others—to join in their annual Hands on Houston Day of Service. And in New Hampshire, three com-panies—Bank of New Hampshire, Providian Financial, and Fleet Finan-cial—underwrote the cash matching requirements for all AmeriCorps programs in the state, while Health Source, a leading national HMO, provided health insurance and first aid training to New Hampshire AmeriCorps members.

Some national businesses and foundations became very involved. IBM, in partnership with the Public Education Network, created Project First, which deployed AmeriCorps members and retired IBM executives to help public schools with their technology needs. The Ford Foundation made a grant of $3 million to the newly created Partnership for National Service and challenged this nonprofit to use the donation to leverage local funds, which it did at a rate of more than two to one. Sony Corporation ran public service announcements on its Times Square "Jumbotron," organized a major concert in New York, and supported public safety programs in New York and Los Angeles. Larry Fish, chairman, president, and CEO of Citizens Financial Network, a New England–based bank holding company, became chairman of the Rhode Island Commission on National Service and soon persuaded each university headquartered in Rhode Island to match each AmeriCorps education award to an income student with one of its own.

In the first year of AmeriCorps, the private sector contributed more than $40 million dollars.[4] Although we regarded this as a success, we thought we could do more. We decided to require, not just encourage, local AmeriCorps sponsors to raise part of their matching funds from the private sector. Although no minimum amount was specified, local sponsors reacted with concern. Historically, some nonprofit organizations had subsisted solely with government funds, never receiving a single dollar from the private sector. Some AmeriCorps sponsors struggled with setting private sector fundraising policies, focusing on the negative—the types of businesses from which they would *refuse* to accept donations. Although we hoped to convince these reluctant AmeriCorps grantees that they could indeed tap this new source of revenue, we were reminded that sometimes the social sector and business sector were worlds apart. Nonetheless, with strong encouragement from the Corporation for National Service, AmeriCorps grantees did attract significant business and other private sector support, and as a group, were ultimately able to decrease the share of funds they derived from federal sources.

Eli left the Corporation in 1996 to test the idea of business–social sector partnerships with a new focus: welfare-to-work. In August 1996, welfare reform legislation was enacted. To help implement the new law, President Clinton called upon the business community to move welfare recipients into the workforce. Six months later, Eli formed the Welfare to Work Partnership with the CEOs of United Airlines, UPS, Burger King, Sprint, and Monsanto. Their mission was simple: to help companies hire and retain welfare recipients without displacing other employees. When the Partnership was formally launched a few months later, the operating philosophy was in place: businesses could better achieve their mission with the help of the social sector. Most businesses had neither the experience nor the resources to do what primarily nonprofit workforce training and readiness organizations had done for decades. The Partnership set out to help its members learn from the experience of others.

By the end of 1998, the Partnership consisted of over 10,000 companies, large and small, across the country. It was working closely with national nonprofits and trade associations like Goodwill Industries, the Council on Growing Companies, the National Retail Federation, the National Association of Manufacturers, the Enterprise Foundation, the U.S. Chamber of Commerce, the Society of Human Resource Managers, and thousands of local nonprofits. And it could point to the hiring of over 410,000 former welfare recipients, largely through the relationships developed with the nonprofit intermediaries.

Shirley left the Corporation for National Service in 1997 to become the founding executive director of a collaboration of a different sort. The nonprofit Learning First Alliance was formed by twelve national education agencies concerned with improving student learning in public schools. Together, the member organizations represented more than ten million individuals engaged in improving, providing, and governing public education, including teachers, parents, school board members, administrators, state policymakers, and teacher educators.

Experience suggested that the challenges faced by Alliance members as they tried to work together to achieve their goals were not unique: agreeing on goals and priorities, ensuring equal ownership, and establishing decisionmaking mechanisms. Nor were they insurmountable, even though the collaboration included labor and management, regulators and practitioners, parents and administrators.

One topic the group wrestled with almost more than any other was working with corporate sponsors. The organizations had widely varying policies themselves—one refused corporate dollars altogether; another received more than $1 million a year from corporate sponsorships. Several had strong concerns about taking money from businesses that had positions on legislation that conflicted with their own, and others were concerned about appearing to endorse a company's products. Again, although the group was ultimately able to raise corporate funding, the issues it faced underscore the many challenges that nonprofits confront in developing business partnerships.

As Shirley discussed her experience at the Learning First Alliance with Eli, we found that we had developed similar ideas about what makes partnerships successful. Our experiences with both business and social sector organizations—we collectively have served on the board or staff of twenty-one nonprofit organizations, fifteen businesses, and four government organizations—convinced us there is a need to demystify cross-sector partnerships. The majority of individuals in the business sector have little to do with their counterparts in the social sector, and vice versa. Business and social sector leaders travel in different worlds, and usually deep suspicion exists. Even individuals with extensive experience developing partnerships and collaboration within their own fields have difficulty applying those lessons across the sectors.

In the course of our travels, we have met visionary individuals whose good instincts, creative energy, and ability to think strategically have made them innovators in the world of cross-sector partnerships. Mission-driven, they have worked to bridge the divide, learning about the other sector and reaching out to potential partners.

The individuals seemed, as we spoke with them, to have followed similar paths to developing partnerships, even though they varied in the kind of business or social sector group they represented. Their stories, we felt, might be useful to others interested in exploring cross-sector partnerships.

In studying these issues further, we also discovered an extensive body of literature describing the creation of alliances within the business sector, and the building of collaborations within the social sector. As we reviewed the literature from both fields, we found common themes and lessons communicated in very different languages that accorded with our own research and experience. But although some of the material we looked at included references to working across the sectors, this was not its primary purpose.

This book introduces businesspeople and nonprofit managers to cutting-edge cross-sector partnerships. It teaches the lessons we have gleaned from our own experience, written materials, and more than one hundred interviews with individuals on both sides of cross-sector partnerships. We chose to focus on the social sector, which we define as including both nonprofit and governmental organizations with a mission of meeting human needs. Nonetheless most of our analysis would apply just as well to other types of government or nonprofit institutions—such as those working in the arts or on environmental issues. We have tried to use the term *nonprofit* when the analysis applies specifically to not-for-profit, nongovernmental organizations.

To help readers understand how partnerships develop and evolve, we chose seven examples of business–social sector relationships that we consider models of innovation and excellence. (In several of these cases, we were already acquainted with one or more of the parties involved.) The seven cases show different ways that organizations work together, illustrating well-known and less-well-known cross-sector partnership arrangements, from strategic philanthropy to social enterprise. They represent large and small companies and nonprofits; national and local organizations; the northwest, south, midwest, and northeast; and different fields. Their experiences, while very different in some ways, demonstrate similar patterns of development. And while none purported to follow a predetermined process, their experiences helped us construct a series of stages, described in chapter 10, that will be useful to others hoping to use cross-sector alliances to create new value for their organizations.

Acknowledgments

Many people made it possible for us share our ideas through this book. We are grateful to all of them.

We especially appreciate the wisdom and patience of our editors, Nicola Sabin, Marjorie Williams, and Lindsay Whitman.

Cameron Hamill got us off to a great start as our first researcher. Eleni Pelikan helped us complete the project. And in between, Anne Ryan Barton went beyond the call of duty to ensure that all the pieces came together.

Many people reviewed drafts of the book. We thank them for their insightful counsel.

Finally, to all the pioneers of cross-sector partnerships who took the time to tell their stories for the common good, we offer our deepest appreciation.

PART I

Getting
Started

1

────────── ❧ ──────────

INTRODUCTION

ALMOST ANYWHERE YOU LOOK you can find evidence of stepped-up business–social sector interaction. Alongside traditional giving—a local store collecting toys for the needy at Christmas, a company participating in a United Way campaign—innovative businesses are creating new arrangements that are as good for the company as they are for the community. This phenomenon may seem to some to be a passing fad. But we see in these exchanges a new paradigm for business and the social sector, one that eliminates barriers between the sectors while preserving their core missions. This new paradigm pairs visionary companies that see how the social context in which they operate affects their bottom lines with a new breed of social entrepreneurs who understand how business principles can enable them to fulfill their social missions more effectively. Together, they are reshaping how communities tackle some of their most intractable social challenges.

If you asked a nonprofit executive in the mid-1980s what business could offer his organization, you would likely have heard one word: money. This hypothetical executive might have spent at least a quarter of his time raising money and maybe a good deal more time thinking about it. Because the organization was likely dependent on government dollars,[1] he almost certainly worried that state or local funds would not offset the recent cuts in federal programs.[2] Although his organization probably never had approached a corporation for funding—and he likely had no professional contacts in the business sector—he may have known that corporate giving was on the rise and had surpassed foundation giving for the first time in 1983.[3] Possibly he would have been aware of local firms' involvement in the public schools or would have heard prominent corporate CEOs calling for more Head Start funding. And he may have become aware of a controversial new practice called "cause-related marketing," in which companies promise to donate a certain amount to a charity for each consumer transaction. Although this executive might have once viewed corporate America as "part of the problem," he might have decided to take another look at corporate funding as a strategy to diversify the organization's revenues during a time of great uncertainty.

Of course, a business leader of the mid-1980s would have looked at the situation differently. She would have been watching some of the nation's largest corporations losing their market position or vanish altogether—during the decade, 230 companies disappeared from the Fortune 500.[4] Her company might have been fighting off a takeover attempt or pursuing a merger or acquisition itself. She might have been looking for ways to streamline the company, seeking efficiencies by downsizing, closing plants, and cutting frills. Faced with declining profits and the need to lay off long-term employees—between 1979 and 1993, the nation lost 36 million private sector jobs[5]—directors and shareholders might have seen the company's philanthropic budget as an unnecessary luxury. In response, the executive might have asked managers to rethink the company's giving policies—not to eliminate donations altogether, but to find ways to make philanthropy serve the company's business objectives.

Given these circumstances, it is not surprising that the nature of the relationship between business and social sector organizations has changed dramatically since the 1980s. Where once the two sectors were worlds apart, with contact between them at best an unequal relationship of philanthropist and charity and at worst one of political adversaries, many businesses and social sector organizations are rethinking how they interact. Significantly, they are looking across sector boundaries for new ways to meet their own needs and, in many cases, are finding more opportunities than they could ever have anticipated.

A New World

The business and social sectors face, with very different implications, challenges posed by rapid technological changes, an increasingly diverse and aging U.S. population, concern about the country's growing social divide, and uncertainty about the economic future of the country.

THE BUSINESS ENVIRONMENT

The 1990s offered private enterprise new opportunities through the opening of global markets and dramatic technological advances. The economic recovery at the beginning of the decade spurred investment and growth, creating new business possibilities, unprecedented profits, and unforeseen challenges. As shareholders came to expect double-digit returns, many companies were tempted to focus on short-term profits at the expense of long-term investments. At the same time, smaller businesses faced takeover possibilities, local retailers faced the threat of category-killer chain stores, and manufacturers faced competition from overseas. Companies from almost every industry found they needed to innovate or be left behind.

The technology revolution fueled this dramatic rate of change and created opportunities unimaginable ten years before. It increased productivity by altering the manufacturing process and made information more and more accessible, allowing for precise targeting of customers, greater customization of products, and flatter organization charts. In many cases, it made it just as easy to do business around the world as across the street, increasing competition here in the United States and opening new markets overseas. It eliminated the need for a storefront in many industries, as one-third of all households had personal computers, and consumers had grown increasingly comfortable with electronic commerce.[6]

Although many predicted that technological advances would decrease the importance of human capital, in fact, a qualified and motivated workforce has become more important than ever. Companies are finding that they need more than workers with technological skills; they need employees who can work together to spur innovation, who can provide exceptional customer service expected by today's consumer, and who are sufficiently motivated by the company's mission and prospects to stay and aspire to higher levels of productivity. The importance of teamwork, loyalty, and skills is becoming doctrine in almost every industry. At the same time, an aging and increasingly diverse workforce, a shortage of skilled workers, and the scars of a decade of downsizing are causing many companies to rethink what they need to do to attract and retain qualified workers and to build a team out of individuals who live in different neighborhoods and come from different cultures.

THE SOCIAL SECTOR ENVIRONMENT

Technology has had an impact on social sector organizations as well, presenting opportunities to improve services, increase access to information, reduce bureaucracy, and customize assistance in ways never before thought possible. But despite its potential, technology's effect has been less significant than in the business sector for a simple reason: high costs put much of the new technology out of reach of many nonprofits and government agencies. In addition, as information access increases in importance in daily life, social sector organizations must concern themselves with "technology have-nots" who risk slipping even further behind their more advantaged peers.

Social sector organizations are being called on to serve more people, with better results, than they have in the past. But they do so with an uncertain resource base, as the number of nonprofit organizations has continued to increase and social sector groups have come to understand that increases in personal income and a growing economy do not necessarily result in proportionate increases in private giving and government spending.[7] Private donors are acting like government funders, increasingly earmarking their dollars for specific programs and purposes and asking that organizations be able to document their results. And nonprofit organizations are operating under increased scrutiny in part as a result of the 1992 United Way scandal in which its former president was found to have been converting charitable funds to his own use.[8] While these demands for greater efficiency, effectiveness, and accountability require staff with exceptional financial, management, and leadership skills, social sector organizations are under pressure to keep salaries and overhead low in order to keep the share of dollars dedicated to program high.

To increase their resource base, some nonprofit organizations are charging higher fees for services and inviting competition from for-profit companies in fields such as childcare, recreation, job training, and home health care. Others have turned to professional fundraisers who use tele-marketing, direct mail, and paid solicitors to produce additional resources for the nonprofit—but keep the lion's share of the donation for themselves. Observes the consulting firm KPMG Peat Marwick in its 1997 report *Organizations Serving the Public:* "After tremendous growth over the last two decades, the market is saturated with nonprofits: there is simply not enough money to go around. . . . Even the best known will have to reinvent themselves, because the financial model of the past isn't working any more."[9]

The Alliance Strategy

Both business and social sector organizations are reinventing themselves by forming alliances. In both sectors, partnerships have been a way to expand capabilities beyond what the organization's own resource base permits. Alliances allow organizations greater flexibility and the oppor-tunity to leverage competencies, improve customer service, and create a wider geographic reach. But organizations in the business and social sec-tors tend to approach alliances differently, which creates challenges in a cross-sector context.

BUSINESS SECTOR ALLIANCES

Business alliances tend to be opportunity focused. After decades of downsizing and rightsizing to improve efficiency, there is now "greater productivity opportunity *between* organizations—in terms of working together more efficiently and effectively—than there is *within* organiza-tions," according to management consultants Neil Rackham, Lawrence Friedman, and Richard Ruff.[10] For example, trucks of company A return home empty after delivering supplies to company B, a manufacturer across the state. Company B has a warehouse in the same town as com-pany A—why not send company A's trucks home with products destined for company B's warehouse? A small efficiency, yes. But the real-life companies in this example have identified and implemented over 200 projects of this kind, resulting in real savings for both companies.[11] It is not surprising that, as a result of the opportunities they present, business alliances grew by more than 25 percent annually from 1990 to 1995, and the trend shows no signs of abating.[12]

Alliances in the business sector take many forms, from technology transfers to joint marketing arrangements. They may be created to co-opt potential competitors, gain access to new knowledge, or move more quickly into new markets. Rosabeth Moss Kanter categorizes business alliances into three types: *mutual service,* in which similar companies in similar industries pool resources to gain access to benefits too expensive to acquire alone (such as advanced technology); *joint ventures,* which enable companies to pursue an opportunity that needs the capabilities of each; and *value chain* partnerships, in which companies in different industries with different but complementary skills link their capabilities to create value (such as supplier–customer relationships).[13]

Although alliances are often very lucrative for business, not all attempts at partnership succeed. Ninety percent of attempts to develop alliances fail, according to Iain Somerville, managing partner of organization strategy for Andersen Consulting.[14] The median lifespan of a business alliance is seven years, and a large percentage of business alliances—nearly 80 percent according to one study—end in mergers or acquisitions.[15]

SOCIAL SECTOR ALLIANCES

Like businesses, social sector organizations often form alliances to improve their efficiency, but instead of framing the purpose of such partnerships as the pursuit of opportunities, analysts in the social sector often discuss the reasons for collaboration in negative terms. "A major source of organizational inefficiency is flawed coordination," according to Seymour Sarason and Elizabeth Lorentz.[16] "There is widespread agreement . . . that [health, education and welfare] services are not enough to meet the needs of a growing number of children, and they are organized and delivered in ways that severely limit their effectiveness," write Atelia Melaville and Martin Blank, who argue for greater collaboration among social service agencies and public schools to improve assistance to low income families.[17]

In the past, funders (particularly the government) have supported narrow categories of services, causing individuals with multiple needs to enroll in an array of programs from a panoply of local organizations.[18] For example, a program might pay for child nutrition but not health services, or drug rehabilitation but not job training. Now funders are increasingly requiring collaboration to help knit together a seamless web of services. Explains one analyst, "Coalitions and partnerships are attractive to funders because they allow leveraging of funds. Coalitions can offer a more comprehensive solution to an issue than individual nonprofits, which usually address only one aspect of an issue, so they give funders a bigger impact for their dollars."[19] Even when collaboration is not mandated, service providers are finding they can deliver better services more cost effectively by working together. "The old model of individual 'silos,' operating independently and providing all services related to particular need, will be too costly and too rigid to survive," predicts KPMG Peat Marwick. "Instead, organizations will shed extraneous functions, moving to shared services based on core competencies, and ultimately, to collaborative alliances."[20]

Seeking to create greater value from fewer donor dollars, organizations serving the same clients might work together to create efficiencies and better services. For example, social service providers serving the same community might jointly commission a needs assessment and agree to share space in the neighborhood, saving all of the agencies money and providing clients with "one stop shopping" for services. Collaborations within the social sector field may be intended to create new capacities by leveraging the resources of individual organizations; make it easier for individuals to access services; resolve conflicts; develop new and innovative solutions that could not be created by a single entity; reduce duplication of services; conserve resources spent competing for clients and dollars; and advocate for policies.

As in the business sector, an extensive body of literature is available on social sector alliances, although much of it is targeted to specific fields, such as community development, early childhood programs, and education. A great deal of the literature emphasizes collaborations among multiple organizations. It stresses the need for a neutral convener or natural leader, inclusion of the right organizations, and the difference between voluntary and mandated partnerships.[21] Invariably, the goals of the coalitions are to correct problems rather than pursue opportunities. They are intended to reform, to eliminate duplication, to break down walls between organizations serving the same community. Much of the literature stresses pitfalls: turf battles, power struggles, differences in philosophy and culture, inadequate resources, overemphasis on consensus. Businesses may in fact be participants in these large, complicated partnerships, but the character of these relationships is invariably defined by social sector norms.

In practice, there are, of course, social sector alliances that resemble business alliances—opportunity focused, entered into for mutual advantage, entirely voluntary. But the essential approach taken by social sector organizations in partnerships reflects the nature of the sector itself. The business sector exists to capitalize on market opportunities to realize profits for owners and investors. The social sector is by its nature compensatory. It exists because of market failures. It remedies, rescues, repairs. For this reason, whereas the stereotypical business alliance creates value by generating new opportunities, the social sector alliance is often a response to a threat—of reduced funding, escalating needs, or hostile forces.[22]

CROSS-SECTOR PARTNERSHIPS

Given the growth in alliances as a survival strategy in both the business and nonprofit sectors, it is not surprising that cutting-edge corporations and social sector organizations are looking outside their own sectors to address specific needs. A 1998 focus group study found that:

> At the same time that businesses are moving beyond traditional philanthropy, nonprofit organizations are recognizing the need to build their own revenue to become self-sustaining. Together they are establishing strategic partnerships to achieve mutually beneficial objectives. Though still in its infancy, the partnership building trend is growing as companies and nonprofit organizations gain experience working together.[23]

Although cross-sector alliances are increasingly popular, both business and social sector organizations bring different expectations to these relationships. Whereas businesses expect all partners to provide value, social sector organizations frequently expect businesses to help them further their social mission without benefiting themselves.

Early cross-sector partnerships typified this approach. The partnerships of the 1970s and early 1980s often addressed education reform, cultural opportunities, or environmental issues in the communities where businesses operated. These relationships went beyond traditional philanthropy as corporations abandoned the old model of check writing. In these cases, the achievement of the social sector goal would also satisfy the business's needs—a company looking to attract employees to the area by improving the local schools would find its need met when student achievement increased; a business struggling with environmental issues would be gratified if a nonprofit helped it reduce waste. As businesses began to engage more deeply with nonprofit and local government organizations, they found greater visibility and recognition. Interest in corporate social responsibility and studies demonstrating connections between good citizenship and the bottom line encouraged more companies to look seriously at ties to the nonprofit sector as a way to improve their image. Cross-sector partnerships became more common, and the press began to cover them, bringing the trend to the attention of other companies.

New marketing campaigns involving causes began to appear in the 1980s, such as affinity credit cards that benefited charities or products tied to specific nonprofit organizations. The growing awareness that resulted from these visible partnerships also fueled interest in cross-sector exchanges by both business and social sector managers, leading to an explosion of new relationships across the sectors, which took a variety of forms and served an ever-wider range of needs of both partners.

These forms or "exchanges" include everything from the familiar corporate grant to a nonprofit to a joint venture by a business and social sector partner. An *exchange* occurs when a business and social sector organization recognize that their needs can be met by the other. For example, when cable TV giant HBO sought to increase its minority viewership, it agreed to make a donation to the United Negro College Fund for each new subscriber. When local business leaders sought to stop the loss of jobs in the rural community of Stanly County, North Carolina, by attracting high tech businesses to the area, Concord Telephone joined with the local schools and universities to increase the technological literacy of the community by creating a telecommunications network linking all the major public and nonprofit service agencies in the county.[24]

These *exchanges* are often called *partnerships*. The term *partnership* has been applied in many different ways to the field of business and social sector relationships. In fact, nonprofit organizations sometimes use *partnership* as a synonym for the traditional relationship between the organization and its corporate and foundation funders. For purposes of clarity, we have used *partnership* to describe the *relationship* between two organizations that engage in one or more *exchanges.*

The major focus of this book is not on different types of exchanges, but rather on the underlying partnerships that make them possible. However, an understanding of the various possibilities for exchanges is essential for both business and social sector organizations to maximize the value of their partnerships. Therefore, the next chapter outlines the major types of exchanges that may form the basis of cross-sector alliances.

2

⁊⧫

EXCHANGES

THIS BOOK PRESENTS AN OVERVIEW of some of the most popular and emerging types of exchanges, which fall into three categories. In *philanthropic* exchanges, a business donates funds, goods, or services to a social sector organization. In *marketing* exchanges, a business affiliates itself with a social sector organization to satisfy consumer or distributor needs.[1] Finally, in *operational* exchanges, a social sector organization helps a business increase its capacity to produce goods or services more competitively.[2]

The *category* of the exchange should not be confused with the *motive* of the business partner. For example, a philanthropic arrangement might be motivated by operational needs—as when a law firm donates to a law school from which it recruits new attorneys—or an operational exchange might have a marketing purpose—as when a manufacturer purchases supplies from a nonprofit social enterprise and makes that fact known to customers. Partnerships, including some featured in this book, may include multiple exchanges falling into two or even all three categories. Some interactions are hard to assign, because they fit more than one category—corporate volunteer programs can be both philanthropic (involving a donation of human resources) and operational (offered as an employee perk or team-building activity). Nonetheless, we use these categories to help readers understand the different forms and advantages of partnerships. Each category is discussed here. Then, in chapters 3 through 9, we profile each type of exchange through a series of case studies.

Philanthropic Exchanges

The Williamsburg neighborhood of Brooklyn, New York, was a pastoral agricultural village when Pfizer was founded there in 1849. After a century of growth, the community began to suffer from urban decay, losing jobs and experiencing increasing poverty and crime and declining schools. When Pfizer moved its corporate headquarters to Manhattan and relocated some of its operations, it decided to invest in the Williamsburg community where it would continue to employ 1,200 people. The company recruited other businesses to the area and joined with the New York City Housing Partnership to construct 280 middle-income homes on Pfizer land. And in a unique partnership with the Beginning With Children Foundation, it transformed its former administration building into a new alternative public elementary school. In addition to receiving several awards for its work, the company has seen the neighborhood improve dramatically and has found a significant increase in the number of qualified workers in the area, enabling the plant to expand operations.

When Afena Akoma, a small importer of African musical instruments and artifacts, moved its retail outlet to Rochester, New York, it needed to establish relationships with the African American community and city leaders. The company's founders had heard about a Texas project called "Drums Not Guns" and decided to try a similar concept in Rochester. In partnership with the nonprofit Action for a Better Community, the company provided free lessons in African drumming and Capoeira (an Afro-Brazilian martial art) to middle-school-age boys. The company also made its gallery and dance studio available to community groups, including the public schools and a sister-cities program important to the mayor. These efforts brought the business to the attention of local media as well as the mayor and provided the nonprofit community with an additional source of constructive activities for inner city youth.

Today's most common form of business–social sector partnership is corporate philanthropy, which began to take hold on a significant scale in the 1970s in response to a demand for greater corporate social responsibility. After a decade of steady growth, corporate donations in 1983 reached $3.67 billion and exceeded independent foundation giving for the first time. Experts commented that "industry seem[ed] likely to displace the former captains of industry [such as Carnegie, Rockefeller, and Ford, who founded major foundations bearing their names] as the major source of institutional philanthropy."[3]

After a brief dip in the late 1980s, corporate giving has continued to increase in real dollars, but not at a pace equal to the growth in corporate profits.[4] Corporate gifts accounted for 1.8 percent of corporate income in 1987 but only 1.1 percent in 1997, a lower percentage of income than the average individual contributes to charity.[5] Most companies have no philanthropic budget; the $8 billion in annual corporate donations is given by just one-third of the nation's businesses.

Corporate donations account for a little more than 5 percent of all charitable giving,[6] which is less than 3 percent of annual federal spending on social programs.[7] However, this figure understates the total resources that businesses provide to social sector organizations. Statistics collected regarding corporate philanthropic budgets do not include, for example, dollars paid to license the name of a nonprofit or donations businesses collect from their customers or employees on behalf of charities.

As the social sector looks for new funding sources and strategies to address community needs, business is thought of more and more as a key partner in efforts to solve critical problems, and demand for corporate philanthropic dollars is at an all time high. Some corporations have identified their philanthropy as a way to distinguish themselves in an otherwise crowded field, hoping to capitalize on increased support for socially responsible businesses. A few companies stand out for their giving—for example, yogurt producer Stonyfield Farms and ice-cream maker Ben & Jerry's donate 10 percent of pre-tax profits to causes; Dayton-Hudson, the large mass market department store chain, gives 5 percent of its pre-tax profits to charity; and Newman's Own, in a category by itself, donates 100 percent of post-tax profits.[8] Other corporations not able to match the volume of these exceedingly generous companies seek greater impact for their donations by:

- narrowing their focus to specific objectives, resulting in support for a limited number of causes or a few geographic areas.

- looking for ways to measure results, such as measuring the increase in the literacy rate rather than the number of literacy tutors.

- tying grants to company business interests, encouraging more synergy with other company departments including public affairs, sales, marketing, human resources, recruiting, and government relations.

- making fewer grants but increasing their size.

- decentralizing community involvement programs and grant budgets to give more autonomy to regional operations.

According to the Conference Board, the greatest corporate benefits of strategic giving are an improved image, greater employee involvement and loyalty, and improved customer ties.[9] Through their philanthropy, businesses have also built better relationships with distributors, franchisees, and shareholders; created training opportunities for their own employees; tapped into a new recruitment pool; improved the quality of life in their communities; and received favorable notice by policymakers and other influential leaders.

One common form of philanthropy is employee volunteering. One-third of companies in one survey reported making community service part of their strategy to address critical business issues.[10] The leanness of companies today has created a need for committed workforces, and volunteer programs have been shown to help companies attract and retain the people they need, and build skills and attitudes that foster organizational commitment, company loyalty, and job satisfaction.[11] One study found employee morale to be up to three times higher in companies actively involved in the community than at other companies, and company community involvement is positively related to financial performance.[12] Another study found that volunteer work increased job satisfaction and commitment to the company.[13] In addition, according to the Conference Board, companies may receive a greater public relations benefit from employee volunteering than other forms of corporate community involvement because the public is less likely to consider volunteer activity self-serving.[14] While conservative theorists and shareholders concerned with maximizing gains have attacked overly generous contributions programs, employee volunteering is relatively noncontroversial.

It is not surprising that nine out of ten companies in one survey report that they encourage their employees to become involved in volunteer service.[15] Social sector organizations that use corporate volunteers well are beginning to find that other donations, including cash, tend to follow the volunteers.

One major trend, documented by the Conference Board and the Council on Foundations, has been the development of long-term partnerships between nonprofits and companies that share a common interest. Local cultural organizations, adopt-a-school programs, and community development and housing initiatives are the most popular causes with U.S. companies.[16] As corporations have thought through how to make their giving more strategic, social sector organizations have found ways to engage their business partners more effectively. Savvy nonprofits know that they are more likely to receive corporate support if they ask for something other than money. As the partnerships we studied demonstrate, today's corporate philanthropy comes not just in cash and "in kind." Increasingly, it comes in the form of loaned executives, donated expertise and advice, raising money from customers or employees, introductions to other potential funders, use of corporate facilities and equipment, and training for nonprofit staff or clients.

Two chapters provide case studies of philanthropic partnerships. In chapter 3, Home Depot becomes the first corporate partner of KaBOOM!, a nonprofit that engages corporate volunteers and community members to build playgrounds in low-income neighborhoods. In chapter 4, Microsoft teams up with the American Library Association to create Libraries Online, distributing computer hardware and software to establish public access to computers through public libraries.

Marketing Exchanges

Hoping to create a hip image for its new "Venezia" line for young women, the large-size women's clothing chain Lane Bryant approached the Campus Outreach Opportunity League—known as COOL— about a marketing partnership. COOL is a national nonprofit organization promoting service by college students. Lane Bryant paid COOL $25,000 for use of its logo to promote the line, with the possibility of additional funds through sales of "V-Girl" logo T-shirts. COOL was *able to get its message out to millions of consumers in its target age group and expand the visibility of its name and attractive logo, which features a Keith Haring drawing. The logo appeared on store banners, a compact disc of popular women artists created for the new brand, magazine ads, the Lane Bryant Web site, and credit card inserts, which also included a reply card for donations to COOL. In addition, a contest to identify "V-Girls" noted that "V stands for Volunteer" and asked applicants, "How do you give of yourself to help your community or act as a role model for other women?"*

When the AmeriCorps national service program was looking for a way to reach its target market of 18- to 24-year olds, it sought a media partner with proven "Generation X" appeal. At the same time, MTV's president was looking to disabuse the public of stereotypical views of young people. MTV had just finished its "Rock the Vote" campaign and was looking for new ways to incorporate community involvement into its programming. Coincidentally, the son of an MTV vice president had just started a term of service with AmeriCorps. MTV agreed to support AmeriCorps by conducting market research and creating a new Public Service Announcement (PSA) to recruit young adults to sign up for the program. The network also covered an "AmeriCorps Alternative Spring Break"—a week-long service project in Florida—as part of its Spring Break 1997 coverage and arranged for the cast of one of its top-rated shows to serve on air alongside AmeriCorps members at an afterschool program. AmeriCorps benefited from the exposure (the PSA alone generated nearly $6 million in free air-time) and from its association with the popular network. MTV gained a way to showcase the social responsibility of the young people who are its primary audience.

Compared to philanthropic partnerships, marketing alliances between businesses and social sector organizations are a relatively recent phenomenon. Sponsorship, in which a business pays to associate itself with an event or property, became popular in the 1980s as businesses discovered they could use it to promote a brand or product to a carefully targeted audience. Unlike traditional forms of advertising, sponsorship is generally viewed favorably by consumers because it *enables* a desired event to occur rather than *interrupting* it.[17] Sponsors often provide product samples, which customers welcome. In addition, press coverage at

sponsored events is a cost-effective way to reach large numbers of consumers. For example, Ben & Jerry's founders write in *Double Dip* about
an arts festival sponsored by the company:

> *Fifty thousand people attended the Minneapolis festival, but it made 9*
> *million impressions through advertising, articles in newspapers, and*
> *radio and TV coverage. It cost us $150,000 or 17 cents per thousand*
> *impressions. A thirty-second TV commercial on the WCCO Min-*
> *neapolis evening news costs $1,800 and reaches 260,000 people, for a*
> *cost of $6.92 per thousand impressions. A full-page ad in the Min-*
> *neapolis* Star Tribune *cost $13,917 and reaches 407,504, at a cost per*
> *thousand of $34.15.*[18]

In the mid-1980s, businesses learned they could sponsor causes the
way they did sporting events or art exhibits and improve their image at
the same time. These practices take many forms. In addition to traditional events marketing, such as sponsoring a 10K race that benefits a
charity, companies can advertise that the sale of a product or other consumer exchange will trigger a donation to a specific charity or cause.
Alternatively, the product itself may be co-branded with the nonprofit's
logo. This type of licensing arrangement usually generates a specified
royalty for the nonprofit.

Marketing deals benefiting causes grew dramatically during the
1990s, with the amount spent by companies on joint marketing deals
with charities increasing from $75 million in 1988 to more than $1 billion in 1999.[19]

Companies spend many times this amount to promote their association with a cause, helping nonprofit partners raise their profile, attract
donors, and build their image through association with a successful business. Other types of common marketing partnerships include social marketing, in which a business joins with a nonprofit or government organization and uses marketing techniques to influence behavior (e.g., a
campaign to promote the use of designated drivers).[20] In addition, cause-
related marketing campaigns of all sorts create opportunities for media
coverage. One company reported six times the usual coverage when it
initiated a social campaign.[21]

Critics attacked early marketing partnerships for undermining the
charitable character of nonprofit organizations, and pundits speculated

that such arrangements would drive away traditional donors. Although these predictions proved to be unfounded[22] (in fact, it is possible that cause-related marketing heightens awareness among traditional donors, therefore inspiring them to give more), marketing partnerships can present problems. Nonprofit organizations may have trouble managing fluctuating income from year to year; they may risk negative publicity if a business partner is found to be engaging in controversial practices; or they may even face legal exposure if arrangements are not structured or promoted consistent with state and federal law. In addition, marketing partnerships may lead organization members and the public to believe that the nonprofit is in fact endorsing the products of the business partner; this confusion could undermine the organization's credibility and cause individuals to purchase products wrongly believing them to be recommended by a trusted institution. Marketing partnerships can be time-consuming and difficult for nonprofit organizations to price. If the campaign fails to meet sales or other economic targets, the nonprofit partner may be blamed.

Despite these risks, marketing partnerships can offer many benefits to social sector organizations. Those organizations most likely to benefit are those that have a strong brand.[23] To have a strong brand, a social sector organization should:

- have a good reputation, promote an attractive cause, and be well known by an identifiable market segment.

- have supporters who are attractive to business.

- be national in scope—most businesses that serve a national market seek nonprofit partners that operate nationally.[24]

- have a well known or charismatic leader or spokesperson.

- be experienced and stable, able to handle any unanticipated impacts of the partnership.

Marketing partnerships are attractive to companies as cost-effective ways to achieve business objectives. Like philanthropic partnerships, marketing alliances can be part of a strategic effort to define and communicate the company's mission.[25] Companies have used marketing partnerships to improve their image and build loyalty among consumers, staff, retailers, and other stakeholders. And of course, such partnerships often have the traditional marketing objective of increasing sales or encouraging other exchanges (such as coupon redemption, credit card use, or establishing new accounts). At least one study suggests that successful marketing partnerships can have both economic goals (such as building brand equity) and noneconomic goals (such as advancing a social cause).[26]

Research suggests that Americans are increasingly receptive to cause-related marketing. The most well-known studies are sponsored by Cone Communications, a Boston-based firm specializing in cause-related marketing, and conducted by Roper/Starch Worldwide. They found growing support for cause-related marketing: 76 percent of Americans surveyed in 1997 said they approve of cause-related marketing, up 10 percent from 1993. When price and quality are equal, 76 percent of consumers reported they would be likely to switch to a brand associated with a good cause, up 10 percent since 1993. The same percentage also reported they would be likely to switch to a retail store associated with a good cause, up 14 percent since 1993.[27]

Like all marketing campaigns, marketing partnerships do pose risks for companies. Salespeople and retailers may object if they believe the advertising is not leading to increased sales. If sales drop during the campaign period, the cause may be scapegoated, undermining the potential for a long-term connection to the nonprofit that might ultimately yield fruit. Key stakeholders may not agree with the social agenda represented by the partnership, creating conflict rather than cohesion.[28] Partnerships may be time consuming to develop and maintain. And, of course, there is a risk that the nonprofit partner will be the subject of unfavorable press or be involved in a scandal that will reflect badly on the company.

Companies that are most likely to be able to overcome these challenges and benefit from marketing partnerships include those that:

- are willing to take risks or have a history of innovative advertising.[29]

- have a "high degree of organizational identification," where employees believe in what the company stands for, and thus are able to find a cause consistent with this image.[30]

- have a history of civic-mindedness.[31]

- can commit to a long-term marketing strategy.[32]

• have a "clean" record without a history of controversy, or at least are engaged in a sincere turnaround effort.

• are able to devote significant resources to the partnership, including product donations.[33]

Chapters 5 through 7 describe marketing partnerships. In chapter 5, Denny's relationship with Save the Children demonstrates how the corporation built its public identity and boost employee morale through a partnership involving cause-related marketing, fundraising, licensing, public relations strategies, and franchise and employee volunteering. In chapter 6, BankBoston's partnership with City Year illustrates an innovative form of sponsorship (as well as philanthropic elements including corporate volunteering, loaned executives, and grants). Finally, in chapter 7, Calphalon's cause-related marketing and licensing partnership with Share Our Strength illustrates how the nonprofit organization leveraged its relationships with influential chefs into a marketing asset for its corporate partners.

Operational Exchanges

Goodwill Industries, one of the world's largest nonprofit providers of employment and training services for people with disabilities and other challenges, supports its programs by selling donated clothing and household goods and providing contract services to businesses. For example, Goodwill has entered into a multi-level partnership with National Van Lines to provide training and jobs for the hard-to-employ. Goodwill trains its clients in direct sales, customer service, and other skills, and National Van Lines provides jobs to program graduates, helping to meet its own need for qualified entry-level employees. As an added bonus for the nonprofit, the moving company encourages its customers who are relocating to donate unwanted items to Goodwill.[34]

New England Electric Systems (NEES) is a utility employing 5,000 people in central Massachusetts. In 1992, in response to chronic labor shortages, NEES formed a partnership with the Worcester Community Action Council (WCAC), a local welfare provider, and began to hire former welfare recipients. For twelve weeks a candidate is trained by WCAC in computer skills, English as a Second Language, and job readiness. Then the candidate interns at NEES for eight weeks. All 40 graduates of the program are still employed. "We can help with a lot of things, like encouraging our female executives to donate old clothes for our new employees," says NEES supervisor Bill Endicott. For employees with greater needs, however, an organization like WCAC can do more than any private company could ever do.

In an operational partnership, a social sector organization helps a business produce quality goods or services more competitively by acting as a supplier, improving training or recruitment services, offering benefits for employees, or serving as a test site for new products. In some ways, this kind of cross-sector partnership closely resembles typical business alliances. However, it brings added dimensions, including philanthropic elements, marketing potential, and the opportunity to further a social mission.

Since at least the 1800s, when the railroads paid YMCAs to provide housing for railroad workers, businesses have turned to nonprofit organizations for needed services. Tax laws discourage nonprofit organizations from engaging in commercial activity by taxing revenues generated through business activities not related to the organization's "exempt purpose."

The law, however, has not barred certain types of nonprofit organizations from acting as vendors for business. For over a century, "sheltered workshops" employing people with disabilities have manufactured products or provided services offered at or below market prices. Education institutions have worked with industry to align their offerings with the needs of employers for workers with certain skills. And social service providers have viewed the workplace as a site to reach potential clients. In each of these cases, nonprofit organizations have found ways to achieve their mission—their "exempt purpose"—by providing goods or services to businesses or customers for a fee, often without paying taxes on the income.

While these kinds of relationships have been in place for decades, nonprofit organizations have in recent years taken steps to improve the quality and value of the goods and services they provide. As nonprofit organizations have become more competitive with for-profit companies, charges of unfair competition have been leveled, and the legal framework that defines unrelated business income for tax purposes has been questioned.[35]

On the other hand, in recent years, for-profit corporations have entered fields previously dominated by nonprofit or government entities.[36] In some cases, businesses have found themselves providing services under contract to local government, a controversial practice known as privatization. For example, for-profit companies now contract with public school districts to run schools and with local governments to provide waste-management services.

Nonprofit organizations best suited to engage in operational partnerships are those that are able to offer goods or services that have value to a business or value on the commercial market. Although most of these goods or services are clearly offered in furtherance of the nonprofit mission, some nonprofits have successfully launched businesses intended to raise money through activities not clearly connected to their social purpose. Nonprofit partners can help address human resource issues such as recruitment, transportation, childcare, or skills training. However, nonprofit organizations may offer other skills that can be valuable to businesses, such as mobilizing fresh thinking and energy, managing diversity, and teaching a company to maintain responsive relationships with its many stakeholders.

Two chapters offer case studies of operational partnerships. Chapter 8 discusses how Ridgeview, Inc., a small hosiery manufacturer, retains workers in a tight labor market by having its employees with school-age children meet with guidance counselors on site. Chapter 9 profiles Boeing's relationship with Pioneer Human Services, a nonprofit organization that has supplied the corporation with aircraft components for more than two decades.

The case studies that follow will provide readers with background information about different types of philanthropic, marketing, and operational exchanges. Where available, we have tried to include solid research evidence relating to best practices for the specific type of exchange. The "what works" sections at the end of each chapter relate specifically to the type of exchange described. This information is useful to organizations looking at cross-sector exchanges, even if a significant partnership is not desired.

The major goal of this book, however, is to change the way social sector and business leaders think about *partnerships*—not the *exchanges*, but the *relationships* that are built between the organizations involved. Therefore, we have emphasized the creation and building of relationships in the case studies to help readers understand how partnerships develop. Chapters 10 and 11 provide a more direct and detailed discussion about these relationships as partnerships by describing the stages in the formation of cross-sector relationships and the characteristics that make certain alliances pay extra dividends for the partners.

To give readers a framework for thinking about cross-sector partnerships, we suggest keeping in mind another type of alliance that everyone can appreciate—a close friendship. Cross-sector alliances arise the way many friendships do—a chance meeting, an introduction by another friend or colleague; or by design, the way a person might join a church or club in order to meet people after moving to a new town. Partnership, like friendship, is most likely to arise when both parties are open to it. The parties must find that they share interests and possess common values. And they must act on their mutual interest in one another, testing the relationship by undertaking an activity together, entering into an exchange the way a new acquaintance might suggest dinner and a movie. If the activity is successful in the eyes of both parties, other plans will follow. Of course, alliances between organizations invariably involve relationships between people so it is not surprising that they track the process of human friendship so well.

In chapter 11, we discuss a unique friendship that we call a "New Value Partnership." We would not advocate that every cross-sector relationship be approached as a significant partnership, just as a company would be foolish to partner with every one of its suppliers and distributors. But it is our hypothesis that most companies and social sector organizations should seek a limited number of these kinds of deep relationships because they yield extra benefits for those who enter into them. The goal is not longevity, although many New Value Partnerships last for decades. A partnership that has ended was a success if it created value for the organizations involved. Rather than permanency, the goal is *impact*— the continuous creation of value for both partners.

Certain elements characterize these New Value Partnerships. They involve communication between decisionmakers and relationship managers, as well as others. They involve opportunities for joint action that meet the needs of the parties, and they involve mutual benefits, resources, responsibilities, power, and accountability. Interaction occurs at multiple levels of the organizations, and the relationship is open-ended, with potential for continual renewal. Finally, the relationships generate new value for both partners, results that often exceed what either originally imagined. Not every relationship profiled in this book is a New Value Partnership, although most are. All are true partnerships, however, and as chapters 10 and 11 will demonstrate, each offers important lessons to those organizations embarking on cross-sector alliances.

PART II

Philanthropic Exchanges

3

❧

CORPORATE VOLUNTEERING
Home Depot and KaBOOM!

Home Depot and KaBOOM! joined together in 1995 when the new nonprofit asked the building supplies retail chain for help building a playground in Washington, D.C. In four years, the partners built more than twenty playgrounds in inner cities throughout the United States.

The partnership works for KaBOOM! because Home Depot helps the organization achieve its mission to "inspire individuals, organizations, and business to join together to build much needed, safe, and accessible playgrounds." The partnership works for Home Depot because KaBOOM! projects use the company's resources well and suit the decentralized, community-focused culture of the company. KaBOOM! engages company employees in meaningful volunteer projects that increase their loyalty to Home Depot while improving community relations. Importantly, the two organizations share a philosophy of social change—"don't do unto, do with."

Home Depot and KaBOOM!

"Moe got shot in the throat." Seven-year-old Ashley Brodie could explain the graffiti on a dumpster that reads "Moe RIP." She could see the dumpster from the barred windows of her apartment, which looked out onto a littered lot. Living in Livingston Manor, a low-income housing project in Anacostia, one of the most depressed areas of Washington, D.C., Ashley amused herself in an abandoned car with a broken windshield, lining her dolls up inside. She watched as her next-door neighbors were evicted. And she prayed for a playground right there, in the empty lot that was her front yard.

So Ashley was not surprised one day in 1995 to see Darell Hammond, the future founder of KaBOOM!, in the lot with a measuring tape. "Have you come to build the playground?" she called to him. Yes, he told her, surprised at the prescience of the slim child. Ashley ran back into her apartment and returned with a thick stack of crayon sketches. "There has to be a slide, and lots of swings, and monkey bars," she told him.[1]

THE NEED

Darell Hammond had a vision for a new way to rebuild communities. He had been mentored by John McKnight, the Northwestern University sociologist and community activist who coined the term "redlining" to describe how banks shun poor neighborhoods.[2] McKnight believes communities should identify their own assets and build from them, rather than point to deficits and demand services from the government to correct them. These "assets" might be a grandmother who knows about infant care, a talented gardener, or a family who helped a child escape gang life. McKnight advocates that instead of looking to "outside experts" to solve problems, people who reside in a neighborhood should work together to leverage their assets in ways that will transform the community.[3]

Hammond had a chance to apply these theories when he participated with volunteers to build a playground when he was in college. He saw the impact it had on the community. This experience motivated him to join the staff of City Year in 1994, where he had the chance to hone his skills organizing service projects in Chicago. He came to believe three things: projects should be grassroots driven, which would mean local involvement even in the case of a national effort; communities need common space; and those from outside the community seeking to help it should adopt a "don't do unto, do with" philosophy, playing a behind-the-scenes role and letting others be recognized. He knew that across the country there were many community-built playgrounds, usually in well-off neighborhoods, organized by a local parent group or other civic association. But the lack of structure and resources in low-income neighborhoods hindered this kind of coming together. Eager to try to play the role of convener, Hammond was ready to try out his theories in the toughest part of Washington, D.C.

THE MATCH

Who would build the playground? Hammond hoped to find a corporate sponsor for the project that would prove to be a long-term partner. Two leading D.C.-area companies turned Hammond down when he asked for their help. Other companies offered a fraction of the $50,000 needed but wanted "to put their name on it" which would make it hard to recruit other partners.[4] And no one wanted to send their employees to Anacostia, a place known for its drive-by shootings, drug dealers, and children who fantasize about their own funerals.

Hammond saw that it would take a company with a real commitment to the community to take the risk of working with a young, idealistic organizer on a project in a dangerous neighborhood. He thought of Suzanne Apple, director of community affairs at Home Depot's corporate office, whom he had met at a housing conference earlier in the year. Apple had worked in real estate marketing, public relations, and "the public affairs side of banking," including administering the bank's Community Reinvestment Act responsibilities. She had developed a sophisticated understanding of the impact businesses have on communities. She too had read John McKnight and was persuaded by his thinking. When she met Hammond, she felt an immediate personal connection with him. And she saw in Hammond, then in his early twenties, "what we see in people who have the commitment of their convictions. I saw enormous possibilities for us to help him meet his vision." Hammond believed that Home Depot's community focus and building expertise made the company a good fit for the playground project, and that the company's excellent reputation would give it credibility. So he researched the hardware chain's volunteer and philanthropic programs and put forward a proposal that incorporated the company's pre-existing structure as much as possible.

Despite the appeal of the proposal and its fit with the company's needs, Apple was cautious. She decided to start slowly, assisting on just one playground: "Having big dreams is important but being able to deliver those dreams is too." Consistent with Home Depot strategy, she enlisted the closest Home Depot store to Anacostia—just two miles away in Oxon Hill, Maryland—to donate materials and provide "Team Depot" volunteers to build Ashley's playground.

THE TEST

Hammond hired Learning Structures, Inc., to serve as the architect for the Anacostia playground, and convinced the Enterprise Foundation and Jubilee Enterprise, the community development corporation that owned Livingston Manor, to put up a share of the needed funds. It was up to seven-year-old Ashley and her neighbors to help rally community members, which they did by the dozens, putting leaflets under doors, speaking at churches, and posting notices around the area. To supplement the donations of Home Depot and other local businesses, community members raised $9,000 through bake sales and car washes. And to provide direction to the architect, the children gathered to fine-tune Ashley's designs. Like Ashley, most low-income children propose traditional playground equipment, because swings and slides are what they have seen. But with a little prodding, the children became creative: There had to be a dinosaur, some kind of boat, and lots of tires.

The first day of the playground build, Ashley's neighbors were out in force along with orange-shirted Team Depot members and other Washington, D.C., volunteer groups. Ashley was up at 6:00 A.M., begging her mother to let her skip school so she could help. "What can I do, what can I do?" she asked the volunteer coordinator. Ashley's mother and stepfather joined the volunteers. Neighbors brought sandwiches and opened their apartments so volunteers could use the bathrooms. By the fifth day, 500 volunteers were on site, including 100 Team Depot members. Tires were sliced, two-by-fours were sanded, cables were strung—and there emerged a 24-foot slide, an enormous swing, the dinosaur Tire-Anosaurus Rex, and the bow of the ship *Tire-Tanic*. There were swings, rappelling ropes, a tire tepee, and a stage. But for Ashley and the children of Livingston Manor, there was something more. A sense of hope.

GROWTH

Suzanne Apple understood the significance of building playgrounds in places where many lack jobs, adequate housing, and other basic necessities. "It's about kids and parents," says Apple. "There is just an enormous need with the cuts in housing and school budgets to provide safe places for children to play. We seem to have lost this in our nation and now kids are playing in empty lots and burned-out cars."

Apple encouraged, and eventually convinced, Hammond to form his own nonprofit organization to apply the expertise he had developed on a larger scale. In 1996, Hammond and his friend Dawn Hutchison founded a nonprofit organization whose mission is to "inspire individuals, organizations, and business to join together to build much needed, safe, and accessible playgrounds." They called it KaBOOM!: "Projects start as a tiny whisper, a rumor, a great idea, or a glistening of hope. From this kernel the project explodes with energy and resources. KaBOOM!"

Initially, Home Depot and KaBOOM! worked together in cities where they had mutual interests. Home Depot shared its community connections with KaBOOM!, which managed the complex partnerships among the store, local community groups, the mayor's office, and other participating national organizations. Together they completed two playgrounds in 1996. The following year, they expanded their efforts to include one playground in each of Home Depot's seven district headquarters cities.

Home Depot has provided KaBOOM! with more than money, supplies, and volunteers. "Suzanne is our mentor," says Hammond. She has linked KaBOOM! with company accountants, and Home Depot's lawyers at King and Spaulding filed incorporation papers for KaBOOM! pro bono.

Interestingly, Home Depot did not seek an exclusive relationship with KaBOOM! Home Depot introduced KaBOOM! to other corporations, including Jack Morton Productions, a marketing agency, and Novus Services, a business unit of Dean Witter, Discover & Co. As a result of these and other corporate partnerships, the nonprofit increased its capacity and helped perfect its process.

Home Depot has not asked for recognition, although Hammond and his colleagues are walking commercials for Apple and Home Depot. "Suzanne gets it," he says. "Home Depot has spoiled us and made us reevaluate every potential corporate sponsorship more closely," says Hammond. Other companies ask, "How much signage will we have? How big will our logo be?" When a rival hardware chain's public relations firm contacted KaBOOM! wanting to "write a check and own us," Hammond was naturally skeptical. "They didn't even have an employee volunteer program," he recalls. "They don't understand what we're about." A volunteer project developed on a trial basis for the company drew just ten employees, compared with the 600 Home Depot associates who helped build a playground in Chicago over a four-day period.

HOME DEPOT STRATEGY

Founded in 1978 by two executives laid off from a regional hardware chain, by 1996, Home Depot had a 13 percent market share in the $134 billion market for building supplies—more than its top four competitors combined.[5] Ranked for six years in a row by *Fortune* magazine as America's most admired specialty retailer, Home Depot expects to be operating over 1,600 stores by 2002.[6]

Home Depot's success is built around combining a warehouse-style format with the same customer service that customers expect from local hardware stores. The company's 160,000 "associates" (a.k.a. employees) are central to the success of this strategy. For this reason, they earn some of the highest wages in the retail industry and share in the company's wealth through stock ownership plans.[7]

When Home Depot moves into a new market, it conducts research with the help of national and local groups to analyze the community, its resources, and its needs. Eighty percent of employees are hired locally for a simple reason: they know what's going on in the area. "Our business is tied to the health of the community," says Apple. This strategy helps dampen the blow communities often feel when local retailers close their doors after the chain store comes to town.

Home Depot makes no secret of the connection between its giving and business strategies. Notes the Home Depot Web site: "The company's social commitments are an integral part of the way we do business. After all, the Home Depot is about people helping people and the relationships we build along the way." This tactic works because the company's philanthropic efforts and business mission are one and the same: putting a comfortable home within reach of the average person.

Although headquarters determines the focus for Home Depot's giving program—affordable housing, environment, and at-risk youth—in this most innovative of companies, store employees take the lead in developing nonprofit partnerships in their own communities, and district managers control half of the company's giving dollars. "Some of the best things we do, I don't know about until we're done," says Apple.

Home Depot's philanthropic activities are closely linked to its volunteer program. One in five company associates, approximately 30,000 people, volunteers as part of Team Depot, the Home Depot employee volunteer program honored by President Clinton with the 1995 President's Service Award and by the Points of Light Foundation with its 1998 Award for Excellence in Corporate Community Service. For the most part, decision-making authority for Team Depot projects rests with the store managers. Corporate asks them to pick three or four organizations to work with on Team Depot projects. Some wait until requests come in. Some collaborate with other stores in the same area.

One employee in each store—sometimes self-nominated, sometimes tapped by the manager—receives two hours each week "on the clock" to coordinate the program, but there is no national policy allowing volunteer work on company time—that's up to supervisors. "You're supposed to sacrifice a little," reminds Apple. Employees learn about Team Depot as part of the discussion of the company's values at orientation and quickly embrace the idea, according to Apple. The number of hours served is up to the employee, as is the choice of projects. Any employee can nominate a colleague to be recognized as a "volunteer superstar" and receive a patch for their orange apron. Each store can issue one patch per quarter. Other items—pins, pens, keychains—can also be used to reward exemplary service.

Even Home Depot's national partnerships are designed to engage district managers and store employees. The company receives more than 7,000 requests a year at the national level, and store managers get six to ten a day. Only a small percentage can be funded. But by partnering with national nonprofits through their local affiliates, the company is able to make its resources go further. It can offer organizations the full range of its assets—cash, training, product, and volunteers—while strengthening connections between its stores and employees and the community.

Home Depot's relationship with Christmas in April, a national nonprofit that renovates homes for the elderly and disabled, typifies this approach: Home Depot's corporate office has provided the umbrella organization $100,000 a year. At the local level, over sixty affiliates benefit from Team Depot volunteers and lines of credit extended by the Home Depot district managers. Christmas in April volunteers have been trained through Home Depot free clinics, sometimes scheduled purposefully around the construction schedule of the organization.

These relationships also benefit Home Depot. The nonprofit affiliate becomes a good customer; according to a company survey, providing

Christmas in April affiliates store credits worth $100,000 resulted in additional purchases of more than four times that amount.[8] Grateful nonprofits may provide excellent exposure for the company: Girl Scouts trained in home maintenance skills at Home Depot became "very loyal customers," according to one store manager. After earning their "Ms. Fix-it" badge, they "won't let their parents shop the competition."[9] And occasionally the company spots talent among community volunteers on Home Depot–sponsored projects, resulting in new hires of committed, connected community members. Three hardworking volunteers at the Anacostia KaBOOM! playground build were recruited to become Home Depot associates.

Perhaps the most important benefit to Home Depot, however, is the sense of teamwork and loyalty that employees develop by serving together. "It brings everybody together . . . the division president with the hourly associate," says Apple. "We never felt forced to help out," says Mike Messina, the store manager of a San Antonio Home Depot, whose store has built three playgrounds with KaBOOM! "We wanted to because we knew we had certain skills that the community needed. The funny thing is, not only did we build a relationship with the people in the neighborhood, but we built a stronger community among those of us who work together every day here in the store."[10]

Corporate Volunteering

Corporate volunteer programs, involving organized service projects, or other efforts to encourage employees to contribute their time and skills to the community, received national attention through the President's Summit for America's Future in April 1997, which brought together all of the living Presidents and an array of celebrities, state and local leaders, national nonprofits, and corporations to rally the country in support of youth. According to Bob Goodwin, president of the Points of Light Foundation and a summit organizer, interest in corporate volunteering is growing. While "on the one hand, many of today's young business tycoons aren't interested, on the other hand, more and more companies are showing up in the civic participation area." Four out of five companies say they sponsor a volunteer program. The number of Corporate Volunteer Councils affiliated with the Points of Light Foundation increased

70 percent from 1992 to 1998, according to Goodwin. Volunteer programs are surviving restructuring and downsizing, as leaner companies find the need to create more committed employees and to counteract the damage to morale that usually accompanies layoffs. Research confirms that volunteer programs can improve employee morale and other factors affecting profitability.

Cash-strapped nonprofits that place fundraising high above volunteerism on their list of priorities are short-sighted. Savvy nonprofit organizations have long been finding ways to engage business volunteers. Providing volunteer opportunities is an excellent way to introduce a company to a community organization it would not otherwise get to know, which can lead to other forms of support as employees become more and more committed. Similarly, more and more companies like Home Depot are linking their philanthropic giving to the causes that engage their employees.[11]

The form of corporate support for employee volunteering varies widely.[12] Most commonly, businesses use rewards or recognition to encourage volunteer service.[13] To help employees find ways to volunteer and to offer nonprofit organizations the chance to recruit, a company may publicize service opportunities or make actual referrals, sometimes in partnership with a volunteer center in the community—the second most common form of support.[14] Encouraging executives to serve on nonprofit boards is also common, as are company-sponsored projects, which often offer at a far lower cost the types of benefits promised by for-profit vendors of team-building and skill-building workshops.[15]

Corporate volunteer projects designed to allow employees to take along spouses and children are increasingly popular, and a way for companies to demonstrate support for both community activities and family life. For example, Target's "Family Matters" program was established in conjunction with the Points of Light Foundation to help employees volunteer alongside family members. More than 90 percent of the "Good Neighbor Captains" involved believed the program improved the chain store's image, and nearly as many believed that employee morale improved.[16] Most corporate volunteer programs are relatively low cost—four out of five companies sponsoring volunteer programs report that they spend less than $50,000 annually on their programs, and more than half report that they spend less than $10,000. Four out of five employ just one person to manage their programs, and a third use a committee or task force with no paid staff.[17]

Costs can go up when companies offer paid leave or contributions tied to service. Employers may match employee volunteer efforts with paid donations, as BankBoston does. Companies may give a limited amount of paid leave to employees; for example, Fannie Mae provides ten hours of paid leave a month for volunteer activities.[18] Timberland grants employees forty hours of paid leave annually for community service and demonstrates its commitment in other ways, including incorporating service projects into company sales meetings and celebrating its twenty-fifth anniversary by closing its headquarters for a company-wide global day of service. According to the Boston College Center for Corporate Community Relations, as many as one in four corporations gives time off to employees to volunteer.[19]

Sabbaticals enabling employees to volunteer full-time with a nonprofit organization are used as a means of enhancing the employee's skills and building community goodwill. For example, United Parcel Service's Community Internship Program places senior managers for up to a month with nonprofit agencies to expose them to the critical factors impacting the American workforce, including illiteracy and drug dependency.[20] Citizens Bank in Rhode Island gives two employees per quarter a three-month sabbatical to work with nonprofit organizations, requiring only that they make a written report to the company and an oral presentation to the board of directors about what they have learned during the experience.

A study by the Corporate Citizenship Company in London found that volunteer placements tied to individual training needs can enhance almost any skill, but particularly communication, teamwork, and creative thinking.[21] The U.S. Conference Board survey confirms that executives believe volunteer participation builds skills and changes attitudes, including respect for diversity, willingness to take risks, and appreciation for benefits provided by employers.[22]

Companies entering into significant partnerships with nonprofit organizations find a myriad of ways to engage employee volunteers. Otis Elevator helps unite its work force around the world through Team Otis, organized in 1994 to support the Special Olympics. Twenty Otis executives serve on the Special Olympics boards of directors for their home countries. Activities around the world range from employees in Russia working a day for free and donating their wages to Moscow Special Olympics, to assisting schools for the mentally disabled in India. When the World Winter Games were held in Toronto in 1997, more than 100 employees from eight countries were on hand to assist the athletes and participate in the "Otis Hosts the World" farewell reception for the athletes and coaches. Although the company requires that activities take place after working hours, it has found that employees are eager to be involved. The company features Team Otis activities in its newsletter, but otherwise seeks no press for its efforts.[23]

The type of support for employee volunteering determines the ways in which a company can benefit. Supporting the employee's choice of volunteer activities through matching programs or paid leave can build loyalty, but not necessarily teamwork or visibility. Long-term placements related to an employee's job can offer professional development opportunities, but may not yield other benefits. Offering a bulletin board or referral system may please community nonprofit organizations seeking volunteers, as well as employees who are affiliated with these groups, but won't do much to improve the company's image with the general public. Short-term, high visibility projects that engage large numbers of employees are a good way to build a sense of community among staff and showcase the company to the community, but these projects take a lot of planning and organization.

Other benefits are possible. To build good relations between employees before a merger, Chase Manhattan Corporation invited Chemical Bank employees to join in their Global Day of Service.[24] When Bank-Boston developed an innovative transition assistance program after a merger, it offered employees the option of working at a nonprofit organization for six months, half time for $10 an hour, paid for by the bank.

Along with the benefits, however, are possible pitfalls. Employees might become so enthused by their service activities that their regular work suffers. A poor performing worker might be a great volunteer, and supervisors may feel that disciplining the employee would send the wrong message. A badly organized project or program may disillusion employees, or a poorly attended project might yield bad publicity.

Planning is the key to reaping the benefits and avoiding the pitfalls of employee volunteering. Experts suggest the first step should be for the company to determine its reasons for establishing the program, taking into consideration its philanthropic, marketing, and human resource needs. Only then should it begin implementation: conducting an audit of the company's existing relationships, forming an employee advisory committee, ensuring senior-level support and recognition for volunteering, involving senior managers on nonprofit boards of trustees, and developing processes for ongoing assessment and reporting.[25] The company should think about its willingness to invest resources in the project and make sure the expectations equal the scale of the investment. Finally, in order to put the importance of volunteering in perspective, the employer should review its other policies, such as family leave, rewards for exemplary workers, and criteria for performance reviews.

The Special Olympics and KaBOOM! have been successful in developing business partnerships, in part, because of their highly developed ability to engage volunteers effectively. Although each has paid staff, both depend on volunteers to achieve their missions. Not every nonprofit embraces volunteers in this way. In most cases, the management of volunteers requires staff to screen, train, and supervise them. Good managers also motivate volunteers, connect them to the cause and to one another in meaningful ways, and recognize them for their efforts. In addition to staff time, volunteers can impose other costs on the nonprofit organization, including background checks for adults who will be working directly with children, liability premiums in the event a volunteer is injured or injures another, or office space and equipment for the volunteer, depending on the type of service involved.

Many nonprofits have found the benefits to more than outweigh the costs. But fear that involving volunteers will undercut the professional identity of regular employees and bring unqualified individuals into contact with clients discourages many nonprofits from engaging volunteers in service that makes a real contribution to addressing community problems. Studies of volunteers show that they are as likely to be placed in administrative tasks or fundraising activities as they are to be placed in service that directly benefits a client,[26] despite the fact that volunteers gain greater satisfaction from service that exposes them to the people they are helping. Good volunteer management can help volunteers play a useful role in addressing almost any community problem. A corporate partner can help make sure that volunteers are screened, qualified, trained, and available on a regular basis—provided the fit is right.

Even when the nonprofit has come to the conclusion that there is no appropriate role for volunteers in its regular program, it may be able to mobilize volunteers for special events that expose them to the beneficiaries of their service: a party for the social service agency's clients, a project to renovate a facility, or a joint service project where the clients of the agency serve alongside corporate volunteers at another community site. In the end, the satisfaction of completing a project and knowing that it will make a difference in the lives of others will keep volunteers coming back, and motivate them to offer other kinds of support. As Suzanne Apple puts it, the best part of Home Depot's relationship with KaBOOM! is just that: "We get to build a playground."

What Works

HOME DEPOT: A CULTURE OF INVOLVEMENT

Culture has a significant impact on a company's ability to implement an effective volunteer program. When employees are expected to work long hours, sacrifice their home lives, or lurch from crisis to crisis, it will be hard to convince them that volunteering is a priority. If senior managers neither volunteer themselves nor reward those who do, an employee interested in advancement will likely conclude that volunteering is not part of the equation for success.

Businesses can create a culture that supports community involvement in many ways. Volunteering can be made part of performance reviews, with volunteer activities a factor in promotions and bonuses. Exemplary service can also be rewarded in the same manner as the company recognizes other excellent employees—through a plaque in the foyer, announcements at staff meetings, or by tangible rewards, such as use of the company's box at a local stadium. The importance of volunteering to the company can be communicated by highlighting a service project at each shareholders' meeting or in the company's annual report.

The company can take every opportunity to inform employees about available opportunities—through an office intranet, newsletter, posters, regularly updated phone hot line, or staff meetings. Sponsoring projects on site—a vegetable garden dedicated to a local homeless shelter, a room set aside for tutoring, or a day a month for local students to shadow employees—helps raise the visibility of volunteer efforts. Information on volunteering can be included in employee orientations and information packages on retirement. Benefits like release time or paid time off for service speak loudly about the company's commitment, as does incorporating service projects into conferences and retreats. Finally, tying corporate contributors to volunteer service helps underscore the broader message of the importance of community involvement.

Home Depot has learned these lessons. According to the Points of Light Foundation's Bob Goodwin, the biggest reason for Home Depot's success "is the expectation created within the executive suite that translates into a culture of involvement." Team Depot is a single facet of Home Depot's commitment to community, rather than its main manifestation. Bernard Marcus and Arthur Blank, company founders, grew up children at risk. According to Apple, "If someone hadn't taken an interest in them" they might not have been so successful. As a result, they have "always embodied a sense of community." Their philosophy is Home Depot's philosophy: "Take care of your people and they will take care of your customers." Apple believes the community is a natural extension of that culture. "We have made community service part of our business. It is the store manager's responsibility and the district manager's responsibility. It is part of our values." As a result, shareholders have never questioned the $12.5 million in donations or the employee time dedicated to community relations.

While the service program was being established, Apple reported directly to CEO Blank, which helped ensure the rest of the company understood its importance. Apple's move to the operations division did not affect the importance of her role or the company's support for community involvement. Blank continues to visit playground sites and meet with employees and residents to underscore the project's importance to Home Depot. Senior executives serve alongside new associates. KaBOOM! is featured in the company's social responsibility report, its annual report, and on its Web site, as are other community partners. In 1998, Home Depot began to promote its relationships with community organizations, including KaBOOM!, in its advertising. All of these efforts help to reinforce for employees and others that the company values community service.

THE RIGHT PROJECTS, THE RIGHT PARTNERS

Not every nonprofit uses volunteers equally well, and not every good project makes sense for every company. Finding the right fit between the company and volunteer opportunities is essential. Beyond identifying the right causes (discussed in chapter 10), a company must find an organization that is able to organize meaningful volunteer opportunities that fit the skills and schedules of employees. Companies should survey employees about their interests and availability for volunteering, organizations they are already involved with, and any barriers to volunteering that they believe to exist. Company-sponsored service projects should not supplant employees' existing commitments to community service, nor should companies attempt to steer employees to organizations they don't support. A good project matches the company's needs and employees' interests and skills with opportunities that are well organized and enable employees to see the impact of their efforts.

Suzanne Apple of Home Depot believes choosing the right partners is "a little bit personality, a lot of philosophy." KaBOOM! and Home Depot share the belief "that you have to build community from within." There are no standard criteria beyond the company's three focus areas (affordable housing, environment, and at-risk youth). "We try hard not to take a cookie cutter approach," says Apple. "We do research to understand what the priorities are in the communities." Home Depot does look for strong local organizations and checks out its prospective partners by reviewing their annual reports and financial statements, conducting site visits, and talking to other funders and partners.

Companies must also be realistic regarding employee availability. A mentoring program requiring regular weekly activities is a poor choice for companies whose employees travel frequently. Saturday construction projects may be difficult for employees with young children.

The structure of volunteer projects must be related to the company's goals. If employee retention is the only goal, an employer will want to give maximum deference to the employee's own interest, for example, by offering time off for volunteering and posting service opportunities that will help the employee find a match. On the other hand, projects intended to foster teamwork and better community relations suggest a different structure. Such projects must be able to be executed in a short period of intensive service. They should allow teams of employees to serve together, side-by-side. The number of companies involved should be limited—having too many partners dilutes the team-building experience. Projects should involve community members who will benefit from the project. Results should be tangible. And while public relations should never be the primary goal, high-impact projects often lend themselves to local coverage.

KaBOOM! playgrounds meet these criteria. "You've got one day to change their lives," is Hammond's philosophy. KaBOOM! uses Home Depot's resources uniquely well. Home Depot donates tools and supplies, and its employees are skilled at building, which helps to engage the energy and enthusiasm found among other community volunteers effectively. Projects can be scheduled during a store's slower periods. KaBOOM! ensures that community members play a major role in every project, that the playground is maintained, and that corporate volunteers can meet the people they are helping. And at the end of the day, employees are able to see the results of their labor: a safe and enjoyable place for children to play.

KaBOOM!: Quality Projects

While a well-planned volunteer project can offer many benefits, a poorly planned, poorly executed effort can alienate employees and community members alike. Volunteers want to believe that their service makes a difference. If they spend long periods standing around while organizers figure out what they can do, or if they are asked to do tasks that appear to be busy work, they are unlikely to return. If volunteers are not given a good orientation to the cause and how the organization advances it, their motivation will suffer. And if they aren't using their skills to maximum advantage, or aren't trained to do what needs to be done, they can easily be frustrated and disillusioned.

To assure this doesn't happen, KaBOOM! developed a step-by-step process, written down in a three-inch notebook, to minimize mishaps. The big things are easy to remember; it's the small things that can ruin a day's build. What happens if it rains? Who will provide cold drinks and refreshments? Where can volunteers use a bathroom? Are enough tools on hand so volunteers aren't standing around waiting to use them? What about first aid? Can volunteers offer child care so parents can help? The KaBOOM! manual, designed for community organizers, includes an evaluation form so it can be improved. It is so comprehensive that for-profit playground companies have plagiarized it repeatedly.

Home Depot could organize its own playground build, but the use of a skilled intermediary like KaBOOM! makes it easier. The nonprofit's expertise minimizes the time that store personnel need to put into planning and ensures that the project runs smoothly. Not every KaBOOM! undertaking has been flawless. But the organization is able to incorporate what it learned on a build in New Jersey into a build in Texas. Because the nonprofit's philosophy is to create connections, not to come between the company and the community, Home Depot realizes all the benefits of the playground builds without all of the headaches.

Regardless of the organizational skill of the nonprofit partner, however, a project must be designed in close partnership with the company, to ensure that it responds to the company's unique needs, culture, and internal systems. Hammond understood early on the importance of getting Home Depot's store and district managers involved, given the company's decentralized community affairs system. "The easiest thing for us would be to make a national contribution, but it is more effective to involve local people," says Apple. Carolyn Smillie, manager of community relations, works out sites and budgets with Hammond and his staff. Then the KaBOOM! field coordinator takes over, working directly with Home Depot's divisional coordinators. There may be three or four decisionmakers involved in a project, depending on the number of partners. With so many people and organizations involved in a playground build, expectations have to be very clear from the start. Roles and responsibilities must be defined and honored. There's give and take. And good communication is essential.

In the case of KaBOOM!, the biggest challenge has been the organization's need to grow quickly without time to invest in organizational development. According to Apple, "Darell has had to slow down. I told him he has to stop chasing the dream long enough to build it." The result has been better planning and a stronger partner for Home Depot.

Home Depot and KaBOOM!: The Impact

When asked to explain the impact of building playgrounds in low-income communities, KaBOOM! cites several factors. Providing well-built, safe playgrounds is one. The need for healthy recreational opportunities for children is another. Perhaps most important, however, is the strengthening of community ties that occurs when a neighborhood comes together to build a playground. That's how the KaBOOM! process, although sometimes cumbersome, delivers perhaps its greatest value.

More than two years after construction, Ashley's playground was free of litter and graffiti. Even on a rainy January day, children—including Ashley and her cousins—could be found playing on the site. In the summer, according to Ashley's stepfather, hundreds of children are at play: "You can't get in here," he says. When a group of drug dealers started hanging around the playground, Ashley's mother and her friends got them to leave. Jubilee Enterprise put in lights to make the playground safer after dark.

On the one-year anniversary of the playground, the Home Depot volunteers joined residents to celebrate and to perform routine maintenance on the structures. A year after that, the community asked for some changes—the tires used to form the bow of the ship were too reminiscent of the piles of old tires that are a blight on the neighborhood. Volunteers tried painting them bright colors, but the residents thought wood would look better. The residents put in the labor to make the change, with help from Home Depot.

In addition to dollars, supplies, and human resources, Home Depot has provided KaBOOM! with savvy business advice, national publicity, and referrals to other potential supporters. Home Depot's support—both financial and moral—emboldened KaBOOM! to launch an ambitious initiative in 1997 to build 1,000 playgrounds in three years. With a three-year commitment of $1 million from Home Depot, and a three-year commitment of $2 million cash and $2 million in-kind commitment from CNA, a leading U.S. insurance company, KaBOOM! is planning to open regional field offices and more than double its staff to fulfill this goal. It is working to make projects more sustainable—to create a national network of KaBOOM! playgrounds, raise money for maintenance fund grants that can be awarded to communities, and leave in place strong local connections that continue long after the last swing is hung.

KaBOOM! and Home Depot built twenty playgrounds together between 1996 and 1998. As for Home Depot, as it rapidly expands, opening stores in new markets, it continues to make KaBOOM! part of its strategy because of the instant connection to the community and camaraderie that develops on a playground build.

Both partners envision further growth in the relationship and expect it to continue well beyond the three-year plan. "It's the quintessential partnership," Hammond boasts.

4
❧

STRATEGIC PHILANTHROPY
Microsoft and the American Library Association

In 1995, Microsoft and the American Library Association (ALA) entered into the Libraries Online partnership. The leading computer software manufacturer donated equipment and technical expertise and supported the development of training materials for the introduction of computers into public libraries in nine low-income communities. After four years, the infusion of a total of $400 million by the company and its CEO, and additional contributions from local governments, the project expanded to over 1,000 libraries.

The partnership was an example of strategic philanthropy (planned giving intended to benefit both cause and company). It was consistent with Microsoft's objectives because giving low-income Americans access to computers would provide the company with favorable publicity and advance its founder's vision of universal access to information technology. For ALA, the partnership would expand the ability of libraries to provide knowledge to people of all ages and backgrounds, and establish ALA as a player in the world of public access computing.

Although the partners had compatible objectives, their cultural differences made for a stressful and comparatively short relationship. Nevertheless, the partnership was successful at achieving its goals.

Microsoft and the American Library Association

Next to the bowling alley, in the strip mall with the Village Thrift Store, Minnesota Fabrics, and Parts, USA, the Essex branch of the Baltimore County Public Library is trying to hold the community together. Essex is the library branch with the lowest circulation in the system—people visit the library but they don't borrow books. "They're afraid to check them out. They move around so much. They're worried about fines," according to Baltimore County Public Library Assistant Director Lynn Wheeler. Twenty-five years ago, Essex was a prosperous, blue-collar community with a stable middle-class population living just outside the Baltimore beltway. Today, with the steel industry gone and urban sprawl, "people are sad about the community," says Wheeler. Crime is high. Families are poorer. Children change schools here more than anywhere else in the district, as their families move from one subsidized housing complex to the next.

In 1995, this library branch was slated for a $300,000 budget cut, despite its participation in a county-initiated partnership to build up the disintegrating community. Then Wheeler got a call one afternoon from the American Library Association. "Did we want to be part of a partnership with Microsoft? Absolutely—Microsoft has such charisma," notes Wheeler. The staff put their application together overnight to meet Microsoft's 9:00 A.M. deadline the next day. They heard by the end of the week that Baltimore County had been selected to be one of nine pilot sites for Libraries Online.

Six months later, Essex opened the first Family Learning Center in the county with seven state-of-the-art Gateway computers, software, Internet access, and networking—a package worth $50,000. The ribbon cutting drew 250 community members. Without a word, the county restored funds cut from the library's budget, with an additional $30,000 thrown in.

Today, the computers are in constant use eighty hours a week. "People literally run to get their names on the list," says E. J. Woznicki, Jr., library manager. "We tried to close the center for maintenance and we almost had a riot," he adds.

On a typical afternoon, the computers are in use by a thirty-something man doing a job search; a 13-year-old boy with backpack at his feet, reviewing the "Television City" Web site; two second-grade boys, regulars here, sharing a terminal playing the "Magic School Bus" game; a fortyish white woman in jeans buying country albums off the Internet; a long-haired teenage girl typing furiously in the Victorian Rose and Garden Society chat room; and a middle-aged African-American woman signing up for a computer dating service. Some might consider these purposes recreational—hardly the stuff that will hold a fractured community together. But behind the seeming triviality of their activities are two children learning science through a computer game; a young man finding information on a favorite TV show but who can also use the Internet to research a term paper; an adult who can find a job listing and update and print a resume; and women who use technology to connect with like-minded peers.

The Essex Library staff is full of stories. A student with behavior problems who started using the computers to join chat rooms has designed and developed his own Web page. A man who taught himself Excel spreadsheet software at the library hasn't been back in two months—staff thinks he found a job that uses his new skill. For researchers, there is information on the Internet that's not in the 100,000 books at the Essex Library: for a homework assignment about funeral customs of the Amish, an article by a funeral director in Lancaster, Pennsylvania; for a woman with a rare lung disease, information describing treatment and prognosis; for a frantic mom, the lyrics to "Here Comes Peter Cottontail." And for anyone searching for resources in the community, there's the Essex Library home page, with listings of 2,500 local agencies, which can be sorted by topics from housekeeping to health care.

This kind of information access seems routine to people with voice mail on their phones, computers on their desks, and fax machines in their offices. But for technology "have nots," home access to the resources available free of charge at Essex Library could equal a year's income for a family living at the poverty line. Microsoft's Libraries Online, created in partnership with the American Library Association, helps to close the technology gap between rich and poor in low-income urban and rural communities where as many as one in five homes may not have a telephone, let alone a computer.[1]

The Essex Library team views its partnership with Microsoft as an unequivocal win. "It's a direction we knew we wanted to go in a vague way," says Wheeler, "but we had no resources." The second round of Microsoft Libraries Online grants enabled four more Baltimore County libraries to open computer centers, along with two satellites: one in a Police Athletic Center that offers a homework club and a second in a support center for teen parents getting their GEDs. Essex Library staff have enjoyed advising staff at the new centers. "We're not anything great," says Woznicki, modestly. "Other branches are busier. But Microsoft put our branch on the map."

THE NEED

Microsoft spent almost a year engaged in strategic planning to move its corporate giving from "random acts of kindness" to a focused program. The basis for Microsoft's earlier giving was one of the most generous employee contribution matching programs in the country—the company matches up to $12,000 per employee per year. "Some of our employees are wealthy," says Chris Hedrick, the former Microsoft manager of Libraries Online. "And they tend to give a lot"—more than $20 million in cash and software in 1997. Other giving by the corporation had been almost exclusively focused on the Seattle area, home of Microsoft. Company officials were feeling the pressure of a public that was beguiled by the new technology but afraid of it, fascinated by the wealth of the company and its founder, but deeply critical of their lack of a major charitable endeavor. Moreover, the company was facing a landmark antitrust lawsuit, and its tactics were characterized in the press as "cutthroat" and "monopolistic."

But what should be its focus? The company hired one of the country's leading experts in strategic giving, Craig Smith, and convened staff from several departments—corporate contributions, government affairs, public relations—to participate in the planning process. Microsoft Public Relations Director Greg Shaw had worked for a chemical company that created a recycling system for the National Park Service, an effort that had transformed waste management in remote areas. Shaw sought a similarly dramatic program for Microsoft. He asked the group, "What's something that Microsoft could do that has significance and that would apply the best of this company to a societal issue?"

Bill Gates (founder of Microsoft) offered the answer: A personal computer on every desktop and in every home—Information At Your Fingertips, referred to at Microsoft as "IAYF." In the mid-1990s, only 15 percent of American households with incomes in the lowest quartile had computers, compared to 68 percent of households in the top quartile.[2] Giving the public, particularly low-income Americans, access to computers and the Internet would advance the broader mission of the company and would be the logical focus of a philanthropic effort.

How and where, however, were not as obvious. Schools, youth organizations, public housing, and homeless shelters all serve disadvantaged communities. Most lack the resources to move into the age of technology. To focus the planning, the team reached out to product groups, district offices, employees who volunteer, consultants, former grant recipients, as well as potential nonprofit partners. "What value could you add to this? What requests are you getting?" they asked.

Schools, a focus of Microsoft's marketing plans, were one natural venue. Schools themselves are a large market and offer an easy way to introduce students and their families to products. Apple's dominance of the school market, supported by an aggressive philanthropic program, had kept the struggling company alive, and many other hardware and software businesses—including IBM, Oracle, and Sun Microsystems—were targeting their philanthropic efforts at elementary and secondary education. To make schools its major focus would not distinguish Microsoft from other high tech companies and would therefore not meet the company's goals for its new giving program. Nor would schools, which serve children not adults, provide universal access.

But there was a second public institution that was almost as ubiquitous as the schools, open to everyone, young or old, and wide open when it came to technology: public libraries. Public relations professionals involved in the project appreciated the obvious analogy between Bill Gates and the great philanthropist Andrew Carnegie, who gave away more than $350 million in his lifetime and used much of his great fortune to build more than 2,500 public libraries.[3] With nearly 9,000 public library systems and almost 16,000 buildings, the United States has more libraries than McDonald's restaurants. In every state and in rural, urban, and suburban areas, a public library is within an hour's drive of most Americans. Open on weekends, weekdays, and evenings and free to people of all ages, races, incomes, and education levels, libraries are unique public institutions.

Created to help people of all walks of life find information, public libraries ought to have been drawn to the Internet. But in the mid-1990s, that was not the case. Although 20 percent of libraries were connected to the Internet, few offered this service to patrons. Libraries used computers for administrative purposes or for the card catalog, but for the most part, were not technologically sophisticated. Out of favor with municipal governments, library budgets were uncertain, declining. When new funds became available, "librarians are trained to buy books so that's what they want to use money for," says Microsoft Director of Community Affairs Barbara Dingfield.

When the planning team briefed Bill Gates in the spring of 1995, he readily agreed to the choice of libraries as the delivery system. He had spent many happy hours in the local public library as a child and saw how public libraries could help realize his vision. He asked his father, William Gates, Jr., to keep apprised of the planning of Microsoft's philanthropic program.

THE MATCH

Having little familiarity with the world of public libraries, Microsoft needed a partner to approach the library community to ensure that the donation would be well received. The planning team had found the American Library Association to be one of the most useful sources of information about libraries. Through its Public Library Association, ALA had an extensive network reaching virtually every public library system in the country. No other nonprofit in the field had as great a reach as ALA, which counted among its members 57,000 librarians and library staff from all types of libraries—public, school, academic, and those serving special populations. And ALA had one additional asset lacked by its competitors: a well-staffed public affairs office.

ALA was receptive to Microsoft. Importantly, ALA shared Microsoft's vision of positioning libraries as a place for everyone to obtain knowledge. "It was clear to everybody that libraries need computers," according to George Needham, the former executive director of the Public Library Association. In fact, that year ALA had set a goal of seeing all libraries "wired" by the year 2000 and had begun planning a technology project of its own. "We had the big idea," recalls Patricia Martin, ALA's former vice president for development and sponsorship. "We were going to do test beds around the country to see how local libraries could become the delivery system for technology." Martin's idea was to knit together partnerships including a hardware company, software manufacturer, and telecommunications corporation to create the system. However, Microsoft offered the whole package, along with a plan for how the program would work.

Despite the generosity of the gift, some association members were suspicious of Microsoft's motives, expecting that the company was using the program simply "to get a toehold in the market," according to Needham. Microsoft officials, from the corporate giving staff to senior management, consistently stressed that their goals were philanthropic, that the company did not intend to use the program for market development. Martin felt that the proposed program would have natural marketing advantages for Microsoft because it would provide potential customers the opportunity to sample software and become comfortable with the Windows operating system. But she did not see potential benefits for the company as a problem, as long as the program helped libraries and did not compromise ALA's integrity.

To preserve ALA's professionalism and reputation, the organization felt strongly that it could not appear to be endorsing a product that it had not evaluated. To respond to this concern, and further underscore its philanthropic intentions, Microsoft agreed to allow libraries participating in the program to choose their own Web browsers and to provide a budget to purchase software from other companies, although the Windows operating system would be used in all donated computers.

THE TEST

The partners set about developing a program to achieve the goal that they shared. But strains in the relationship quickly arose over who would control the design. ALA looked at Microsoft as a typical corporate donor that would provide the financial backing and step aside, leaving the program design to them. "They make the contribution, attend the opening, get their name on a bronze plaque, and never talk to you again," explains Needham. In contrast, in order to learn from the process and ensure it met the company's high standards, Microsoft intended to be involved with its development.

Eventually ALA agreed to work with Microsoft on the project. But the company's approach made the nonprofit uncomfortable. ALA staff found Microsoft's way of operating—gathering information, huddling among themselves, and then unveiling their proposal—not conducive to teamwork and joint planning. Nor was Microsoft forthcoming about its own needs, according to Martin, who believed the company hoped to use the program "to evolve a more benevolent company identity."

The ALA team became uncomfortable with what they understood to be their lack of control over program materials, which would be issued under their name. The association had run into the issue before with a fast food company planning a literacy program. In the thick of negotiations, it had become clear that the company intended to develop the content of the reading material that would feature the logo of the ALA. "The day you let me do the hamburger recipe is the day I let you prepare the reading material," one of ALA's negotiators, a Ph.D. in reading, told the company. As it had in this case, ALA considered walking away during negotiations with Microsoft, despite the importance of the program.

Despite these challenges, "it wasn't 'getting to yes' that was the hard part," according to George Needham. Even after the deal had been sealed, cultural differences presented major problems. Microsoft was unhappy with the pace of ALA's work on the project. Microsoft employees worked evenings, weekends, all the time. In contrast, "librarians have a lot of interests," explains Needham. "They have personal lives. If Bill Gates wanted you to have a personal life, he would issue one to you," he jokes. In contrast, ALA staff, in keeping with the culture of the government-run public library system, worked regular business hours and were accustomed to planning based on its budget cycle. As a result of these differences in work styles, "we were impatient," explains Barbara Dingfield. "We didn't have enough respect that nonprofits work with constituencies, use consensus decision-making, and take more time." ALA staff tried to adapt to Microsoft's fast pace—"nanoseconds versus geologic time," says Needham. "They helped us see some of the vulnerability of our bureaucracy.... You can't wait six months between board meetings to say yes to someone with a check."

Microsoft "came with so much money for R&D and travel—the library staff was shocked," according to Needham. Librarians are conservative, he notes. "We've never had more than we need, and we squeeze every nickel until the eagle screams." Consistent with its intention to think big, Microsoft wanted to start with 500 libraries. ALA pushed for far fewer. The result was a compromise—a pilot program that would allow for a quick roll-out while a larger program was developed. It would give Microsoft something to point to and give the team time to work out any problems before going full scale.

The team defined goals for the program carefully. The program would expand public access to computers in low-income neighborhoods and build capacity in libraries to provide those services over the long run. The team would handpick the initial pilot sites. Microsoft sought libraries serving low-income communities, including some in major media markets, places where it had a major staff presence (Seattle and North Carolina), Washington, D.C., and rural communities. ALA sought libraries that were entrepreneurial, forward looking, and that would provide a fertile ground for the program, hoping to avoid those with an inflexible board or management, or without the money to sustain the program.

Nine libraries were selected as pilot sites in the following areas: Brooklyn, New York; Seattle; Charlotte, North Carolina; Jackson, Mississippi; Los Angeles; Pend Oreille, Washington (serving the Kalispell Indian Reservation); Pierre, South Dakota; Tucson-Pima, Arizona; and Baltimore County. Microsoft supplied specially designed Gateway hardware and Microsoft software for business, reference, and children's use. No library would be required to promote Microsoft or its products, other than posting a small Libraries Online poster to signify participation in the program. ALA would create an advisory committee from the library field, and convene the grantees at its annual conference, creating an opportunity for them to share their experiences. It would promote the program through its publications and Web site, and organize press conferences at the opening of each site. The team took a lesson from Andrew Carnegie, whom they discovered had required communities receiving buildings and books to buy the land and pay for staff. To ensure that there was this type of local "buy-in," the project required grantees to pay for telecommunications, furniture, and staff support.

Neither of the partners was in a position to provide the technical knowledge necessary to implement the program. Microsoft had hoped that its employees would become involved in the program as volunteers, but it was "not anyone's job" to provide technical support to the project, according to Chris Hedrick, and it would be a drain on Microsoft resources to take on that responsibility. Implementing public access computing was different from working with business or individual users. Computers would need to be configured to accommodate many users at different skill levels. There would be security issues. Every library would have slightly different needs, and that would require customization. In addition, library staff would need training to be able to assist patrons. These factors had likely kept the computer industry from viewing public libraries as a profitable market. But they would nonetheless need to be addressed for Libraries Online to succeed.

"We needed that expertise and someone who wouldn't be perceived as pushing the company's interest," says Hedrick. That someone turned out to be close at hand. Willem Scholten had set up a technology resource center at the Seattle Public Library and had helped Dingfield and Hedrick think through their philanthropic project. "Willem was part of blind good luck," says Dingfield. He proved to be an invaluable member of the team, providing ad hoc advice first to project staff and later to grantees. "Because of his knowledge and willingness to work long and hard, he became a major resource," according to Dingfield. With backing from Microsoft, Scholten ultimately set up a nonprofit organization, the Technology Resource Institute, that could serve the library project.

With all the parts in place, ALA and Microsoft were ready to launch the Libraries Online program publicly.

Strategic Philanthropy

Libraries Online helped Microsoft be named the most philanthropic corporation in America in 1995, a distinction that prompted online magazine *Salon* (a competitor to Microsoft's own online magazine *Slate*) to question Microsoft's real motives.[4] "Now free software is a grand thing. I wouldn't mind having some free Microsoft software myself, maybe that cool new version of Word with the fully customizable Toolbar," the author noted. "But free software—even $62.1 million of it—ain't philanthropy, not if the word is to have any meaning."[5]

Comparing Microsoft founder Bill Gates unflatteringly to Andrew Carnegie, who also had targeted libraries as the beneficiary of his major philanthropic endeavor, *Salon* took on the Libraries Online program. Eighty-five percent of Microsoft's donation was in the form of free software, which costs Microsoft a fraction of what it charges retail customers. And not only that, the software was directed to libraries, educators, and others in ways that provide Microsoft a strategic advantage, according to *Salon,* by opening new markets, increasing market share, developing future customers, and widening "Windows' lead as the dominant operating system."[6]

It's not surprising that a company known as a master innovator and fearsome competitor should be on the cutting edge of *strategic philanthropy*—planned giving intended to benefit both the cause and the company. And it's also not surprising that critics question the practice—Microsoft's success has caused everyone from journalists to the Justice Department to scour its marketing practices for improprieties. As they had earlier in negotiations with ALA, Microsoft people involved with Libraries Online contend their motives were philanthropic. "We're giving to the most disadvantaged people—if we were looking for a competitive advantage, we'd be in the suburbs," notes Chris Hedrick. "Libraries are an inconsequential market." But Hedrick agrees that Microsoft's support of the library program is a good example of strategic philanthropy.

Ironically, during the time that Andrew Carnegie was building up his company, it would have been illegal for U.S. Steel to make charitable gifts from company profits *unless* the donations would benefit the company.[7] It was widely believed that the sole responsibility of a company was to its shareholders—philanthropy was the province of wealthy individuals, not corporations. Consistent with this policy, the lasting monuments and institutions built with the fortunes amassed by turn-of-the century Captains of Industry (or Robber Barons) were funded by the men who built the railroads, banks, and the steel industry, but not their companies. Although these donations in many ways defined the field of philanthropy (the Ford, Rockefeller, and Carnegie Foundations were created by these men), they too were not free from reproach: "He had no ears for any charity unless labeled with his name," noted one critic of Andrew Carnegie. (Carnegie sent out architectural plans along with each library grant and did not object to having his name carved on the building.)[8]

World War I brought new pressures for charitable giving on the part of business. To support the war effort, companies issued dividends to shareholders that they were to pass on to the Red Cross. Still, in 1919 Congress refused to reverse the law and allow corporations to give without regard to their own interests.[9] It was not until 1953 that the law finally changed, giving corporations freedom to broaden their charitable efforts.[10]

The late 1960s brought pressure for greater corporate social responsibility. Many companies increased their philanthropic efforts and established foundations. Most contributions were spread broadly to community groups, and companies rarely sought recognition for their gifts. Gifts that related to the company's line of business were more the exception than the rule: a pharmaceutical company might give to the ballet; a clothing manufacturer to a hospital.[11]

And then came the 1980s. After a decade of declining productivity and stagflation, the economy did improve. But other forces put pressure on companies to watch their bottom lines. The fear of leveraged buyouts, new technology, and new foreign competition—as well as opportunities in foreign markets—appeared. Corporations downsized, and more and more shareholders called on companies to justify their philanthropic efforts in a business context. At the same time, demand for donations began to grow exponentially, as nonprofits reacted to deep cuts in the federal government's domestic spending.[12]

Business responded. Giving became more focused and specialized in ways that were related to the goals and interests of the company. The field of corporate giving, which had been the responsibility of whichever senior manager showed an interest, became a profession. The number of corporate foundations grew dramatically, although most companies continued to make direct gifts. Whatever the form of the philanthropic program, greater selectivity and larger grants allowed businesses to expect donees to demonstrate the impact of contributions on the community. Companies began incorporating their charitable efforts into their business plans, and giving became more strategic—tied to business interests and designed to have greater community impact and visibility. Today, 86 percent of corporations that make charitable contributions in one survey claimed to use strategic philanthropy.[13]

GENERAL MILLS

General Mills is fairly typical of corporations that have taken a more strategic approach to philanthropy. The company's foundation budget increased dramatically from about $6 million in 1989 to more than $16 million in 1993, then flattened. Nonetheless, Foundation Director Reatha Clark King expects the corporation's giving to have a greater impact than in the past.

She attributes this trend to three important changes that have occurred since she joined the foundation in 1988. First, giving has become more proactive—the company began soliciting proposals from specific nonprofits, instead of sitting back and waiting to see what comes in. "After so many years of being reactive, we see problems getting worse," she notes. Now the foundation actively seeks partners that share its interests and works with them to create solutions to identified community needs.

Second, the foundation has increased its efforts to address serious social problems, rather than to support primarily "the prestigious side of community activities." Although General Mills maintained its funding for the arts and culture, its 1997–2000 strategic plan targeted education, providing safe and nurturing environments for children, and health and nutrition, a first for this breakfast cereal giant. The plan also called for greater emphasis on determining the impact of grants and a strong focus on innovation.

Third, like many companies hoping to improve community relations outside its corporate community, General Mills for the first time has allocated a third of its philanthropic budget to the twenty-one communities where its plants are located.

To engage employees who live and work in those communities, funding decisions are made by employees serving on Community Partnership Councils, with priority for groups employees are involved with—"the best indicator of likely impact," says King.

The company is also aiming to increase the share of employees volunteering through its Volunteer Connection. And General Mills has reached out to retired employees to volunteer. "They bring great skills and they are available full time," notes King.

HALE AND DORR LLP

Like Microsoft and General Mills, the Boston law firm Hale and Dorr LLP also used a strategic planning process to reengineer its charitable giving. The firm had long been a leader in Boston for its pro bono legal work and its financial support of legal services organizations and the United Way. But while other giving was business-focused—the firm would buy a table at a charity dinner or make a donation if an existing or prospective client was associated with an organization—it was impossible to determine the impact of these gifts on either the firm or the community.

To address this issue, the managing partner appointed a task force of partners and staff members who had experience in the social sector and a good knowledge of firm culture. The managing partner appointed Jack Regan as chair; he was a natural leader who had been active in the community and, importantly, a partner who had the respect of everyone in the firm.

After researching the firm's philanthropic activities, the group was "surprised at how much money we were giving away and where it was going," according to Regan. The committee decided that the firm needed to maintain its leadership position with the United Way and legal services for the poor, as well as its business-focused giving, but that the rest ought to be more focused for greater visibility and impact.

But what organizations should the firm support? Eventually, the group settled on inner-city youth and education, believing the topic would engage the most people. The committee decided to select several different organizations in order to provide a menu of options for involvement—"some people want a sustained relationship, others want to come and go." The group used its own knowledge to generate an initial list of potential organizations and asked nonprofit leaders, a major foundation, and another law firm to help them narrow down the list.

To make a final decision, the group visited the organizations, looking for evidence of entrepreneurial leadership, which they felt would be a good fit for the firm—"dynamic people with a vision and a model for helping kids in need." They also sought organizations that were young, but not in their first or second year, so the firm could "add value" by helping with infrastructure building.

Each of the four organizations selected was offered $250,000 over three years—with no strings, except a responsibility to report on how the money was used. Teen Empowerment, a program that "involves inner-city youth as agents of positive change" used funds to open a new site; Jumpstart expanded its corps of work-study students working with Head Start children; Citizen Schools, an afterschool enrichment program for middle-school students taught by community members, used funds for staff salaries; and Cathedral High School, a parochial school serving low-income students and the only organization selected that was more than five years old, used funding for its library, for educational software, and to hire a psychologist.

The firm assigned a team to work with each of the four organizations. Each team held planning meetings with its partner to generate ways for firm employees to become involved. "It was very time consuming," notes Brenda Fingold, a partner on the Jumpstart team. "After a two-hour meeting, we would have twenty new ideas on the table . . . and someone would need to follow up." In order to solve this problem, to convey a seriousness of purpose, and "carry on a more in-depth dialogue with organizations to find out about their needs," the firm hired a full-time community services administrator.

With a structure in place, the "in-depth dialogue" has yielded a rich array of opportunities for involvement. For busy lawyers and staff, every effort is made to see that their time is not wasted. They can volunteer on company time, as long as they clear it with their supervisor, which helps send the message that the firm isn't asking employees to spend even more time away from their families. Activities have included a fundraising drive to buy college application guides for low-income students at Cathedral High School (each book had a name plate inscribed with the name of the employee who purchased it for a student), reading to Head Start children served by Jumpstart, tapping the firm's network for career day workshops at Cathedral, and board recruitment. In a single summer, 100 employees volunteered. Students from Teen Empowerment and Cathedral High School interned at the firm during the summer, increasing the visibility of the programs, which were also promoted at staff meetings and on the firm's intranet.

The result of Hale and Dorr's well-thought-out planning process has been stronger ties among lawyers and staff. "When you're working together to teach skills to kids, titles don't matter," according to Fingold. "You begin to see your colleagues in a new light." In addition, Regan hopes the new program will give new lawyers "a significant point of differentiation between us and our law firm competitors. Hiring, recruiting, and training young lawyers is a tremendous cost," he notes. "Turnover can be costly and destructive to the fabric of the place." The real benefit "for the organization is not only the moral good being done for recipients, but the bonding between the employer and employee. . . . Employees sense that this is a good place to work, it has values beyond productivity and profit."

What Works

MICROSOFT: DESIGNING FOR IMPACT

Microsoft, General Mills, and Hale and Dorr all used sound internal planning to develop their strategic philanthropic programs. The most visible and often successful efforts of this type involve a partnership between the donor and donee that enables the nonprofit organization to benefit from the expertise of the business. Such arrangements create natural linkages between the organizations at many levels and departments, and often provide meaningful volunteer opportunities for corporate employees. Relationships that allow for real engagement by the corporate partner often fill a knowledge gap common to many nonprofit corporations and strengthen the nonprofit's overall capacity.

Philanthropic partnerships designed for social impact must involve the transfer of sufficient resources. Traditional philanthropic practices often resulted in a large number of small donations enabling the company to reach the largest possible number of nonprofit organizations. This practice may have won the company many friends in the community, but it didn't necessarily result in significant social change. Increasingly, companies are limiting gifts to a few organizations within a targeted field and increasing the size of each individual donation to increase the social impact of their giving.

All cross-sector partnerships, particularly philanthropic alliances, must have the advancement of a social mission as a major goal. However, other goals are also appropriate, such as increasing employee loyalty, raising the profile of the company in the community, improving the organization's image, or making connections to key constituents. Partnerships of this sort require careful planning, involving staff from all relevant departments (the corporate foundation or corporate giving department, human resources, marketing, public relations, planning, and other operational units). Involvement of these units also helps to leverage additional resources for the partnership that would be out of reach of the corporate giving office alone.

Finally, it is critical for the company to seek out a partner that can deliver a quality program. No matter how well conceived or compelling a program, if the organization that manages it is weak, the program will suffer over time. A company may find it needs to address or otherwise compensate for the problems of its partners, and over time, such a relationship is not sustainable.

Libraries Online represents an excellent example of strategic philanthropy for several reasons. It clearly benefits a social cause—it is easy to see the value of Microsoft's donation to disadvantaged communities who use the computers, and to the library profession itself, which had been falling behind technologically. The donation was strategic in the sense that the team identified a compelling need it could help fill, conducted research, and looked for ways to use the assets of the company—in this case software and technical expertise—most productively. It found the right partners—the premier public library association—agreed upon vision and goals, and provided sufficient resources to achieve its goals. Although the company was at times overly controlling of the program, it agreed to ALA's sensible suggestion to roll it out with an initial pilot effort. It wisely funded an evaluation before going to scale. Finally, it took the additional step of structuring the program to be sustainable by local communities, by training the librarians to work with the new technology. Ultimately, the Libraries Online program inspired local governments and other funders to contribute to the effort, expanding the pool of resources available for public access computing.

Furthermore, Libraries Online offered Microsoft specific benefits. First, Libraries Online enhanced Microsoft's image as a good corporate citizen. The opening of the centers was covered by the media in almost every state, giving Microsoft the kind of uniformly favorable exposure it rarely gets from the press.[14]

Second, the program enabled millions of library patrons, many of whom will one day purchase their own computers, to sample Microsoft software and become familiar with the Windows operating system.

Third, it broadened public access to the Internet, helping to expand the number of people who can contribute to the growth of technology. A key finding of the Libraries Online evaluation determined that "Once people were exposed to computing power, they became strong advocates." Pat Martin, now president of the Martin Resource Group, also believes that Microsoft factored into its selection of pilot sites its need to cultivate certain lawmakers. "My assessment is they got out of it a government relations overlay," says Martin. "It was not communicated to us, but it seemed obvious."

Fourth, the giving program connected employees with volunteer opportunities that utilize their technical skills. While volunteer projects have been hard to implement at a company whose culture puts employees on call seven days a week, employee volunteers in Charlotte and Seattle have assisted the program. Fortunately, the success of Libraries Online was not dependent on the involvement of volunteers—they proved very helpful to the program, but had they not been available, the program could have gone forth, as it did in many communities. Companies whose culture and work demands leave little time for volunteering can focus on developing volunteer opportunities that do not require a steady commitment of time or that can be completed according to the employee's own schedule.

Finally, to accommodate Libraries Online, Microsoft made changes to its products to make them more suited to public access. Staff involvement in the program enabled Microsoft to apply product adaptations it developed for public users in libraries to a larger and more profitable market of public access users: schools and universities.

AMERICAN LIBRARY ASSOCIATION: KNOWING THE FIELD

Social sector partners must stay true to their mission as they attempt to meet the needs of business partners. Particularly in the case of trade associations or granting agencies, it is essential that the organization understand the culture of its constituency groups and prepare them to participate effectively in the program. Sometimes this will require that the organization find those constituents that are most likely to be receptive, working with them first before involving a broader field.

ALA set a goal for wiring public libraries based on its own assessment of the best interests of its members. It sought to provide its members with an important benefit—a significant donation of computer software, hardware, and training—that they would value highly. Trade associations constantly must assess whether they are providing their members with enough value to justify their paying membership dues—the lifeblood of organizations like ALA. The sizeable donation represented by Libraries Online, with the possibility of additional resources becoming available over time, was an important benefit to ALA members. Although the bulk of the new resources went to local library systems, not ALA itself, the association did acquire significant new expertise and credibility in the area of technology.

In securing the donation, ALA applied its deep knowledge of the culture of the public library and made sure the program was a good fit. With a conservative membership largely unfamiliar with new technology, early failures could have spelled disaster for the program. ALA's advocacy of a pilot program instead of a large-scale start-up, selection of entrepreneurial libraries as sites, and internal publicity about the program, achieved through sessions at its annual conference and articles in its member publications, were key decisions that made the program a success.

ALA was also correct to insist that if its name was to be associated with the program, it should have a role in developing it. In addition, aware that it would appear to be endorsing the company's products—even though no actual endorsement was made—ALA worked with

Microsoft to soften potential criticism by ensuring that libraries could make decisions about the Internet browser and some software. Finally, while ALA worked to adjust its manner of operating to respond to Microsoft's desire for speed, it did not ignore the needs of its members or put aside its own substantive concerns. As a result, the program was widely embraced by the public library community.

Microsoft and the American Library Association: The Impact

Although Libraries Online had been carefully planned, with the involvement of experts at every stage, some members of the team had nagging doubts about how the program would work in practice. "Is this going to be the Coke bottle in 'The Gods Must Be Crazy'?" wondered Greg Shaw, referring to the South African movie in which a bottle dropped from an airplane created bewilderment in a remote village. "Here it is, what do we do with it?"

The first libraries to receive assistance from Libraries Online proved that rather than a mere curiosity, the computers were a sought-after resource. Demand was so high, many libraries were forced to ration use, limiting patrons to forty minutes a day.[15]

The pilot program surfaced many issues. Some were technical—for example, a large number of "technologically challenged" users who didn't know how to "double-click the mouse" would click slowly over and over, necessitating hardier hardware. Others related to personnel—for example, it turned out the more junior library staff adapted more easily to the new computers than the more senior staff who had been targeted for training. And still others involved usage—for example, because it was common for two people, especially children, to share a terminal, the space between workstations was often inadequate. For the most part, users were not malicious, but security was also an issue, as was the temptation on the part of teenage boys to change the home page on the computer to pornography. Software had to be loaded on the hard drive and the CD-ROM drive turned around, to prevent patrons from putting disks in upside down or using the circular drive as a coffee cup holder. These technical and usage issues could be readily addressed because the key partners possessed the necessary expertise among them.

Despite the kinks, grantees reported "phenomenally positive public response," according to an ALA press release. The program seems "to have made serious inroads in its stated purpose of bringing information technologies to economically disadvantaged communities," according to the ALA report, and despite the fact that the first few months of the project were difficult, library staff indicated that they were happy with the results. An evaluation of the pilot program found that users mirrored the ethnic diversity of the community, and that 87 percent had no Internet access at home. Eighty-five percent were under the age of 21, and a majority was male. Ninety-eight percent said they would be repeat users, and 83 percent said they had accomplished the task they set out to do. At the Brooklyn site, which monitored usage closely, more than a third of library patrons used the computers, with 29 percent coming to the library solely for this purpose.[16]

The successful first round of grants led to a second round in 1996, expanding the program to thirty-two additional library systems and providing additional assistance to the initial nine sites. In Brooklyn, at the announcement of stage two, Mayor Rudolph Giuliani joined Bill Gates to unveil a public/private initiative to connect all sixty branches of the borough's public library, the city contributing $5.5 million to augment Microsoft's contribution of $2.2 million. "Today's national launch builds on our vision of information at your fingers by empowering people with access to the Internet and the World Wide Web," said Gates.

Ultimately, Libraries Online was regarded as such a success that replicating it became the first major philanthropic effort of Bill Gates himself. Having been involved from the beginning, visiting several sites, engaging in online chat sessions with users of the library computers, and meeting with staff to understand the implications of the program fully, Gates donated $200 million towards its replication. He and his wife established the Gates Library Foundation, managed by former Microsoft Vice President Patsy Stonesifer and, early on, Chris Hedrick, to take the program to half of the nation's public libraries. When it was announced in 1997, the program drew praise from the White House. It "will do more than connect libraries," said Vice President Gore. "It will connect worlds and minds. This is living proof that, in America, we do not just await the future, we must prepare for it."[17]

Unlike many philanthropists before him, Gates provided the money not as an endowment, with investment income to be spent each year, but rather as a lump fund to be spent over five years. The foundation, rather than the ALA, is responsible for making the grants, and Willem Scholten and the Technology Resource Institute is providing the technical help. Microsoft matched Bill Gates's contribution with $200 million in software. The foundation's first large-scale effort was to wire the entire state of Alabama, selected because it is a poor state, according to Scholten, and because it had an enthusiastic cadre of librarians ready to make it happen. When complete, no one in the state would be more than an hour and a half from a public access computer.

More than 1,000 libraries in America received funds for new computers and Internet access in 1998. The Gates Library Foundation and its Technical Resource Institute were renamed The Gates Learning Foundation and Gates Center for Technology Access and became part of the Bill and Melinda Gates Foundations. ALA is no longer part of the program; with its legitimacy within the library community and knowledge base established, Microsoft and The Gates Learning Foundation determined it no longer needed the library association as a partner. ALA was nonetheless supportive of the Gates donation, which tracks closely ALA's own vision for a grander effort and made the whole library field and, therefore, ALA "a viable key player in the information and access industry."[18] "Carnegie changed the physical landscape," according to former ALA Executive Director Elizabeth Martinez. "This will do the same for the twenty-first century."

In 1998, ALA considered granting Bill and Melinda Gates honorary membership. According to ALA reports on the meeting, "while the board felt that the Gateses' $400-million gift to libraries was clearly an extraordinary commitment to ensuring equal access to information, the detractors felt they needed time for the Gates gift to play itself out and allay their suspicions about the business motives behind it." Nonetheless, the nomination of the Gateses was approved by a large margin.

PART III

Marketing Exchanges

5

---—— ❧ ——---

IDENTITY BUILDING
Denny's and Save the Children

In 1993, during a period of negative publicity and low employee morale, national family restaurant chain Denny's entered into a partnership with Save the Children to help build a positive public identity for the company. Five years later, all of Denny's company-owned restaurants and one-third of its franchisees were engaged in the program. Together, they sponsored more than 1,000 children, provided many hours of volunteer service, and contributed more than $3 million to Save the Children.

Trust and communication enabled the partnership to flourish. The choice of the well-known children's organization was sound for the restaurant chain because the cause resonated with its employees and customers, and because Save the Children had the history, culture, and personnel to meet the needs of its business partners without compromising its mission. Save the Children's decision to partner with Denny's made sense given the chain's sincere commitment to improve the lives of children, significant pledge of resources, and ability to put the cause before millions of potential donors—Denny's employees and customers.

Denny's and Save the Children

It was 1993—a tough year for Denny's. On the very same day that Denny's settled a federal discrimination suit, six African-American Secret Service agents went public with allegations that the restaurant had denied them service. National media ran with the story and "Denny's became, almost overnight, a national symbol of big-business bigotry," according to *Fortune* magazine.[1]

Denny's new president and CEO, Ron Petty, brought in to turn around the financially ailing company, moved aggressively to wipe out discrimination at the company. Believing the lawsuit would eventually be settled, Petty wanted "to be able to stand up and tell the press what we've done." Working with Denny's parent company, Flagstar, Petty developed a policy of "zero tolerance" for discrimination, implemented diversity training for all staff, and created a process for all claims of discrimination to be investigated by an independent third party. The company created a "Fast Track" program to prepare minority candidates for franchise ownership, and increased contracts with minority-owned companies.

In addition to its public relations and legal problems, the restaurant chain suffered a crisis of morale among its employees and franchisees. Petty was enthusiastic about the brand and its potential and believed that the vast majority of people who were part of the company were good at heart. For more than two decades, local Denny's had participated in "Community Cheer," collecting change for local causes. But although the company had raised millions of dollars for charity, it had no national partners and could not quantify the impact it was having. Petty thought a focused program would raise their spirits.

He would have developed a more strategic philanthropic program regardless of the company's current troubles because a large company "can make a more meaningful impact if you get behind a single cause." But with the crisis in morale among employees and franchisees, Petty moved with even greater urgency to find for Denny's its own Ronald McDonald House. He sought a "well-known charity that did something with kids" that would "instill pride in the employee base and help get the company back on an even keel."

IDENTITY-BUILDING PARTNERSHIPS

Companies seeking identity-building partnerships often seek both to engage their many stakeholders—employees, franchisees, suppliers, customers—and to tie their public image to a cause or charity. McDonald's affiliation with Ronald McDonald House was one of the first and probably the most well-known identity partnership. Interestingly, the first Ronald McDonald House was developed not by McDonald's corporation, but by Philadelphia Eagles football player Fred Hill, whose daughter had developed leukemia. Tired of camping out on hospital chairs and eating food from vending machines, Hill enlisted the help of his teammates and local McDonald's franchisees to create, in 1974, the first temporary housing facility for families of hospitalized children to carry the Ronald McDonald House name.

Building on this early success, by 1999 Ronald McDonald House Charities had in place a network of over 150 local charities serving 27 countries. In addition to operating almost 200 Ronald McDonald Houses, the charity had awarded over $200 million in grants to nonprofit organizations that work in the areas of education or children's health. At least one expert calls the Ronald McDonald House program "the most fully developed and successful example of a corporate philanthropy project that provides a rallying point for stakeholders."[2] The company is able to leverage its donation significantly by engaging others in the charitable endeavor that bears its name. While the corporation makes seed, expansion, and emergency grants and provides in-kind goods and services, operating funds are donated locally. Customers support the project by donating spare change; vendors are corporate contributors; and franchisees are the primary fundraisers, and often serve on the boards of local houses.

Companies seeking identity partners are wise to follow McDonald's example and use a full spectrum of resources to engage with their chosen cause. This approach can generate additional volunteers, cash, and in-kind resources. It can also have a positive impact on the company—uniting different parts in a common cause and building morale as a result. And finally, by reaching out to customers and ensuring a strong local presence, a company can improve its public image. Once the company's effort has continued for a period of years, it can, like McDonald's, safely tout the relationship in national ads without fear of a backlash.

THE NEED

Petty had seen firsthand the benefits of creating an identity-building partnership with a nonprofit. As a regional vice president for Burger King, he had been involved with a center for abused children and a burn center in Miami, and he had seen what these efforts meant to the company's employees. Franchisees had told him they were eager for a national program with local activities that would make the public aware of how much Denny's restaurants were giving back to the community. But it was not easy to identify an organization that would enable employees to demonstrate their generous spirit, inspire franchisees, and at the same time, foster a favorable identity for the company.

Several years before, Denny's director of promotions and community relations, Susan Schneider, had explored the idea of working with a national nonprofit partner. The company had been losing market share. Flagstar was experiencing financial problems, with $2.3 billion of debt after a series of leveraged buy-outs. Fast food chains with lower prices and casual dining chains that were more expensive but offered liquor and ambiance threatened Denny's base. Recognizing that family dining was its niche, Denny's had for the first time hired a marketing agency specializing in the family market and had begun advertising on television. But Denny's needed to do more.

Schneider went to her boss and urged him to consider working with a nonprofit partner. She believed a national nonprofit partnership with an organization that helps children would bring focus and visibility to Denny's efforts.

Schneider began to call well-known national nonprofit organizations that helped children, telling them that Denny's wanted to raise money for them. But her cold calls failed to draw a bite. "Maybe I wasn't talking to the right people" at the organizations, she says. In some cases she was passed to four or five different people at the nonprofits she called. None of them followed up. When Schneider's boss left the company and financial problems grew worse, the project was set aside.

Then in 1993 when Petty sought a national philanthropic partner, he decided to house the effort in his own office, believing that "if something like this is going to work, the CEO has to be thoroughly behind it—you can't just turn it over to marketing." Soon, he got a lucky break. He had asked Nancy Gaines, then an employee in the operations division, to create new uniforms for restaurant staff that looked less institutional. To gather information about uniforms, she met with local restaurant employees, who expressed interest in "fun" neckties. When she came across colorful ties decorated with children's artwork, she discovered that the ties were indeed designed by youth, and that their sale benefited a charity, Save the Children. Excited, she bought samples to show her boss. "They're outstanding," Petty told her. "Tell me more about the charity," said Petty, giving Gaines the assignment of planning the new philanthropic program. He was hopeful that Save the Children might be the answer to Denny's search for a partner that would help demonstrate its commitment to the communities it served.

THE MATCH

Founded in England in 1919, Save the Children helps approximately nine million children in forty countries through education, health and nutrition, emergency relief, and economic development. The organization pioneered the idea of child sponsorship: Individual donors provide funds to help identifiable children, who communicate with their sponsors by letter. Save the Children's advertisements, featuring actresses Sally Struthers and Roma Downey and other celebrities, gave the organization 80 percent name recognition in the United States despite its overseas focus. But child sponsorships, which are priced at just $20 a month for each donor, are costly to secure and maintain—they require cumbersome tracking mechanisms and high levels of staffing to support. As a result, they provide just a quarter of Save the Children's budget. Therefore, the organization actively seeks innovative partnerships and other arrangements to supplement these funds.

The Save the Children neckties were the result of a partnership with Salant Corporation, a menswear company interested in developing a line of novelty ties featuring children's artwork. In 1992, the two organizations held a children's art contest to choose the designs. The smiling children of many races sketched by the first winner, 12-year-old Dana from New Jersey, became Save the Children's signature design, to be followed by hundreds of other patterns created by children across the country. The ties were a hit, generating significant sales revenue and contributions for Save the Children and inspiring a trend of cause-related neckwear. In the next five years, the newly created licensing group at Save the Children signed up three dozen companies to put children's artwork on mugs, bedding, cookie tins, shoes, and silver jewelry, with 5 to 10 percent of the wholesale price going to the organization to help children.[3]

Denny's, attracted to Save the Children because of its ties, offered the nonprofit "the world's most perfect situation," recalls Diane Whitty, the former associate vice president for corporate marketing for Save the Children. Typically, Whitty would spend months or even years cultivating a prospect; here, a major corporation was calling out of the blue. To maximize involvement of its restaurant employees, Denny's wanted to support Save the Children's work in the United States. Coincidentally, Save the Children's 1993 strategic plan had targeted the United States for expansion, and the organization had recently created a position of executive director of U.S. programs.

But Save the Children's new CEO, Charles MacCormack, was wary. Companies looking to improve their image had approached the nonprofit before. MacCormack had found that corporations seeking an association with the organization were not always sincere in their commitment to the cause. Was Denny's only interested in helping itself, or would it be a true partner in Save the Children's effort to help children?

"When a company is in trouble, you look those people in the eye and see if they are going to turn lemons into lemonade—or not," says MacCormack. Ron Petty and MacCormack hit it off immediately. Petty liked Save the Children's businesslike approach. MacCormack liked Petty's heartfelt concern for children. Denny's met Save the Children's written standards, which required that its partners not be engaged in activity that harms children. Although some members of the Save the Children board and employees had concerns about the partnership, MacCormack felt strongly that it should go forward. To make the case, MacCormack's team looked into all that Denny's was doing to reach out to minorities and concluded that the efforts were sincere. "Being part of the change of heart is okay," he explains. "One of the good things about American culture is it appreciates learning from experience and positive responses to crises."

The two organizations found that they shared basic philosophies about helping children and their families: "Enabling, equipping, and encouraging low-income people to solve their own problems" is how the Save the Children's statement of beliefs frames the sentiment. After eight months of discussions, the two organizations decided to work together to implement this shared philosophy to help U.S. children. Denny's would raise $750,000 using its network of 1,600 restaurants, 70,000 corporate and franchise employees, and the nearly one million customers who eat at Denny's in a day. In return, the company would enjoy the distinction of becoming Save the Children's largest corporate sponsor.

THE TEST

The Denny's/Save the Children partnership was announced to the public on National Children's Day, October 9, 1994.[4] The company used a video to roll out the partnership to employees and franchisees and distributed promotional materials. Employee newsletters began to feature information on Save the Children and its programs. Denny's servers would sport Save the Children ties, a practical way to engage customers in discussions about the nonprofit organization. Each company-owned restaurant and participating franchisee would sponsor a child, sell Save the Children ties and note cards, and engage in other local fundraising activities. These activities would not supplant local restaurants' existing charitable programs—a key element to ensuring the support of employees and franchise owners.

For its part, Save the Children, which operated primarily in rural areas of the United States, agreed to accelerate development of its planned urban programs, beginning in key Denny's markets: Los Angeles, San Francisco, New York, and Phoenix. "If they stayed in the rural areas of Mississippi, that wouldn't have worked for us," explained Susan Schneider.

The U.S. program plan, developed by new Executive Director of U.S. Programs Catherine Milton, would focus on improving and expanding afterschool programs for school-age children. It would provide funding, training, publicity, and other resources to existing local children's organizations so that they could offer youth a "web of support"—caring adults, safe places, and constructive activities, such as music and arts programs, community service opportunities, or homework assistance. By building on programs already operating in the community, Save the Children could leverage its resources and capitalize on the knowledge and contacts of local organizations.

As an added bonus, because no new organizations had to be established to carry out the program, the "web of support" could be put in place quickly. But not as quickly as Denny's would have liked. Denny's efforts to promote diversity and make its charitable activities more visible had succeeded in "changing the dialogue with the press," according to Petty. But the company still had work to do with internal stakeholders.

For the partnership to achieve its full potential, franchisees, which operated nearly half of Denny's restaurants, would need to participate. Franchisees wielded a great deal of influence with the corporation, and their cooperation would be essential to the creation of a coordinated national philanthropic effort. Marcia York of Fort Myers, Florida, was a leader among franchise owners, and Petty believed her support would help persuade others to follow. He asked her to represent franchisees in the development of the Save the Children partnership.

While concerned about the plight of poor children, York was a tough sell. She researched Save the Children on her computer; then she flew to the nonprofit organization's headquarters in Westport, Connecticut, to "see if they walked the walk and talked the talk."

"I went as a skeptic and returned as a believer. They were everything they said they were and more," says York. "I started making speeches and approaching franchisees. Ron [Petty] and Nancy [Gaines] named me National Franchise Spokesperson." This role landed York, along with Petty and Gaines, an invitation to meet with First Lady Hillary Rodham Clinton at the White House with a group of seventy-five advocates for children.

Not every franchise owner could fly to Save the Children's headquarters for a personal pitch. They wanted to know that the money they raised would help children in their own communities. Denny's asked Save the Children to accelerate its program development in targeted areas. "Denny's was so anxious to be able to engage their employees, they didn't realize the effort that it takes to put those kinds of programs in place," recalls Save the Children's Whitty.

To show progress and engage the restaurant chain, Save the Children hired a consultant to review programs in the Los Angeles area. The consultant asked Denny's corporate and L.A. restaurant personnel to help with the needs assessment. "They had a lot of market information," Whitty recalls. Because of their previous involvement with Denny's Community Cheer program, "they could point out what organizations were good, and point us to smaller organizations" that Save the Children did not know.

Because Fort Myers was the location of Marcia York's restaurants, Catherine Milton also sent a staff person there to see if that community met Save the Children's criteria. She discovered that the extreme poverty of the Pine Manor neighborhood in Fort Myers made it an appropriate place for the nonprofit's planned program. York introduced Milton's team to Judy Saint Somers, director of a local Big Brothers/Big Sisters program, and Save the Children agreed to make Fort Myers one of its new urban sites.

Milton believes there were advantages to rolling out the program quickly and credits Denny's with causing that to happen. "The reasons for pressure from Denny's were well understood by key people at Save the Children and gave me the license to move ahead as fast as I could," she says. "It also forced the program staff to spend time designing a national program that would produce, within a reasonable time, tangible, positive results for children. That is good pressure."

In order to maximize the potential of the partnership to result in a new public identity for the company, it was important to make the relationship more visible. Borrowing from Save the Children's partnership with Salant Menswear, Denny's elected to sponsor a children's art contest. Fourteen-year-old Sharon Clay from Blue Springs, Missouri, submitted rows of watercolor children resembling chain paper dolls. Hers was one of twenty chosen from more than 8,500 entries.

Press coverage of Denny's ceremonies for the national winners was excellent. Sharon and her artwork appeared on three local networks. Local anchors sported the ties she had designed; Denny's regional director appeared on one station; other stations noted that the ties were on sale at Denny's or filmed the segment on location. Winners in other areas received similar press coverage. State and local officials were invited to each of the local events along with school personnel and the winning child's family. The tie or T-shirt featuring the artwork was sent to local reporters, editors, and producers and to fifty selected media celebrities in other markets.[5] "It was a really special and touching time for everyone," according to Denny's franchise operations manager, Leslie Duggins, in the "Denny's Today" employee newsletter. "The event went a long way to building community awareness of the Denny's/Save the Children partnership."

GROWTH

The success of the art contest, Save the Children's presentations at the national franchisee conference, Denny's mailings and newsletters featuring the program, and Marcia York's passion for the charity helped convince a large group of franchise owners to join the partnership. The franchisees had asked for two things: assurances that the funds they raised would eventually be used to help children in their own backyards, and "turnkey" programs that were easy to implement. With these conditions met, a half dozen franchise owners signed onto the program.

By the end of 1995, $750,000 had been raised by Denny's restaurants across the country. Save the Children honored Ron Petty with its Distinguished Service Award. Then, in early 1997, Petty left to become CEO of Peter Piper Pizza, and John Romandetti, head of El Pollo Loco, another Flagstar chain, became president of Denny's. While such transitions can spell the death of partnerships, in this case, the strong support at many levels in the company, including Senior Vice President for Marketing Jon Jameson, allowed the Save the Children partnership to weather the change of leadership. Susan Schneider took Romandetti to Westport, Connecticut, to meet the people behind the program. "He was supportive before, passionate after," Schneider recalls.

The new president took a more practical approach than Petty, according to Diane Whitty. He moved responsibility for the program from the executive office to marketing, with a view toward maximizing the partnership's potential to attract families to the restaurant. And he wanted to make Denny's participation simpler for the restaurants to manage. Because sale of Save the Children merchandise had created problems for restaurants not equipped to secure the products, retail sales were discontinued.

Romandetti replaced the sale of merchandise with a coin collection canister. In addition, in 1997, five cents of the proceeds for each package of Denny's popular holographic baseball cards and ten cents of every All American Slam meal, a low-priced breakfast platter, went to Save the Children. To respond to concerns raised by local restaurant managers, Denny's and Save the Children redesigned the uniforms, replacing with colorful aprons and caps the silk ties that were so easily stained.

To encourage local restaurants to work aggressively to raise funds, Denny's held a national "Lend a Hand" competition. Winners included a restaurant that raffled off a hand-crocheted wreath and quilt and one that sold paper dolls for $1 each. One franchise winner, Carl Ferland, decided to forego the $500 banquet offered to winners and used the money instead to sponsor a child. By the spring of 1997, Denny's had contributed more than $1.5 million to Save the Children and had pledged to raise up to $1 million a year for the next three years.[6]

While Denny's worked to fulfill its commitment to Save the Children, the nonprofit organization proceeded with the development of its $20 million urban U.S. program. Through a series of working partnerships at the local and national level, the "web of support" would connect children's service providers to one another and give them a stamp of approval of sorts. It would inspire them to develop a broader vision, and bring them together to focus their energy. It would fill gaps, creating new services where needed. Finally, it would reward excellence and provide leadership training to community-based staff. Using the needs-assessment process it had piloted in Los Angeles and Fort Myers, Save the Children lined up local partners around the country who agreed to be part of the "web."

But Save the Children had one more challenge. Denny's was counting on restaurant employees to participate in the local programs they were supporting, as had happened in Fort Myers. Would local children's organizations welcome the participation of Denny's in their activities?

In early 1998, Save the Children learned the answer to this critical question. The organization assembled staff from the community organizations participating in its fourteen pilot sites for an initial training at a 4-H Center in Maryland. The staff who attended included leaders from African American, American Indian, and Latino communities. Denny's was invited to make a presentation about the partnership. The turnout of key players underscored the importance of the session to both parties. Denny's Vice President Jon Jameson, Nancy Gaines, Susan Schneider, Marcia York, and a half dozen franchise owners were on hand, along with Save the Children's Vice President of Global Marketing George Guimaraes, Director of Corporate Marketing Paula Madsen, and Catherine Milton. But behind the scenes, staff from several local organizations were concerned about having a relationship with Denny's—the discrimination case loomed in their minds. Opening applause was polite but unenthusiastic.

Denny's unveiled its new Save the Children promotional video and new television commercial, featuring a diverse group of young children dressed in the gear of various jobs:

> *Children grow up regardless of us. How they grow up is up to us. At Denny's, we believe one of our biggest responsibilities is making sure every child is loved, nurtured, healthy, and educated. So we're the largest corporate sponsor of Save the Children all around the country. Because children are 35 percent of our population but 100 percent of our future.*

Marcia York spoke of her commitment to the program. She told stories: A young employee, Sean, applied to become a mentor with Big Brothers/Big Sisters after he played Santa at a Christmas party for the children of Pine Manor. After Timmy, an 11-year-old who was sole caregiver to his disabled father, was hospitalized, York took him into her own home to recuperate. Funding from Denny's provided 11-year-old Antonio, a victim of sexual abuse who had become an abuser himself, with in-home counseling because his abuser status caused him to be turned away from the children's center.

For the audience, hearing from Schneider and York and meeting the other Denny's executives had a powerful impact. The company had a human face that Save the Children's local partners could connect with. Almost all left persuaded of the company's good intentions and motivated to explore the potential of the relationship.

THE CHALLENGE

A dark cloud loomed in the back of the minds of both Save the Children and Denny's officials at the 4-H Center, however. The *Chicago Tribune* had begun an investigation into international child sponsorship programs, with journalists sponsoring a dozen children. Two years later, the reporters traveled to visit their sponsored children. One was a young Malian girl sponsored through Save the Children. But when the reporter arrived in the child's distant village, she discovered the little girl had died three months after the sponsorship began.

Thinking the case to be an aberration, Save the Children launched its own investigation. The internal review turned up other problems in Mali, including twenty-two other deaths of sponsored children that had gone unreported by local part-time staff hired to manage the program. Save the Children moved quickly to address the problems. In a spirit of cooperation, the organization turned over its internal report to the *Tribune*.

While waiting for the story to run, the organization began to inform its allies—child sponsors in Chicago, the community agencies it worked with, and its corporate partners, especially Denny's. Both Denny's and Save the Children had been through similar experiences over the years of their relationship. A *Prime Time Live* story on Save the Children in 1995 had claimed that benefits were not reaching children in Save the Children's southwestern program. In 1997, Denny's was back in the news when several Asian Americans alleged racial discrimination, claiming they had been denied service in Syracuse, New York (it was later refuted in an investigation by the District Attorney's office). In both cases, the partners had kept each other informed and the relationship survived. During Denny's troubles, Save the Children had "never questioned the partnership," according to Nancy Gaines. "They feel like we feel about them—that we will make it right."

When the *Tribune* story finally broke many months later, it caught the partners off guard. The article used Save the Children's own investigative report to expand its own negative findings and went on to include a sidebar about Save the Children's corporate sponsors. "Like it or not, you may be donating to Save the Children," warned the headline.[7] Accusing the organization of "selling its name," the article pointed out that "[i]n effect, people who eat at Denny's, buy a necktie or make a call on AT&T [another of Save the Children's corporate partners] are also making a small donation to Save the Children."

The wake-up call offered by the articles had parallels to the wake-up call Denny's itself had received when allegations of discrimination surfaced. Denny's had taken active and immediate steps to eradicate discrimination in its restaurants. Similarly, Save the Children made significant improvements to its program in response to the report.[8] Under the new protocol, all sponsored children were to be contacted by Save the Children staff on a regular basis. Deaths would be reported within two days of staff receiving notification, and sponsors would be informed immediately thereafter. Together with other child sponsorship agencies, Save the Children helped to create a new panel to examine programs and recommend standards. Finally, modeled on the government's "inspector generals," a new internal auditing function was installed to give future sponsors and corporate partners assurance that even if the regular system of oversight broke down, there would be a mechanism to check up on the organization's operations around the world.

Despite the unfavorable publicity, Denny's did not reduce its support. "They opened their records, gave them everything," observes Schneider. Her personal experience adopting a child from Romania had given her an appreciation for the difficulty of doing business with less developed countries. "I didn't know the age, name, or weight of the girl I was adopting until I saw her in person." While impressed with Save the Children's response to the crisis, Denny's staff also relied on their faith in MacCormack and his team. Schneider prepared a recap for franchisees, stating that Denny's was confident that Save the Children had taken measures to fix the problem. "There was *no* backlash," stresses Schneider. "We are sure they are doing the right thing. Their heart is in the right place. If there is a problem, they will fix it."

What Works

DENNY'S: FINDING THE RIGHT PARTNER

A business seeking to build an identity through social sector partnerships, particularly in the wake of adverse publicity, should seek a partner with a good reputation, high name recognition, and experience working with companies. A company under stress, even if it is contemplating a long-term relationship, cannot afford to take the time to help a less well-known nonprofit build its name recognition. Nor will it achieve its objectives if the nonprofit lacks credibility or is unsophisticated about helping the partnership succeed. At the same time, a nonprofit that has many corporate sponsors may not be a good fit if it is unable to give significant attention to its new partner. In addition, in identity-building partnerships, as in other marketing relationships, the cause should not appear self-serving, but should bear some relationship to the business and have wide appeal, particularly to the target customer base.

Denny's did contribute to civil rights groups in the wake of the discrimination lawsuit. But choosing a civil rights organization as an identity partner would have served to remind customers of the lawsuit and confuse the public, which might have viewed the partnership as part of the settlement. As a family restaurant, Denny's customers and employees alike had strong ties to children, which made a children's organization the logical choice. But which one? Schneider had been very impressed by Children's Miracle Network, but recognized that the organization was working with dozens of other companies and thought Denny's might not stand out among the many sponsors. Save the Children, on the other hand, did not have any other major sponsors for its U.S. program. The fact that Save the Children did not have its U.S. programs operating in Denny's target markets when the partnership was formed made it less than ideal for Denny's, which wanted a quick start. Nonetheless, Save the Children's decision to involve Denny's in the establishment of its new program created greater "ownership" on the part of Denny's and ensured that the program met the needs of the restaurant chain.

In identity-building partnerships, each partner must look into the other, both face-to-face and through background research, before signing a deal. Meetings should occur at several levels—including top-level executives, line staff who will manage the relationship, and program and marketing staff. In addition, a business should use the Internet and other sources to research potential partners (see chapter 10). It should also check on whether the organization is a member of trade groups that require adherence to quality or ethical standards.

Could Denny's have done more research and unearthed the problems reported in the *Chicago Tribune* articles? Unlikely. The newspaper spent two years and significant funds on the investigation, well beyond the ordinary "due diligence" searches that should be done about prospective partners. Save the Children had been rated a top charity by *Money* and *Parents* magazines, and conformed to the Better Business Bureau standards for charitable organizations. Nonetheless, had Denny's asked questions about the nonprofit's ability to monitor its far-flung network, requested that Save the Children disclose any past complaints, or probed where the organization itself felt vulnerable, it might have exposed weaknesses in the organization.

SINCERE COMMITMENT

Companies facing public relations crises often reach the conclusion that a partnership with a credible nonprofit organization can help improve their image. When McDonald's came under fire from environmental groups for its plastic packaging of fast food meals, the company agreed to work with the Environmental Defense Fund to develop alternative packaging that was more earth-friendly.[9] After a heavy rain created an oil slick on the Charles River near its Boston railway yard, Conrail joined with the Charles River Watershed Alliance to create a tool for monitoring water quality. Both companies were successful in changing their dialogue with the press through their efforts.

Although partnerships developed following adverse publicity can be an effective way to restore a company's reputation, they are even more effective as a preemptive tactic, according to strategic philanthropy expert Craig Smith. Smith's 1994 *Harvard Business Review* article recounts the unhappy experience of Exxon, whose philanthropic efforts had been "thoroughly insulated from Exxon's corporate policies."[10] In contrast to competitor Arco, which had partnered with environmental groups and had learned to respond quickly when accidents occurred, Exxon supported only charities unrelated to its industry. This policy left the company on the defensive with nowhere to turn when the Exxon *Valdez* oil spill occurred in 1989. The company took ten days before running ads apologizing for the spill, and its chairman did not appear on the scene until three weeks after the disaster.[11]

How a company behaves when it is at fault in a crisis ranks third after quality and service in consumer buying decisions, according to a survey by the public relations firm Porter/Novelli.[12] The experience of Odwalla, after its fresh unpasteurized juice was found to be tainted with bacteria, demonstrates the value of doing the right thing—and of having credits in the bank of public goodwill. Odwalla responded quickly to the news that contaminated juice had killed one child and put dozens of others in the hospital.[13] The company immediately took responsibility, expressed concern for the victims, and moved to recall not just apple juice, which had been identified as the source of the bacteria, but other juices as well. A rapidly created Web site—operational the day after the outbreak— enabled the company to communicate directly with the media and its customers about the recall.

Prior to the outbreak, Odwalla had received a *Business Ethics* magazine award for its environmental efforts.[14] In partnership with a community coalition, the company had created a special juice with information about a proposed dam on its label, with profits going to the coalition to fight its construction. The company provides scholarships for women pursuing health-related studies, supports an education and research program to reduce pesticide use in Costa Rica, and pioneered a system for leasing farmland and then contracting for fruit grown on it according to its own standards for organic produce.

When Odwalla faced a public relations disaster that could easily have forced it into bankruptcy, it enjoyed the continued support of many customers and shareholders who were aware of Odwalla's track record and therefore believed the company would respond responsibly. They were right—Odwalla moved quickly to build a state-of-the-art bottling room, to implement a system of "flash pasteurization," and to add food safety experts to its board.[15] Although the company lost more than a third of its value, Odwalla's recovery from the recall was more rapid than anticipated. Former Odwalla chairman Greg Steltenpohl attributes this quick recovery to a "combination of being forthright and having some type of ethical responsibility backed up by a track record of commitment. It made core consumers buy more than before," he says.

For companies in identity-building partnerships, the essential question must always be "What more can we do to support the cause?" not just "How can we improve our image?" Both parties must be committed to the stated social goal. Making a significant dollar commitment is one way to demonstrate the company's sincerity—Denny's should benefit from being able to describe itself as Save the Children's "largest corporate sponsor." Denny's interest in involving its employees in the partnership should also pay off—not just in a more loyal and motivated workforce and franchise community, but also in the court of public opinion. Research suggests that direct, hands-on assistance is less likely to be viewed by the public as self-serving than cash donations.[16]

Finally, sophisticated companies hoping to gain favorable public relations through good works are wise to wait until they have made a significant investment in the project before they try to tout their efforts. Even then, public relations should be focused on the cause, not the company. Denny's had been involved with Save the Children for three years before it developed ads featuring the charity. Public relations efforts up to that point had been focused on children winning an art contest, with Denny's contributions a secondary element. Especially in the case of a company that has experienced unfavorable publicity, the press and the public will be quick to question its motives. Before going public, the business needs to have something to show beyond good intentions, and that will likely take time.

SAVE THE CHILDREN: THE RIGHT BALANCE

With more than a decade of experience with business partnerships, Save the Children has a well-developed ability to work productively with corporations to meet their needs. Save the Children CEO Charles MacCormack places a high value on being an entrepreneurial organization— fast-moving, learning from the best practices of business, and knowing how to engage with the marketplace. "Nonprofits tend to overinvolve people in decisionmaking. They're slow, bureaucratic, inefficient," according to MacCormack. Businesspeople "won't work in these environments." To build its capacity to work in parallel with business, Save the Children actively seeks to combine the best elements of business and the social sector.

The nonprofit has been able to attract very senior businesspeople to the staff, including Vice President of Global Marketing George Guimaraes, a former vice president with the advertising giant Saatchi and Saatchi, and board member and volunteer Bill Haber, co-founder of Creative Artists Agency, one of the most powerful talent agencies in

Hollywood. "They won't work slow," says MacCormack. "We need to leverage their time." Half of the U.S. program staff has business backgrounds, which Catherine Milton believes has helped the program be more effective in achieving its mission. "The staff with business backgrounds have sharp analytical skills and creative approaches to producing positive, measurable results for children and developing new sources of income," she says. "As an extra bonus, they also have a lot of great contacts which have enabled us to build new corporate partnerships."

Because of the constant need for resources, program staff have learned to temper their creativity with reality. "We can't just look at whether it programmatically makes sense," says one program staff person. "We have to ask, 'is it fundable?'" To seek new sources of funding, the organization has assembled a staff to manage relationships with the business sector, including a six-person corporate partnership staff and a five-person licensing group, both headed by highly skilled women from the business sector.

"We get in the door and show how their image or market access or product differentiation or goodwill will be enhanced. How it might make them more, or at least not cost them any money," explains MacCormack. A threshold issue for the corporation is whether its resources will achieve social good. But pitches to companies are "two minutes about us, and 58 about how to help them," since they've done "due diligence" too, says Paula Madsen. "We listen first to what their needs are before we pitch what we can do," she adds. This process is time consuming, but effective. "Blue chip partnerships take a long time to cultivate, between the letters and visits and persuasion," she advises. "Start small—a single promotion or event. But the only way you get benefits is to be in for the long term."

While the resources Save the Children generates in the business arena speak for themselves—in 1997 the organization raised over $2 million from licensing revenues and over $3 million from other corporate partnerships, the equivalent of more than 20,000 individual sponsorships—Save the Children must make sure that such ventures enhance its programs, or at least don't undermine them. Save the Children follows a careful protocol when it approaches a business. The organization has written standards, and very often seeks out companies that it believes will meet its own needs instead of waiting for an approach. Companies are screened through internet searches and consultation with groups like Businesses for Social Responsibility, and in the case of major or controversial partnerships like Denny's, the board of trustees is involved. Face-to-face meetings are essential and should occur at many different levels to determine whether there is a synergy between the organizations and a reason for the partnership, for example, a common interest in children. "We basically look at the costs and benefits—how much good are we going to do versus what will the cost be," according to MacCormack. Save the Children has turned down lucrative partnerships offered by companies that are engaged in activities that harm children—for example, a manufacturer of infant formula that was not in compliance with the World Health Organization's guidelines. Although Save the Children is eager to help its partners achieve their goals, it will not compromise the integrity of its programs.

Denny's and Save the Children: The Impact

Although neither Denny's nor Save the Children has conducted an evaluation of the partnership, both believe the relationship has been a success. "A lot was intentional and a lot accidental," according to Nancy Gaines, but the fact that the relationship was grounded in shared values about how to help children helped the partners to make decisions that would benefit both parties. Both organizations regard the relationship as a work in progress and will continue to "push down to the local level what was in the early stages a national relationship," according to MacCormack. "The course we have mutually set is most likely to become more and more fruitful because we have laid down a geographic face that is more likely to meet the needs of both organizations."

Having Denny's as a major corporate sponsor enabled Save the Children "to conceive of an ambitious program for U.S. children," according to Catherine Milton. In addition to contributing over $3 million dollars in five years, Denny's raised awareness of Save the Children and helped the organization recruit additional individual and corporate sponsors. With Denny's support, the organization provided children in eight cities and forty-two rural areas of the United States with safe places, caring adults, and constructive activities. As a result, 96 percent of youth in the program in Duncan, Mississippi, improved their reading comprehension level. In Covington, Tennessee, participating youth increased their academic proficiency by 12 percent. In Madison, Arkansas, the number of youth in the program who completed almost all of their homework assignments more than doubled.

Denny's relationship with Save the Children withstood staff changes at both organizations, Save the Children's public relations challenge, and the financial problems and restructuring of Denny's parent company, renamed Advantica. In 1998, one-third of franchisees were participating; the company's goal is 100 percent. Both partners hope to see more restaurant employees become involved with Save the Children programs. Save the Children would like to help Denny's receive more public attention for its efforts. It made its 100,000 individual sponsors aware of Denny's commitment through a calendar prominently featuring Denny's logo and through mailings urging sponsors to "Head to Denny's for a great meal, and the great feeling when you make a difference in the lives of children."

Denny's efforts to eliminate discriminatory practices also yielded results. After the settlement of the lawsuit and the company's aggressive efforts to improve its civil rights record, the number of franchises owned by African Americans increased from just one in 1993 to 114 by 1998, contracts with minority-owned companies increased from none to $125 million during the same period, and the company formed partnerships with the Hispanic Association on Corporate Responsibility and the National Association for the Advancement of Colored People (NAACP). In 1997, Advantica received the Fair Share Award for Minority Business Development from the NAACP, and in 1998, Advantica was named by *Fortune* magazine as number two on its list of the fifty best companies for Asians, African Americans, and Hispanics.[17]

As for its partnership with Save the Children, Denny's brought one additional asset to the relationship. In 1998 Denny's conducted for Save the Children's local program partners the diversity training that it developed after the lawsuit. "The trainers were very candid about Denny's experience," says Catherine Milton. "It was received very well by participants, including the young people." Unlike the session at the Maryland 4-H Center, there was no discernable tension among participants.

"It's one thing to give money," notes Milton. "But it's another to integrate programmatically with us. The trainers were candid about the company's experience, and asked the programs to think about what changes they wanted to see in their community.

"Because of Denny's, we can have big dreams," she adds.

6

❧

SPONSORSHIP
BankBoston and City Year

In 1988, Bank of Boston became the first team sponsor of City Year, a fledgling nonprofit organization committed to uniting diverse young people in a domestic Peace Corps. A decade later, City Year had scores of corporate sponsors based on the original model, permitting 1,000 young adults to serve their communities every year, tutoring children, teaching violence prevention, and otherwise helping neighborhoods in need.

The relationship has permitted BankBoston* to build closer community relationships, redefine its charitable giving philosophy, reinforce a new image of public spiritedness, and connect with its employees in a fresh and meaningful way. For City Year, sponsorship by the bank gave it access to good advice, positive media exposure, and the credibility to land other corporate sponsors.

The partnership works for several reasons: Both partners have similar values about teamwork and diversity, they respect each other, and both are willing to go the extra mile to meet the other's needs.

---

* Bank of Boston became BankBoston after acquiring BayBank in 1997. In 1999, BankBoston announced plans to merge with Fleet Financial Group to become Fleet Boston Corporation.

BankBoston and City Year

The Bank of Boston conference room had a long, polished mahogany table and dark paneling, and would not, under normal circumstances, be an unusual place for young lawyers to find themselves pitching a deal. But in the winter of 1988, the proposal on the table was singular in almost every respect. Alan Khazei had recently graduated from Harvard Law School, and his partner, Michael Brown, was in his last year there. But unlike most of their classmates, they were not planning to head for corporate law firms. Instead, they hoped to pursue their vision of a national service program—an urban Peace Corps that would unite a diverse group of young people in a year of full-time community service.

Brown had worked on youth corps legislation for Congressman Leon Panetta during a year's leave from college, and Khazei, as a congressional intern in college, had researched national service as an alternative to the draft. Both had developed an interest in national service as a strategy to build active citizens and unite diverse young people in a common purpose. They knew skeptics did not believe it could work—that young people from all economic and racial backgrounds would, for poverty-level stipends, serve side-by-side to rebuild their communities. Few if any existing programs fit the bill. The handful of youth corps around the country typically engaged only at-risk youth. VISTA, the anti-poverty volunteer service program enacted under President Lyndon Johnson, fielded individuals, not teams, and had lost some of its early spirit.

Before law school, Brown spent a year at the new City Volunteer Corps (CVC) in New York, which he thought might serve as a model. He admired the team structure of the program and its focus on human service in an urban environment. But CVC had difficulty achieving its goal of diverse membership, and had been unable to attract private sector funds.

Brown and Khazei, who had been roommates, began planning their version of national service while in law school. The corps they envisioned would recruit teams of ten or twelve young adults aged 18 to 24. Each team would include people of different races, educational levels, urban and suburban residents, and men and women. A junior taking a year off from college would serve alongside a single mother working on her GED. A high school graduate from South Boston would serve with a Vietnamese refugee. All these people would learn from one another and would come to appreciate what unites them, rather than what divides them. The teams would take on projects that would strengthen the community—painting over graffiti, planting a community garden, organizing afterschool activities for children. And all corps members would practice good citizenship. They would vote, learn first aid, speak in public, and give up their seats on the subway if others were standing.

THE NEED

Because they would serve full-time, middle- and low-income corps members would need living allowances in order to participate. Resources would also be needed to pay staff to organize and lead the teams. Brown and Khazei believed that private sector funding would best help them achieve their goal of creating a model program that might eventually draw public support. The limited government funds available came with too many restrictions. Brown had learned through his CVC experience that early government support could deter other funders. Brown saw the need to involve donors in the corps, beyond just writing a check, so they would maintain their interest and help the program achieve its goal of civic engagement. The new corps would need a mechanism to connect funders with the young people so they could see the impact of their support.

The 1984 Olympics in Los Angeles provided Brown and Khazei with the inspiration for such a mechanism. Thanks to Peter Ueberoth's marketing team, these were the first to be a commercial success. Companies (called sponsors) paid to be the official soft drink, official car, even official noisemaker. In contrast to the baggy sweat suits and plain T-shirts worn in earlier competitions, every U.S. team had a sponsor, with athletes wearing the name of its corporate funder on specially designed uniforms.[1]

Brown and Khazei considered how to use sponsorship to raise funds for their new organization. They wrestled with the idea of putting corporate logos on youth, and concluded that it would be all right as long as they stayed away from tobacco and liquor companies and corporations operating in apartheid South Africa. Keeping the Olympics' framework in mind, they decided to ask foundations, corporations, and groups of individuals to sponsor teams of corps members. Team members would wear the name of the sponsor on their uniform, providing visibility for the company wherever service was performed.

Although Bostonians would see the corps in action in their neighborhoods, unlike the Olympics, the corps would not be in a position to put its sponsors before hundreds of millions of viewers around the world. Khazei and Brown understood that they would have to deliver other benefits to companies in order to attract sponsors. In the nonprofit world, sponsorship is sometimes used in a different sense. For example, Save the Children and other children's charities sign up individuals as sponsors for specific children. Although this form of fundraising is very costly and hard to administer, it provides sponsors a personal link to the children they are helping. This emotional bond keeps child sponsors donating for years, and sometimes inspires them to make payments for special gifts for the child, to exchange letters, and even on occasion make a visit.

THE MATCH

It was this kind of personal connection between the corps members and their benefactor that Khazei, Brown, and their colleagues Jennifer Epplett, recently arrived from EF Hutton, and Neil Silverston, a young graduate of Harvard Business School, had in mind when they approached Bank of Boston in 1988, hoping to land their first team sponsor.

Their arrival in the bank's conference room had been preceded by a simple exercise. "You're only twelve handshakes away from anyone in the world," was Silverston's philosophy, Khazei recalls. Ira Jackson, Bank of Boston's executive vice president, turned out to be only two—a law school classmate of Khazei's and Brown's was working with a professor at Harvard's Kennedy School where Jackson had been associate dean. Jackson had come to the bank after five years in Governor Michael Dukakis's administration as Massachusetts Commissioner of Revenue. He had been brought on board to improve the image of the bank, which had a history of public relations missteps and was experiencing increased competition in the newly deregulated banking industry.[2] In charge of government relations, public affairs, marketing, philanthropy, and community investments, Jackson was the man to see, even though he had been on the job just a month.

"They were young, eager, passionate," says Jackson. "I pushed back hard." He questioned the "rainbow of diversity" they painted, when the four of them were white, middle class, and well educated. "Color me skeptical," he told them. "You've never done anything before." He felt the name of the new corps, "City Year," intended to follow the "junior year" and "senior year," was too limiting. But he liked the concept, thinking, "it's an idea whose time perhaps has come."

At the end of the meeting, Jackson's colleague, Director of Corporate Contributions Judith Kidd, took Epplett aside and asked that she come up to her office. "Ira's excited about this idea and this is what you've got to do," Kidd advised. "You've got to demonstrate that young people are interested. You need to broaden your board and diversify your staff. And show that you've got community support." She gave Epplett names of people to call—other funders, African-American leaders, community activists.

The City Year team responded. They had raised only $1,000 so far and needed a major sponsor to give the project credibility and entree to other companies. Bank of Boston was a 200-year-old financial institution, a pillar of the community, Boston's largest corporate donor. It could provide that heft.

For Bank of Boston, City Year was a risk. Although Jackson felt the concept was sound, it would take a "huge leap of faith, given how eager and Harvard they were," he recalls. Bank of Boston was used to assessing risk and making investments. In this case, the return, at least in the short-term, would not be financial. Indirectly, the bank would benefit from a stronger community, a more committed work force, and a positive image if all went well. Things could go wrong. But Jackson sensed promise. He wasn't sure what authority he had to offer them funds, but he decided to take the leap.

THE TEST

In the spring of 1988, the phone rang in the tiny office in Cambridge the seven members of the City Year staff shared. At that time, only one staff person was working for pay, and none of the funders they had approached had yet made a commitment to sponsor a team.

On the phone was Kidd, for Epplett. The bank would invest $25,000 to sponsor a team during the summer pilot program, she said. The City Year staff was "ecstatic," according to Khazei. "With our first team sponsor in hand, the program was definitely going to happen."

Once committed, Jackson and Kidd became very involved. "Maybe he saw himself in us," Khazei speculates. Jackson joined the City Year board of directors. Jackson and Kidd talked Bain and Company, General Cinema Corp., and Equitable into sponsoring teams, and Bank of Boston's seal of approval gave City Year the credibility to be taken seriously by other potential sponsors.

The summer program was launched in July with five teams of ten young people, who would receive $60 a week to live on and a $1,000 scholarship at the end of the summer. Jackson was a featured speaker at the well-publicized opening day, appearing on almost every station in Boston. The bank paid for a ¾-page ad in the *Boston Globe* introducing City Year and its diverse corps members to the greater Boston community. During the eight-week program, the corps started each day doing calisthenics on Boston Common in their City Year uniforms emblazoned with the names of their sponsors—a highly visible way to gain the attention of Boston's citizens. Calisthenics were followed with community service projects, and every Friday was a day for education and reflection. To help connect the team to its sponsor, Bank of Boston brought its ten corps members to headquarters for a day-long overview of the bank's history and sessions on finance and banking. "The corps members loved Ira," recalls one City Year staff person. "He didn't treat them like kids." In August, about fifty Bank of Boston employees volunteered for City Year's fundraiser, a "serve-a-thon," helping to paint schools, renovate homeless shelters, and clean up parks. The summer culminated with a half-hour local television feature, again with Jackson as principal spokesperson.

GROWTH

With a summer program to its credit, City Year was ready to plan for a nine-month program to be launched the next year. But by September, the group had only $6,000 in the bank—enough money for just a month's payroll. Jackson heard the group was dispirited. "I knew we had a 'beta site' initiative that had been a success." He recalls, "I thought as an initial investor we should send them money to encourage them to step up to the plate. I was thinking very much of it as analogous to the kind of venture capital investments the bank makes."

He sent $50,000—enough to sustain the program for three months—with a message: "write a business plan and get a hot meal." He insisted the City Year team work with the same kind of discipline that any business would use to approach this phase of development. "You can't usually get this done for fifty grand, but Alan and Michael did," recalls Jackson.

Twelve months later, City Year was launched as a nine-month program with fifty corps members. Although minor improvements were made to the summer program, the model was the same. The teams would have corporate sponsors, they would start their days with calisthenics, and then work together on community projects. For $100,000, Bank of Boston again sponsored a team. Kidd personally recruited bank employees to be mentors to the Bank of Boston corps members, and she herself chose to mentor the team leader. One of Kidd's recruits, Mark Vasu, a loan officer, took a special interest in the project. He volunteered to serve on the steering committee for City Year's now annual serve-a-thon—through which teams of community members served for a day, collecting pledges from friends and colleagues to make donations to City Year—and to organize a group of Bank of Boston employees, including Ira Jackson and his daughter, to participate.

The serve-a-thon became a valuable tool to unite diverse groups at the company, from bank tellers to executives, including those in remote locations. Bank of Boston fielded the largest volunteer team at the event. The message used to recruit employees was "responsibility and an obligation to share," recalls Vasu. It had a profound effect on the employees involved. "Here's a stodgy Brahmin institution out there encouraging its employees to get involved in something that's new, hot, different, fun, electric," explains Jackson. "For those involved it was a source of pride that their company logo was on the jackets of the team members, that they were a part of something new." Recalls Vasu: "The afterglow was people wanted to do more."

Vasu saw the potential of City Year to do even more to market itself. He made a pitch to Jackson: he would join the City Year team for a year as a loaned executive, at Bank of Boston's expense. He framed the proposal in business terms. A year of dedicated time to help with marketing and the structure of involvement would translate into other investors for City Year. It would enable the bank to be a leader in the community by using its expertise of investing in start-ups. "Sending over a $50,000 employee wasn't at the top of my hit list," says Jackson. The bank was losing money at the time. Nonetheless, Jackson approved the placement.

CITY YEAR SPONSORSHIP STRATEGY

As corporate development director at City Year, Mark Vasu used his business knowledge to good effect. Using the Bank of Boston relationship as a model, he refined the sponsorship program. His goal was to help each company understand how it could benefit from an association with

City Year. Although sponsorship continued to be the structure for major corporate partnerships, marketing and visibility in the community was often of less importance to companies than the opportunity to engage employees, support diversity, or be part of an organization "with a big vision for the future." "We had to listen to what they needed most and position the organization to serve that," explains Vasu. "Almost every company was investing for a different reason."

When some companies thought $100,000 for a sponsorship was too high to be sustained year after year, City Year reset the price at $70,000—half of the annual cost of a team. It hoped to make up the difference with government grants and individual donations.

The minute a company decided to sponsor a team, it was an opportunity to make the sponsor's leaders spokespersons with the media, to ask them for help with other funders, to involve employees with the team and the serve-a-thon, and to ask for advice. Two staff people were responsible for supporting the relationship: the City Year team leader, who was expected to stay in contact with the company, and a senior person, like Vasu, who could make decisions. Sponsorship would be recognized in many ways—on the colorful T-shirts and jackets of corps members, with signage at events, in publications, and with the media. When sponsors sought more visibility, City Year tried to provide it.

Although City Year's philosophy was "Find a sponsor for everything,"[3] the program turned down some offers of sponsorship, particularly if the company tied its support to requirements that weren't strategic or sustainable. For those companies whose offers were accepted, City Year sought to deliver value to the sponsor. Unlike many nonprofit organizations that angst about corporate support compromising their missions, City Year leaders believed company sponsorship enhanced their work. It "has a huge impact on corps members in understanding corporations aren't evil," explains Khazei. And secondly, according to City Year's handbook, *Putting Idealism to Work*, "By building a direct link between a private sector sponsor and the service work, we share idealism, engage more people in service and build a stronger democracy." The 1998 version of the handbook lays out the City Year belief system in 180 numbered points. Distributed to all corps members, the handbook helps create a "Tao" known to every corps member. Items range from the mundane to the philosophical: "Courtesy is a powerful skill for social change." "Everyone needs to do things that are not in the job description." "Remember,

<u>everyone</u> always needs to be prepped." "It's a privilege for all of us to serve at City Year." "Develop a 'core theory' for what you are doing, and narrate it through every aspect of your task." "Pay very close attention to City Year's 'look and feel.'"

As a self-defined "action tank," City Year designed its visitors program to win the support of corporate sponsors, national leaders, and policymakers. From its early days, the program hosted an average of ten to twenty guests a week. Visitors were invited not just to observe, but to participate in calisthenics, address corps members, visit a project site, and engage in a roundtable discussion with a team. While corps members were never told what to say, their comments to visitors were clearly heartfelt and invariably consistent with the City Year message.

Mark Vasu used the visitors program to engage potential sponsors. "People knew I was a loaned exec," he recalls. "I used business language to describe City Year: customers, marketing, sales, franchise, return on investment. . . . We created the sense that City Year was trying to operate with business principles."

While Vasu and others in the development office worked closely with the sponsor, the team leader and a designated corps member had responsibility for ongoing interaction with the sponsor on a more frequent basis. At a minimum, this interaction would consist of a meeting at opening day to discuss goals, participation in the serve-a-thon, a team visit to the company offices, and participation in the graduation ceremonies. Most sponsors went beyond these activities. By 1992, the Boston-based corps was attracting twenty major sponsors a year, almost all of whom renewed their sponsorship in the subsequent year.

BANKBOSTON: CHALLENGES

As private sector support for the program grew, the opportunity for federal funding became a reality. City Year had intended its program to be a model for national service supported by both the public and private sectors. Khazei, Brown, Jackson, and others had spoken before congressional committees about the program, and City Year had hosted many influential political leaders through its visitors program. This effort paid off in 1990 with the passage of federal legislation sponsored by Massachusetts Senator Edward Kennedy to provide grants for model national service programs.

City Year was poised to grow, eager to take advantage of the new national funding. Khazei and Brown turned to Bank of Boston for support and advice. But Jackson was concerned that City Year was growing too fast, without much research about what worked and what didn't. The bank was facing its own challenges. Financially, Bank of Boston, like many other financial institutions in New England and across the country, was in trouble. Its stock had dropped to under $3 a share, and the company lost $400 million in a single year.[4] Despite his reservations and Bank of Boston's own financial problems, Jackson agreed to increase the bank's contribution, paying $100,000 to become a founding sponsor of City Year in Rhode Island.

When the bank turned a corner financially—by diversifying its business, writing off bad loans aggressively and early, and slashing expenses—"we decided we had to come out of it a different company," according to Jackson. And with this came the need to change their image from what *Forbes* magazine called "certainly one of the snootiest" banks in the country,[5] and find ways to emphasize its core values of "teamwork, initiative, integrity, and diversity."

Instead of the bank's annual golf outing, Jackson thought a community service project might meet the company's need for an event that would build team spirit. He called Khazei and Brown for help, and together the bank and the corps planned a project to rebuild a lakeside camp for low-income children.

Corps members led the bank executives in jumping jacks and toe touches. The bank supplied a catered lunch, bug spray, tools, funds for materials, and a nurse—just in case. Bank executives pulled an old diving dock from the water, built shower stalls, and patched the rotted roof. At the end of the day, they celebrated with a barbecue.[6]

Unlike the traditional golf outing, the experience was transformational, according to Jackson. "It was a metaphor for the company we wanted to become." Over the next five years, BankBoston (Bank of Boston changed its name in a 1997 acquisition of retail powerhouse Bay-Bank) regained its financial footing, growing from a market value of $500 million in 1993 to $16 billion in 1998. But it did not walk away from its commitment to "manage for value with values." The bank played an increasingly visible role in the community. It became the first major Massachusetts bank to earn an outstanding rating from bank regulators for its compliance with the Community Reinvestment Act.[7] It made all employees shareholders. In 1996, it formalized its corporate volunteer program, which drew on its City Year experience, naming it the "Eagle Corps and offering incentives like paid time off for service and "service stars" to recognize employees who volunteer. It expanded its program to match employee charitable donations and became one of a few companies to offer cash matches for employee volunteer time with an organization.

Principally a commercial bank, Bank of Boston had never had a strong retail franchise. When it acquired BayBank and its two million customers, community activities became even more important to its success. The bank gained public acclaim for the generous and progressive Employee Transition Assistance offered after it acquired BayBank. It was similarly recognized for its support of long-time customer Malden Mills—when the owner announced he would keep all employees on the payroll after a devastating fire destroyed the factory, BankBoston made an unsolicited $50,000 donation to the employees fund and committed $150 million in financing to rebuild. The bank's reputation as a good citizen brought it 5,000 requests a year for funding. It has "significant relationships" with more than sixty organizations. In 1997, the bank made a major commitment at the Presidents' Summit for America's Future, promising to dedicate $5 million and 5,000 volunteers to help at-risk youth and to provide 500 inner-city teens with a job, a mentor, and at least one volunteer in their schools. Even more dramatic was the bank's decision to co-sponsor a Massachusetts volunteer summit with its then archrival Fleet Financial Group: "We called it the Miracle on Federal Street," comments Ira Jackson.

CITY YEAR: CHALLENGES

Visibly identified with City Year, BankBoston was betting that the program would succeed. As a start-up, the corps received good local press and national attention. But as Jackson had predicted, rapid growth put strains on the nonprofit. Financial management issues that surfaced in a government audit created a minor flurry in 1996, resulting in a feature story in the *Boston Globe*, headlined "City Year Slips as It Rushes to Grow."[8] Despite the bad press, BankBoston stuck with its partner. "As with companies that evolve, there are large and traumatic transitional issues," according to Jackson. "We need to watch that the O-rings don't break." "Ira was wonderful," says Khazei. "He was one of the first people we called when the story broke, and he helped develop the organization's strategy to respond. 'Own what you need to own, but get your side of the story out,'" was his advice, according to Khazei. While the story lasted for a few days, it culminated with a favorable *Boston Globe* editorial that called attention to the challenges of what City Year was trying to do and stressing that the program is "greatly needed to offer strength to neighborhoods in decline."[9]

Over the years, BankBoston and City Year have weathered other challenges. At times, City Year's vision and reality have been out of synch. City Year service projects involving BankBoston employees have not always been as well planned as they needed to be. The bank has raised concerns that the program should do more to help young corps members from the inner city develop job skills. In some cases, efforts to tie the corps members to the bank were unsuccessful. For example, the bank had provided corps members with free checking accounts, consistent with City Year's message that good citizenship includes financial responsibility. But it turned out to be a "major pain—kids always lose their checkbooks," says Kidd. Suggestions by the bank were not always heeded. City Year kept its name, despite Jackson's admonition that it was too limiting. The program rejected Jackson's advice to grow slowly. And City Year declined to focus on youth entrepreneurship, although Jackson had encouraged this focus. Khazei and Brown are "courteous, diligent and attentive, solicitous and gracious." But they are also "headstrong visionaries" who are not always great listeners, says Jackson.

Although the personal bond between Jackson and the City Year leaders clearly has helped to sustain the relationship during challenging times, the need to keep revenues ahead of expenses at a better than the industry average doesn't allow the bank to be frivolous. The bank is "excessively generous relative to our peers and competitors," according to Jackson, but looks for a return. "They ask for the moon, and we drive a tough bargain. We've got an accounting scheme that looks for equivalent benefits." For example, when Khazei called looking for funding for a video to be shown at their annual conference, Jackson didn't hesitate to respond, but insisted that BankBoston's logo appear at the end of the tape in return.

In the end, however, City Year's ability to generate positive PR for the bank may not be its most important benefit to the bank. Rather, explains Jackson, "in a commoditized business," in an area with low unemployment, "we are coming to the realization that having a heart, making a difference not just a profit, helps us feel good about ourselves."

Sponsorship

Sponsorship began to take off in the 1980s. It is defined as *"a cash and/or in-kind fee paid to a property (typically sports, arts, entertainment or causes) in return for access to the exploitable commercial potential associated with that property."*[10] In contrast, advertising involves the direct promotion of a company through print space or airtime bought for that specific purpose. Advertising, according to IEG, a leading sponsorship agency, is sold and evaluated in terms of cost per thousand readers. Sponsorship, in contrast, is a qualitative medium, creating a tie between the company and the team, cause, or event.[11]

Sponsorship has traditionally meant associating a company with an event or property (a stadium, theater, or sports team). Cause-related sponsorships have followed this pattern. Typically businesses pay to put their name on a sporting event (the AIDS ride or Race for the Cure), fundraiser (a reception or dinner, like the Taste of the Nation discussed in chapter 7) or, occasionally, an organization (Denny's is the largest corporate sponsor of Save the Children). Both traditional and cause-related sponsorships expose the company, brand, or product to its target audience in a context that communicates a particular lifestyle or set of values. The connection may be stronger than advertising—a company that buys an ad in a magazine is trying to reach a target audience of readers, but readers don't interpret the ad placement as implying an endorsement of the magazine. In contrast, a sponsorship implies an endorsement of sorts—the company paid to make the event possible. In addition, sponsorships often create opportunities for direct involvement by employees, who might attend an event or volunteer with the organization.

A business might choose sponsorship over advertising to take advantage of an opportunity for visibility with a narrowly targeted audience or to associate itself with a particular lifestyle. It might use sponsorship to provide consumers direct exposure to its product through free samples, or to obtain benefits that can be shared with clients, employees, or others it hopes to influence. For example, when Wendy's, a fast food chain, hoped to enhance student interest in employment opportunities and increase restaurant traffic in one of its major markets, it sponsored the North Carolina High School Athletic Association. The sponsorship package provided Wendy's "presenting status" at championship games for eleven sports, mention on a weekly sports television show, and the opportunity to distribute 3.75 million tickets for school sporting events preprinted with coupons for free hamburgers, fries, and a drink.[12] When Fruit of the Loom's BVD brand sought to set itself apart from other underwear marketers that use sexy or goofy advertising, it sponsored Big Brothers/Big Sisters, which similarly includes 23- to 35-year-old males among its target markets.[13]

Unlike advertising and many other forms of marketing that consumers find annoying and intrusive, sponsorship positions the company as the benefactor, the entity that makes the event possible. It also can provide better value—sponsorship often yields press coverage and other types of "public relations exposure," which typically costs 10 percent of what straight advertising costs.[14] At least one study suggests that whereas advertising can be more effective at communicating specific product attributes, sponsorship can be a superior way to improve a corporate image, create a propensity to purchase, and increase brand awareness.[15] Annual sponsorship spending in North America (not including dollars spent to promote the sponsorship) increased from $850 million in 1985 to about $6.8 billion in 1998.[16] And whereas early sponsorships went almost exclusively to sporting events, today arts festivals, fairs, and entertainment tours receive about a quarter of sponsorship dollars; causes receive between 8 and 9 percent.[17] Nonprofit organizations receiving sponsorship payments do not have to pay taxes on the revenue in most circumstances, a policy clarified by a federal law passed in 1997 exempting "qualified sponsorship payments" from unrelated business income taxes (UBIT).[18]

What Works

CITY YEAR: SPONSORSHIP REDEFINED

City Year's innovation—putting a company name on a team of young corps members—created an instant link between the company and the specific young people they sponsored. Potential sponsors know how their dollars will be used and can identify the young people they are supporting and the good they are doing for the community. City Year uses the visitors program, funders roundtables, and other events to attract new sponsors and inform them about the program. Then, once the company has made a commitment, City Year uses time-tested activities to connect sponsors to their team—from the serve-a-thon to visits to the headquarters.

This new model of "relationship" rather than event-based sponsorship demands different metrics for determining success. Traditional sponsorship arrangements can be evaluated based on the number of "impressions"—how many people attended the event or saw it advertised. With appropriate baseline information, a sponsor can measure awareness levels achieved, attitudes changed, or even sales results. But in the case of a nontraditional sponsorship with multiple goals, the mere "naming" and "viewing" may not generate the intended benefits. Rather, the social sector partner will need to support the sponsorship in other ways—by promoting it through the media, informing its donor and volunteer network, and creating opportunities for the sponsor's involvement with the organization. And it will need to come up with appropriate ways to report on results, both traditional (the number of people in its network who were informed about the relationship) and nontraditional (specific projects completed using the resources provided by the sponsor; ways that employees became engaged with the organization). In no case should the organization overstate the potential or resulting impact of the sponsorship, regardless of the metric used.

City Year does not pretend that sponsorship will convince customers to flock to BankBoston. It does, however, work to see that the bank receives press attention for its role—valuable favorable publicity that the bank could not obtain on its own. It has placed Jackson in front of powerful audiences to speak about why the bank supports City Year, which benefits both partners. It has agreed to appear in BankBoston advertising, again allowing the bank to underscore its community leadership while creating awareness of the youth corps.

Because City Year understands that the goal of sponsorship is not always visibility, it is able to meet the unique needs of each organization that takes on a team. In the case of BankBoston, City Year has helped the company internally. "Increasingly our motivation is to become a cool place to work," explains Jackson, who estimates that a majority of employees are aware of the City Year relationship. "People get turned on when they see City Year in action." The number of BankBoston employees signing up for the serve-a-thon remains high. Employees often choose City Year as the recipient of their United Way contribution. And it is not unusual for a BankBoston employee to inquire about getting a son or daughter into the program.

Experience with City Year helped the bank "develop templates that apply to other major partnerships," according to Jackson. The bank began to apply to other relationships the "social venture capital" model it developed with City Year, investing modest dollar amounts early and going beyond financial support and board participation for "value added partnerships." The City Year partnership also "taught us a lot" about how to structure volunteer efforts, according to Jackson. City Year has supported the bank's own volunteer projects, such as its annual "Holiday Gifts for the Homeless" program and Walk for Hunger. The program arranged for the BankBoston City Year team to be placed at the Quincy School in Chinatown, where bank employees volunteer. The bank credits City Year with helping to weave service into its culture. As a result of the bank's commitment to community, it is easier to retain and motivate employees, and in return, they give better service. In these ways, Jackson believes the bank is doing right by all its stakeholders—employees, shareholders, and customers alike.

AN EXCELLENT PROGRAM

A strong program is an essential ingredient of a strong sponsorship relationship. The Salt Lake City Olympics scandal of 1998, in which Olympics officials were found to have accepted bribes from prospective host cities, reminds us that even long-standing, highly regarded organizations may face problems that challenge their ability to attract corporate sponsors. All organizations should get their own house in order before reaching out to potential partners.

If the program is a start up, it will not have a track record, balance sheet, or existing projects that can be evaluated. In these cases, greater emphasis must be placed on assessing the founders and leaders of the organization. Their background and track record become essential to any assessment of a potential partnership, as does the logic of the proposed program.

Both of the start-up organizations we have examined—KaBOOM! and City Year—were forced to go through difficult periods of systems building. City Year offers an important lesson that a strong program does not obviate the need for financial strength and management capacity. The inadequacies of City Year's financial system jeopardized its core funding and brought it the only negative press in its history. Ultimately the problem was corrected (City Year's corporate partners played an important role in responding to the crisis), and the organization seems to have been made stronger for the challenge because it responded quickly and with integrity. But the lesson holds.

One way to increase a sponsor's confidence in a program is to be candid about challenges and aggressive about meeting them. Over the years, City Year has asked for and received a great deal of advice from its sponsors, sometimes good, sometimes not. Asking for advice is an excellent way to engage company executives, helping them become personally invested in the program's success. Advice need not always be heeded—in fact, blindly acceding to the sponsor's wishes can spell disaster as easily as failing to heed good advice. What is important, and a skill that City Year leaders have learned from experience, is the ability to listen to the sponsor and weigh the suggestions, using their own judgment about what to do. Declining to respond to the sponsor's wishes, from Jackson's admonitions about the City Year name to his concerns about the growth plan, has not undermined City Year's relationship with BankBoston—a relationship in which the bank helps City Year to succeed, the way an investment bank advises new ventures.

PRICING

Pricing can be troublesome to social sector organizations new to sponsorship. Organizations seeking sponsors for traditional events or properties can set prices based on comparable events or properties. According to IEG, variables that impact price include the tangible (the value of on-site sampling rights, expected media exposure, the face value of tickets, and the value of the mailing list); and the intangible (the prestige of the property, the recognizability of property marks and logos, and the level of audience loyalty); the reach or impact (the size and scope of the market); and price adjusters (degree of sponsor clutter, size of sponsor's promotional commitment, and networking opportunities with co-sponsors).

Organizations seeking nontraditional sponsorship arrangements often must rely on supply and demand based on their own cost structure and what the market will bear. It is often helpful to be able to tell sponsors precisely what their dollars are buying. City Year's pricing for a team sponsorship was calculated based on the actual cost of fielding a team divided by two (with government money covering the other half). The program decreased its prices after the first year after hearing from sponsors that the initial price of $100,000 was too high to allow companies to continue to sponsor a team year after year.

We suggest organizations set a floor for sponsorships, given the hidden costs involved in seeking partnerships and maintaining relationships. Don't forget to factor in staff time and overhead as well as direct costs. Testing the figure with trusted advisors from either sector can help an organization determine if its pricing structure is viable.

BankBoston: Strategic Investment

Strategic use of sponsorship involves combining the best practices of cause-related marketing and strategic philanthropy. Sponsorship resembles cause-related marketing because it is externally focused, contributing to a public image for the company and influencing potential consumers. For this reason, businesses are wise to limit the number and types of major cause-related sponsorships in which they engage and to support the sponsorships with advertising or public relations efforts. Sponsorships should be promoted weeks or months in advance to an audience that goes beyond those who will experience the event or program directly.

Sponsorship is similar to strategic philanthropy because it makes possible the advancement of a cause or delivery of a social program, and therefore can appeal to internal stakeholders. For this reason, companies should seek opportunities for employee involvement and linkages with the organization's overall philanthropic program in order to strengthen the social sector partner. A company's ability to sell the program internally will directly affect the value it derives from the sponsorship.

Sponsorships should align with business needs—be targeted to the right markets and create a desired image. Finally, companies should also seek longer-term relationships—changing partners too often is confusing to internal and external audiences alike and reduces the potential that an individual sponsorship will contribute to the company's public image.

BankBoston's early and sustained support for City Year has given it a special relationship with the nonprofit. The bank has invested strategically, sponsoring teams in the cities where it does business, encouraging employee involvement, and funding City Year's innovations. "We're the provider of risk capital for their newest venture," explains Jackson. Because new ventures are likely to generate press attention, being the first funder to step forward generates significant press attention for the bank. In addition, by being supportive when City Year undertakes new projects and providing additional in-kind resources—corporate volunteers, bank accounts for corps members, service on City Year's advisory boards, and most important, management and public relations expertise—Bank-Boston maintains its position as one of the organization's most valued sponsors. In return, City Year likes to give BankBoston visibility and other benefits, even though other sponsors have provided more money.

BankBoston and City Year: The Impact

A decade after his first meeting with Brown and Khazei, Jackson reflected on the beginning of BankBoston's involvement with City Year: "In retrospect, it's as sound and successful an investment as BankBoston has ever made in 214 years." With BankBoston's early investment, and the legitimacy, advice, and positive publicity it brought with it, City Year expanded in a decade from a fifty-person summer pilot to a national program with 1,000 corps members in ten cities.

Created to serve as a model for national service in which the government and private sector share responsibility, City Year proved that it was possible to recruit diverse teams of young adults and played an important role in the passage of President Clinton's AmeriCorps program. Although federal funds helped fuel its expansion—City Year received $9 million in AmeriCorps funds in 1998—the organization keeps government funds at no more than 50 percent of its budget to preserve its private sector roots. Other corps have been created based on the City Year model.

In keeping with its regional focus and self-defined role as a "provider of risk capital to new enterprises," BankBoston declined to become a national sponsor of City Year, deciding instead to focus on the Boston and Rhode Island sites.

BankBoston has sponsored a City Year team every year since the program began. The bank consistently fields the largest serve-a-thon team each year, and in some years, bank projects were so full, employees joined other companies' teams. It has helped to sustain the program in other ways, hosting corporate breakfasts to introduce colleagues to City Year and testifying before Congress on behalf of national service legislation. And it has provided more than $1 million in support. After it announced plans to merge with Fleet Financial Group, the company announced an additional $1 million gift toward City Year's endowment, a testament to the strength of the partnership.

Using the BankBoston relationship as a model, City Year developed equally strong relationships with other companies. Bain and Company, a management consulting firm, sponsors a team every year and developed strategic plans for every major turning point in the program's ten-year history. Digital, which developed City Year's technology platform and Web site, agreed to become a national founding sponsor, and after being acquired by Compaq, made a substantial gift of computer equipment. Timberland, a second national founding sponsor, began its relationship with a donation of seventy pairs of work boots for the corps. It became the official outfitter in 1993 and had given or pledged over $5 million in cash or services by 1998.

Staying true to Brown and Khazei's vision, City Year has ensured that the corps is racially, ethnically, and socioeconomically diverse.[19] The focus of the corps' work is with children. From 1997 to 1998, corps members served more than 68,000 children through school and community-based educational programs. In addition, corps members also assisted more than 9,000 people in disaster relief efforts; laid 21,000 feet of trail; and assisted 21,000 adults in shelters, nursing homes, hospitals, and other social service organizations. The corps developed an innovative program to engage eighth graders in service, taught an HIV/AIDS prevention curriculum in English and Spanish at public schools, and designed and ran school vacation camps and afterschool programs for more than 5,000 children in Chicago's Cabrini Green and other low-income housing projects. They recruited and led 35,000 other volunteers in service projects, and collaborated with hundreds of community organizations from the Red Cross to local churches. Corps members themselves have benefited by receiving about $5,000 toward college expenses and, where necessary, by obtaining a GED. Ninety-five percent of corps members felt they learned leadership skills in problem solving, negotiating, planning and organizing events, crisis management, and public speaking.[20]

The BankBoston City Year team received training from Reading Recovery and a local reading organization, and together provided nearly

8,000 hours of tutoring at the Quincy School in Chinatown. In 1998, the school received the highest scores in Boston in statewide assessments, despite the large number of children whose native language is not English. In addition, City Year corps members and BankBoston volunteers worked together on Chinatown beautification efforts, a geography education project, and a playground for the school.

On the doors of the auditorium in the Quincy School is a mural of yellow sunflowers on a blue background that was painted at the October 1997 serve-a-thon. It was designed by the wife of a BankBoston employee; painted by kids from the school, their parents, a dozen BankBoston employees and their families; and organized by two City Year corps members. It is a permanent, visible product of a complex collaboration and an optimistic reminder of what is possible when different communities open the door to cooperation.

7

૨▲

CAUSE-RELATED MARKETING
Calphalon and Share Our Strength

In 1994, Calphalon, a mid-sized manufacturer of high-end cookware, agreed to co-host an event held in a New York City department store organized by Share Our Strength (SOS), a national anti-hunger group. After five years and many joint projects showcasing Calphalon and its products, the partnership had produced significant cash resources and visibility for SOS.

Cause-related marketing worked for the company by encouraging sales of its products; strengthening its relationships with retail, catalogue, and online distributors; and distinguishing the brand for its target market. For SOS, the revenue from Calphalon was used to sponsor Taste of the Nation, a series of food and wine events, which raised nearly $5 million in 1998. Through its partnerships with Calphalon and other prominent companies, SOS has become one of the most visible and credible practitioners of this new, yet growing, form of cross-sector partnership.

Calphalon and Share Our Strength

Monique Barbeau was running late. A young-looking 28, backpack over her shoulder, she hardly looked like one of the nation's top chefs. She was returning to Seattle after attending an event for visiting chefs at Harvard Business School—which had paid for her first class ticket. She had recently won the 1994 James Beard Foundation Award for the best chef in the Pacific Northwest and had been featured in a cookbook, an important professional milestone. The cookbook, *Home Food,*[1] was edited by Share Our Strength (SOS) staff Catherine Townsend and Debbie Shore. SOS, a leading anti-hunger organization, would use all profits to support its network of food banks, soup kitchens, and nutrition programs.

Dean Kasperzak was pleased to have an open seat next to him on the flight to Seattle. The Calphalon executive, son of the late founder of the company, was on his way to Seattle to meet with executives from the department store Bon Marché. For Calphalon, a top-of-the-line manufacturer of cookware, relationships with retailers are critical both to position the product with consumers and ensure adequate shelf space.

Kasperzak's father, Ron, had taken the company from a "job shop" turning out aluminum components in the early 1960s, to one of the leading cookware brands and a pacesetter in the trend toward gourmet cooking. Ron Kasperzak's vision of offering professional-quality cookware to the public had been realized by making cookware from anodized aluminum and by an innovative marketing philosophy. The philosophy, now widely copied, called on retailers to emphasize open-stock pieces rather than sets, discouraged price promotions, required salespeople to be knowledgeable about the product, and featured product support including training, educational literature, in-store demonstrations, and advertising. Although this strategy proved successful with the public, allowing the business to grow about 20 percent each year for a decade, it required high levels of cooperation from retailers that were unaccustomed to operating their housewares departments like specialty stores.

When Monique Barbeau dashed onto the plane as the doors were closing, Dean Kasperzak was sorry to see what looked like a "college student with a rich father" toss her backpack into the seat next to him. For an hour, they didn't talk. "He has an attitude," thought Barbeau. Then the flight attendant came around with the lunch selection. "Have the sandwich," Barbeau told Kasperzak, with great authority. Intrigued, Kasperzak asked her how she knew so much about food. "I have a restaurant in Seattle," she said. After establishing that it was not "the one that's really well known that's not so great," but rather, the "great one in the hotel," as Kasperzak recalls the conversation, she then asked what he did for a living. He replied nervously. "Chefs are very opinionated," he explains.

"Chefs either love Calphalon or hate it." "I have every single piece that you ever made," Barbeau replied.

They talked nonstop the rest of the flight, Kasperzak sharing his family's love of cooking, Barbeau recommending the best restaurants in every city. She told him about events that helped increase her exposure, like Share Our Strength's Taste of the Nation, a series of food and wine benefits held in major cities around the country to raise money to support SOS's anti-hunger and nutrition education programs. "The steward probably thought we were some pick up," recalls Barbeau.

That night, Kasperzak brought the Bon Marché executives to Barbeau's restaurant—Fuller's at the Seattle Sheraton. It was "like a love-in," says Kasperzak, and the talk turned to Share Our Strength and the Taste of the Nation. As a result, Bon Marché decided to support the Seattle "Taste" event. And Kasperzak, seeing the potential of a partnership that could strengthen his company's relationship with retailers and appeal to high-end consumers, decided to contact Share Our Strength to explore a possible tie.

THE NEED

Share Our Strength was Bill Shore's brainchild, conceived "on a hot and lazy August morning in 1984 . . . when a brief article in the *Washington Post* carried the headline '200,000 to Die This Summer in Ethiopia.' I'd had no previous knowledge of this tragedy in the making and was stunned by its enormity and the matter-of-fact nature of the reporting."[2] Shore, an aide to then-Senator Gary Hart, and his sister Debbie used their political organizing skills to recruit chefs to raise money for the anti-hunger cause. "We built our network one chef at a time. For instance the most influential chef in Dallas, Stephan Pyles. We corralled him in a hotel. We'd read about him, wanted to meet him, and heard he was in town for a March of Dimes event. We staked him out in the hotel and waited until he got there."[3] Influential chefs like Alice Waters of Chez Panisse in Berkeley, California, and Jimmy Schmidt of the Rattlesnake Club in Detroit, recruited other chefs. By the late 1980s, SOS had lined up hundreds of top chefs in major cities across the country.

Operating on a shoestring budget in a one-room basement office on Capitol Hill in Washington, D.C., SOS experimented with ways to engage the chefs they had recruited. They discovered early on that restaurateurs preferred to donate food and participate in events that gave them exposure than to make cash donations. In 1986, SOS moved to Denver as the Shore family prepared to assist Gary Hart's second presidential run. There, leaders of the restaurant community helped Shore organize a food-and-wine benefit that became the model for the Taste of the Nation.

Taste of the Nation is based on a simple formula. Local committees of chefs, food professionals, and other volunteers organize a dinner benefit, usually in the spring. Local chefs and restaurateurs provide "tastes"—an appetizer, dessert, or signature dish. It "is an opportunity to do what I do best and help others at the same time," explains Rick Bayless, a prominent Chicago chef. Distributors provide samples of wines and corporate sponsors underwrite the cost of the event so that all ticket proceeds can go to benefit local agencies. In its first ten years, the event raised more than $23 million with events in more than 100 cities involving more than 5,000 culinary professionals.

While Taste of the Nation proved to be an attractive event for chefs eager to increase their visibility with upscale, food-oriented patrons, it also proved to be appealing to companies interested in associating themselves with these chefs and restaurants. In 1988, MasterCard paid $30,000 to become the first national sponsor of Taste. In 1990, *Bon Appétit,* a magazine focusing on gourmet cooking for the home cook, offered to become a sponsor for significantly more money, an amount MasterCard wouldn't match.

The next year, as part of its examination of its relationship with restaurants, AmEx approached SOS about a partnership. At the time, American Express needed something to boost its image among restaurants, where it was in danger of losing market share because of its high fees. AmEx's then vice president Karen Aidem met with SOS. "I was being pitched five to ten times per week for philanthropic donations," she recalls. "What SOS did, which nobody at the time was doing, was pitch it in a business sense—why this made sense for American Express." They would ask, "How are we going to help you improve the relationships you have out there? How can we make this event important to your company?"

Bill Shore's philosophy of working with corporate partners is spelled out in his book, *Revolution of the Heart.* "To find the intersection of public interest and private interest that will work for your partners, begin by sitting down with them to learn about their needs before telling them about yours," he writes. "When you are asking people to buy something that they might want or need, you are in a stronger position than when you are simply asking them to give you something for nothing beyond the warm feeling of giving." And after the relationship is underway, "[d]on't assume they will see the benefits on their own. Instead identify them, measure them, quantify them, and communicate them. Also make sure your partners not only hear from you, but from their customers, other local businessmen, and civic leaders."[4]

In keeping with this philosophy, SOS listened to AmEx's concerns and objectives. AmEx did not want to look like they were taking over the event with banners and signage. So instead, SOS arranged for the company to have its representative speak at the briefing for chefs held before each event—a more subtle way for the company to reach its target audience of restaurateurs. Initially, the reaction of the restaurant community to American Express's sponsorship of Taste of the Nation was mixed, but by the second year, chefs who had been critical had come around.

Impressed with SOS's business sense and pleased with the success of its involvement with Taste of the Nation, American Express explored new ways of partnering with the organization. A group exploring ideas for increasing use of the card suggested donating a portion of every transaction during the holiday season to a cause. Although SOS did not yet have a well-known "brand name," AmEx executives felt it was a natural fit. The company offered SOS $15 million over three years to participate in a new cause-related marketing promotion: Charge Against Hunger.

CAUSE-RELATED MARKETING

American Express had pioneered the *cause-related marketing* concept in 1983—it had even coined the term to describe the *marketing of a product or service by using commercial exchanges to trigger donations, thereby raising money and visibility for a cause.*[5] In contrast to strategic philanthropy, which boosts a company's image but is not intended to increase its revenue, the success of cause-related marketing activities can often be measured in the short-term in dollars and cents. American Express's first large-scale cause-related marketing program donated one cent for every transaction with the card and $1 for every new card issued to the renovation of Ellis Island and the Statue of Liberty. Compared with the previous year, use of the card increased 28 percent and the Statue of Liberty Foundation received $1.7 million for the renovation projects.[6]

The success of the Statue of Liberty campaign prompted other credit card companies to follow suit and helped give rise to the affinity card—credit cards, issued to nonprofit organization members and donors, that rebate a percentage of charges made to the charitable group. Other companies also got into cause-related marketing in the mid-1980s. For example, Scott Paper Company created a "Helping Hand" product line, purchase of which generated funds for charities involved in childhood diseases; the exact amount of the donation to each individual organization was determined based on the funds it raised from the general public. The Easter Seal Society received a dime for every Pepsi consumed during the month of the charity's telethon. Purina created Pets For People through the Humane Society to help senior citizens adopt cats and dogs, with donations based on the redemption of coupons during the last quarter of the year.[7]

The spread of cause-related marketing programs created controversy. One critic charged that "companies, in the guise of giving charitable assistance, exploit philanthropic causes for their own financial profit, commercializing the causes and threatening their traditional sources of long-term support."[8] In 1986, the National Association of Attorneys General issued a model law addressing commercial co-ventures and charitable sales promotions.[9] The next year, the Better Business Bureau conducted a survey to determine consumer receptivity to cause-related marketing and discovered that the practice enjoyed a great deal of support. Four out of five people said they might choose to buy a product that helps support a charity if they were familiar with the quality of the product. Forty percent said they might choose to buy such a product if it cost the same or less as their favorite brand, with a substantial minority (17 percent) saying they would pay more. Almost half said they would like to see more joint-venture marketing.[10]

Growing 10 to 50 percent per year, by the early 1990s,[11] cause-related marketing was considered one of the hottest trends in marketing.[12] A 1991 follow-up to the earlier Better Business Bureau survey found the public no less willing to give, but more sober about charity–business marketing and eager for information about how much of the purchase would go to the charity and how it would be spent.[13] Importantly, contrary to the warnings of critics, the survey found that only 5 percent of those surveyed said they would reduce charitable contributions as a result of cause marketing.[14]

Launched in 1993, Charge Against Hunger, American Express's marketing promotion with Share Our Strength, was similar in design to the Statue of Liberty campaign. During November and December, for each charge, American Express would donate three cents to SOS, up to $5 million—ten times the amount of money SOS had received from American Express through its Taste of the Nation sponsorship and an amount that would represent almost half of SOS's annual budget. American Express developed a three-part approach to appeal to different constituents: a compelling marketing campaign to card members; opportunities for merchants to participate in the program; and employee volunteer opportunities tied to the issue of hunger.

The company began Charge Against Hunger with $15 million of advertising support, including television ads featuring Bill Shore talking about hunger. The program was a success for both AmEx and SOS. For AmEx, it increased charge volume by 12 percent and improved perception of the company by merchants, card holders, and employees. Charge Against Hunger changed SOS dramatically. In addition to growing the nonprofit's budget and staff, the partnership increased SOS's and Bill Shore's name recognition significantly, helping to build SOS's brand. The additional funding caused the organization to increase the sophistication of its grantmaking process and to expand its public relations staff, which helped make Shore's book possible. The close relationship between the two organizations also helped refine SOS's understanding of business and how to reinforce a partnership.

It also helped develop Bill Shore's own evolving view of how nonprofit organizations ought to respond in an era of declining resources. "The nonprofit sector of society is rich in compassion and idealism, but it is entrepreneurially bankrupt, stuck in the posture of settling for that tiny margin of the financial universe that consists of leftover wealth—the excess funds people are willing and able to donate after their other primary needs have been met," he writes. The solution, according to Shore, is for nonprofits to run for-profit businesses by providing a product or service that people want to buy for reasons independent of their charitable intentions. SOS's *Home Food,* the cookbook featuring Barbeau and other Taste of the Nation chefs, is one example; making the SOS name available to American Express for use in its advertising is another. Both involve a "sale" of something of value in exchange for funding that benefits the cause.

SOS had two constant needs—to raise money for anti-hunger efforts and to build its brand through increased visibility. It sought to meet these needs by adding new corporate partners, which Shore and his colleagues attracted and sustained by trading on its assets—its name and logo and network of chefs.

THE MATCH

Charge Against Hunger had been running for a year when Dean Kasperzak approached SOS about a possible partnership. Before meeting with Kasperzak, Townsend and her colleagues brainstormed ideas that would respond to Calphalon's business needs. They knew that Calphalon was a high-end cookware company, that Calphalon marketed itself as "the professional cookware," that Kasperzak was "a big food guy," and that relationships with retailers were the lifeblood of a brand like Calphalon. SOS did not ask for money. Instead, SOS floated several possible joint projects with a range of price tags, including a kickoff event for *Home Food* with SOS chefs at Bloomingdale's in New York. Kasperzak loved the idea.

THE TEST

Calphalon agreed to host the Bloomingdale's event and purchased 2,000 copies of *Home Food* to be offered as a gift for customers making a $50 Calphalon purchase. SOS flew in twenty chefs, and together Calphalon and SOS sponsored the most successful event the 59th Street Bloomingdale's housewares department had ever held. Excited, Kasperzak and his colleagues agreed to attend SOS's annual Conference of Leaders and to sponsor the awards dinner, complete with certificates framed in anodized aluminum.

A last-minute program change made Kasperzak the co-emcee of the dinner with writer Richard Russo. "We ended up doing Rowan and Martin," he says, referring to the comedy duo from the 1960s television show *Laugh-In*. "I'm meeting writers!" SOS sensed Kasperzak's enthusiasm. "And then they ask us to co-sponsor the Taste of the Nation with American Express," he recalls. "I said, are you kidding? We're a little cookware company."

GROWTH

SOS had discussed with American Express the possibility of Calphalon as a second sponsor of Taste. American Express liked the idea. Calphalon was not an AmEx competitor. Calphalon hoped to appeal to consumers through its sponsorship; American Express sought to influence restaurateurs. American Express, a Fortune 100 company, had payed $600,000 to be sole sponsor of Taste, and would pay $400,000 to co-sponsor the benefit with another company; this amount was beyond the reach of the privately held cookware company with sales estimated at $100 million. SOS offered the sponsorship at $300,000. Calphalon said no. SOS countered at $150,000, conditioned on a commitment to increase the amount over time. This time the answer was yes.

Calphalon chose to raise the funds by borrowing the strategy that had proven so profitable for American Express: cause-related marketing. The company would designate a pan per season for co-branding with SOS—the first year it was a two-quart sauté pan—and donate $5 for each one sold. Half of these funds would come from retailers, who would participate in local promotions.

"Did this thing have legs? Overwhelmingly," according to Kasperzak. The sauté pan, which became the communications vehicle to engage retailers, had real appeal. Calphalon sold four times the number of two-quart pans as it had sold the year before, and Calphalon's first check to SOS was in the amount of $180,000. They presented it to Bill Shore at the first "Taste of Toledo," organized by Calphalon and held in its distribution center. "We had no idea how many pans would sell," recalls Townsend. "Dean was very soft-spoken about it—he wanted to wow us." When SOS staff expressed excitement about their windfall, Kasperzak would reply, "If we're giving you $180,000, can you imagine how much *we* made?"

Reflecting on SOS's work with Calphalon, both Kasperzak and Kathleen Rarey, the former director of marketing who managed the relationship on a day-to-day basis, point to the nonprofit's willingness to work hard to meet the company's needs. Kasperzak finds "a lot of similarities between SOS and an ad agency." Rarey observes that "they're drastically understaffed, but they worked hard to get me what I need. . . . They have a good grasp of reality that there's a business side of it."

Calphalon's contribution to SOS grew in the ensuing years, through the sales of additional pans and in other ways. Calphalon encouraged its regional sales reps to join local Taste committees around the country and donated a pan to each committee for use as a door prize or reward to dedicated volunteers. It also opened the door for SOS to forge new relationships with retailers, including Burdine's, Bon Marché, and Bloomingdale's department stores, Chef's Catalog, and the online Cyber Shop.

Sales reps and in some cases SOS volunteers and staff worked with retailers to promote SOS and the Taste event. For example, Burdine's, a major department store headquartered in Florida, developed promotional materials, including a video, posters, and a public service announcement featuring Lauren Hutton; created a recipe packet, free with purchase of a Calphalon pan, featuring participating chefs; held demonstration events in the stores; and took out a half-page ad in the *Miami Herald*. Bloomingdale's, taking a different approach, organized simultaneous Sunday brunches in 21 stores featuring Taste chefs. Calphalon paid for a free trip to anywhere in the continental United States for the sale associate who sold the most $15 tickets to customers. Customers who bought a ticket also received a discount in Bloomingdale's housewares the day of the brunch. The brunch became an annual event almost as popular as the Taste dinner itself, raising nearly $50,000 for SOS in 1998 alone.

Of course, Calphalon benefited from the involvement of retailers in promoting SOS and Calphalon. They also benefited from the implicit or explicit endorsement of Taste of the Nation chefs who were involved in the events—using Calphalon pans at the Bloomingdale's brunch or at demonstrations in Macy's housewares departments. To make sure that the chefs also benefited, Calphalon and SOS sought to find ways to showcase them and their restaurants: handing out recipe cards including information about their restaurants and promoting them in advertising for the Taste of the Nation pan.

In 1998, Calphalon and SOS created the Chef's Alliance to formalize the company's relationship with a team of eighteen SOS chefs, including Monique Barbeau, Claude Mann of TBS Dinner and a Movie, and Jeffrey Buben of Vidalia in Washington, D.C. These chefs agreed to showcase the hard-anodized Calphalon line with demonstrations of classic cooking techniques in targeted department stores. Retailers took advantage of this opportunity to host celebrity chefs because it would increase traffic in their housewares departments and enhance their reputation as good corporate citizens. In return, the stores guaranteed a minimum donation of $5,000 to SOS, agree to promote the nonprofit, and display Calphalon during the event. In this way, everyone involved benefited.

It is not surprising that Calphalon's venture into cause-related marketing in the mid-1990s proved successful. As an innovator in the marketing of cookware, Calphalon was ahead of its main competitors in tying its product to a cause. Studies have found that cause-related marketing, while acceptable to a broad spectrum of the public, holds most appeal for the type of consumers who comprise a large segment of Calphalon's target market: employed women, white-collar professionals, and "influentials"—the 10 percent of the adult population who are identified primarily by their social activism and their role as opinion makers and group leaders.

Over the period from 1993 to 1997, Cone/Roper surveys found that early skepticism about cause-related marketing had faded, decreasing from 58 percent of consumers who in 1993 suspected the practice was just for "show," to just 21 percent in 1997. Only 2 percent said they would have a less favorable opinion of a company engaged in the practice, which suggested that companies could proceed with minimal risk. And importantly, the study found that three out of four people said they would switch to brands or retailers associated with a good cause when price and quality are equal; again the figures were higher for influentials and women.[15]

A related Cone/Roper study conducted in 1995 found that building deeper relationships with customers and enhancing a reputation or image are the main reasons companies engage in cause-related marketing. Nine out of ten executives rated their own programs as successful. Those who were most pleased had set specific goals from the outset. Interestingly, most companies did not measure their cause-related programs in direct relationship to sales, but described their program results in terms of enhanced corporate image, increased loyalty among customers, higher employee retention, and increased customer satisfaction.[16]

Alan Andreasen writing in *Harvard Business Review* suggests there are three types of cause-related marketing campaigns.[17] In *transaction-based promotions,* the most common form, a company donates a specific amount of cash, food, or equipment in direct proportion to sales to one or more nonprofits. Calphalon's donation to SOS for each Taste of the Nation pan sold fits this model, as does Procter & Gamble's Special Olympics promotion, one of the longest running cause-related promotions. Procter & Gamble donates ten cents to the nonprofit organization for each special coupon redeemed by a certain date.

In *joint issue* promotions, a corporation and a nonprofit organization tackle a social problem through tactics such as distributing products and promotional materials and advertising. Health-related campaigns of this sort have become increasingly popular, contrary to the views of early naysayers that associating one's product with a disease might cause customers to keep their distance. The advent of AIDS—and the involvement of popular celebrities like Elizabeth Taylor—convinced marketers of the value of mobilizing around an illness.[18] Avon's Breast Cancer Awareness Crusade is one of the most well known and most successful examples. Using its 450,000 person sales force to talk to women about early detection and to sell $2 pink ribbon-shaped pins to benefit breast cancer prevention programs, Avon has distributed more than 48 million educational brochures and raised $25 million for the cause.

Finally, in *licensing partnerships*, a nonprofit authorizes use of its name and logo to a corporation in exchange for a fee or percentage of revenues. Even more than other forms of marketing partnerships, a licensing arrangement implies that the nonprofit organization in fact endorses the product, in addition to benefiting from sales. Save the Children's popular ties featuring children's artwork is one example. Share Our Strength's licensing of the Taste of the Nation name for gourmet food products is another. Again, health-related partnerships—the Arthritis Foundation put its name on pain relievers by Johnson & Johnson, the American Cancer Society put its name on SmithKline's Nicoderm smoking-cessation patches—have been common in this area, and have been among the more controversial.[19]

A 1997 partnership between the American Medical Association and Sunbeam, under the leadership of "Chainsaw Al" Dunlop, illustrates well the downside of poorly considered cause-related marketing partnerships. When the AMA agreed to endorse Sunbeam's home-health-care products, it neglected to establish a process to test the effectiveness of the products. Although the deal would generate millions for the medical society to fund a variety of public-health programs and expand the distribution of the AMA's educational materials, consumer groups and the AMA's own members denounced the arrangement, forcing the AMA to try to break the deal. When Sunbeam sued the organization, five AMA staff members lost their jobs and the nonprofit paid $9.9 million to settle a lawsuit with Sunbeam.[20]

In partnerships like this, where a nonprofit's name becomes identified with a product, consumers may believe it has been evaluated by the nonprofit. Should the organization fail, as the AMA did, to develop a process to assess the products that receive its implicit endorsement, and should the product turn out to be harmful, the nonprofit could be exposed to tort liability. These risks can be minimized if an organization exercises reasonable care in selecting its partners and evaluating their products. Disclaimers may also be appropriate to make clear the nonprofit's limited role with respect to particular products. In fact, the attorneys general of sixteen states jointly issued a preliminary report in April 1999, recommending practices to end misleading cause-related advertising. The report recommended that ads clearly state whether the nonprofit endorses a product, whether the nonprofit was paid for the use of its name and logo, and whether an exclusive arrangement exists.[21]

Despite these potential problems, consumer demand and the business community's growing awareness of research supporting the practice have helped create a proliferation of cause-related marketing campaigns. IEG estimated that North American corporations would spend nearly $1 billion for cause-related marketing partnerships in 1999 (not including advertising dollars used to promote the tie-in), and there is every reason to believe that the popularity of these programs will continue for the foreseeable future.[22] Ninety percent of executives surveyed by Cone/Roper in 1996 said their company's commitment to cause-related marketing will continue, with more than half saying they expected it to increase.[23]

Although national campaigns are more visible and well known, small businesses and local grassroots organizations can also develop cause-related promotions. For example, My Sister's Place, a shelter for battered women in Washington, D.C., received funds from a local beauty salon for each appointment during a slow period. The clothing line Goober Pea, named for its owner/designer's dog, donates 5 percent of profits to an animal protection organization (the dog, which is featured on the clothing, was rescued from an animal shelter). Even an Alexandria, Virginia, street performer—a mime who performs only *after* change has been deposited in his cup—notes on a cardboard sign that a share of his take will go to support a disabled child.

The flexibility of cause-related marketing allows for almost any company to make such an arrangement. In some cases, it may be more advantageous to affiliate with a single nonprofit organization. However, if the desired cause lacks a well-known nonprofit organization with a solid reputation, the cause itself might be the visible tie, with funds going to several different less well-known organizations (Avon's breast cancer campaign fit this model). The tie may be between the cause and a company, a brand, a group of products, or a single product. It may be time limited (the Charge Against Hunger took place during the last quarter of each year) or continuous (Working Assets, a long-distance reseller, donates 1 percent of revenues to causes selected by its customers). The transaction generating the donation may be a coupon redemption, use of a credit card, return of a survey, or retail sale.[24]

What Works

CALPHALON: A MULTIFACETED CAMPAIGN

Like all advertising, cause-related marketing campaigns require multiple impressions to create awareness and influence consumer behavior. Simply labeling a product with a tag indicating that a share of the purchase price will go to charity may yield modest funds for the organization but will not likely drive sales, build an image, or create loyal customers for the company. Many companies conducting cause-related advertising campaigns spend five or ten times the amount donated to charity on advertising to promote the partnership.

Beyond advertising, the campaign can be reinforced in many other ways that are likely to be effective for both partners. This process works best if a company has a genuine interest in the issue, a success factor underscored in Cone/Roper's study of corporate executive views on cause-related marketing. A "top to bottom" commitment throughout the organization and the dedication of sufficient financial/human resources were also repeatedly cited by executives as being vital to the success of a cause-related marketing program.

Although the main cause-related tie was between SOS's Taste of the Nation trademark and a selected hard-anodized Calphalon pan, individuals familiar with either the charity or the business would see a "top to bottom" commitment by both partners. In 1998, SOS promoted Calphalon's national sponsorship at its Taste of the Nation events, at its annual conference, in its publications, on its Web site, to its other partners, to its Taste of the Nation volunteers, to its network of chefs, and through staff speaking engagements. Calphalon provided SOS or Taste of the Nation information on recipe cards included with each pan, linked to SOS through its Web site, created point-of-sale information cards and posters, and promoted the pan to retailers, some of whom included it in advertising circulars. It also arranged for Bill Shore to brief its regional sales reps, who became familiar with the organization first hand by volunteering on local Taste committees.

MAXIMIZING POTENTIAL

Focusing on the consumer as the sole target of a cause-related marketing campaign may limit its potential to create value for the brand or product. The campaign can be made more effective, and yield greater benefits, by engaging retailers and other possible stakeholders. The campaign creates an opportunity for retailers to attract customers by holding events, featuring the cause in its advertising, and engaging its own employees in cause-related activities. The company can create a rewards program to motivate retailers and their employees. It can also encourage the participation of retailers by agreeing to target its donations to programs in the retailer's community. In this way, the company, the retailer, and the social sector partner all benefit.

Calphalon offers a good example of using cause-related marketing to strengthen its relationships with retailers. Department stores were receptive to doing SOS events proposed by Calphalon, having seen how they can benefit by bringing more customers to their often out-of-the-way housewares departments. Calphalon was well equipped to support these events logistically and was able to offer incentives, for example, to department store employees who sell the most tickets to an event. Its partner SOS contributed volunteers and chefs. In this way, Calphalon received extra promotion at the retail level in advertisements, displays, and by motivated salespeople.

Calphalon also used its SOS relationship to boost its placement in mail-order catalogs. The former owner of Chef's Catalog, Marshall Marcovitz, became a strong supporter of SOS. Chef's Catalog offered featured placement to the SOS-licensed Calphalon cookware and even designated three additional Calphalon pans as SOS promotions—for each of the pans sold SOS received $2.50 from the Chef's Catalog. In 1997, it gave Calphalon the cover of its holiday catalog for the first time, along with more pages than were dedicated to any other manufacturer.

MAKING A COMMITMENT

Cause-related marketing appears to be most effective when a company or brand focuses on a single cause over a period of years. Lurching from cause to cause from year to year won't establish a link in the minds of consumers. Trading partners often, even if they work in the same field, limits opportunities for richer relationships that involve additional activities that reinforce a marketing campaign and provide other benefits (the New Value Partnerships discussed in chapter 11).

Calphalon began its relationship with Share Our Strength with the possibility of a long-term partnership in mind. It found a partner that made sense—hunger works well as a cause that is related to cookware. Its support for the cause was not implicitly self-serving, and the brand's association with SOS's network of leading chefs affirmed to consumers that the cookware is high quality. Calphalon allowed the relationship to develop over time, engaging in new transactions, and dropping or modifying activities that didn't work as well as others. Calphalon has also benefited from its role in the larger SOS family—when American Express included a Calphalon pan in a magazine advertisement featuring the household goods of political pundits James Carville and Mary Matalin.

SHARE OUR STRENGTH: DEVELOPING AN ASSET

Social sector organizations seeking cause-related marketing partnerships must begin with a strong brand—including name recognition, an appealing cause, and a good reputation (see chapter 2). Beyond brand, many of the national organizations that have been most successful in attracting cause-related marketing deals have local operations—such as Goodwill, Red Cross, Special Olympics, Boys and Girls Clubs, and the Children's Miracle Network.

In addition to the basic requirement of brand, an organization's ability to promote the partnership is of particular importance. A strong public relations operation, an articulate and sought after spokesperson, and a large network of volunteers and donors are good assets for this purpose.

SOS founder Bill Shore is a sought-after speaker for social sector and business organizations. He commonly uses these opportunities to talk about SOS's corporate partners, including Calphalon, thereby giving the company additional credibility and exposure among influential audiences. SOS has an in-house PR department that generates significant coverage for the organization and its partners. The organization works with a network of thousands of local volunteers who put on Taste of the Nation and other programs, and it maintains a mailing list of individuals who have supported the organization in the past.

One asset that makes SOS stand out from other anti-hunger organizations is its network of accomplished chefs. "It is a natural fit for chefs to get involved in the fight against hunger," Shore explains. "For chefs to 'share their strength' with those who are struggling to feed their families on limited incomes has a profound impact on the chef and their community." This network made the nonprofit attractive to partners seeking ties to restaurants (like American Express) or companies looking for a gourmet image (like Calphalon and Bon Appétit). In addition, instead of simply asking chefs to donate money, SOS involves them in ways that are more meaningful to them, such as preparing food for events. In this way, SOS gives them and their restaurants visibility and connects them to other chefs and community members who are involved in the cause. As a result, the chefs are willing to maintain their relationship with SOS, even when it imposes significant costs. Without the important asset of the chefs network, SOS might have had a difficult time developing some of its major corporate partnerships.

INTEGRATING CORPORATE PARTNERS INTO THE FAMILY

In order to engage multiple corporate partners, an organization must have the capacity to meet each of their individual needs. A dedicated staff helps—these individuals may be responsible for ensuring that enough is being done to support the partnership and can navigate within the organization to get things done. Of course, in the case of a cause-related marketing partnership, the marketing department must be integrally involved. But the relationship need not be limited to a single unit—in fact, the more the corporate partner can be integrated into the social sector organization, the more likely it is that additional opportunities to create value will arise for both partners.

SOS continually seeks to ensure that its partners' needs are met. In the case of Calphalon, Taste of the Nation and public relations staff at SOS kept in touch with marketing staff from the company on a day-to-day basis. In addition, an annual planning meeting involving senior managers from both organizations set the direction for the year. Other staff became knowledgeable about the relationship and became involved as opportunities arose. SOS's familiar refrain—"Are you happy? How are we doing?"—let Calphalon know that the organization was always ready to make adjustments to meet the company's objectives.

SOS's ability to work with its partners effectively has enabled it to benefit from more than a dozen business partnerships over its fifteen-year life span, including relationships with Barnes and Noble hosting SOS-affiliated authors at book readings, and The Motley Fool, Inc., as the beneficiary of its groundbreaking online holiday donation drive.

SOS works to make its corporate partners part of its network, on an equal footing with its other funders, volunteers, and grantees. SOS sponsors a by-invitation-only annual Conference of Leaders for its network of chefs, Taste of the Nation volunteers, corporate sponsors, grantees, and SOS staff for three days of gourmet meals, panel discussions, and inspiring speakers who reinforce the importance of the mission and build community among the diverse participants in the conference. Involvement in this event convinced Kasperzak to develop a larger partnership with SOS, and Calphalon became a visible regular participant at the conference, with staff featured on the program.

Calphalon and Share Our Strength: The Impact

As the amount of money directed at the partnership grew, Calphalon senior executives and board members raised the issue of measurement. Can outcomes be quantified? When SOS asks, "Are you happy?" does the company have enough information to respond? Although the organizations constantly evaluated the partnership informally, they had not done a formal evaluation. For example, the company tracks sales of the Taste of the Nation pans, but has been unable to determine if the brisk sales of the item relate to the SOS tie-in or to the promotional pricing of the pan.

In the spring of 1998, Calphalon was bought by Newell Co., a multinational manufacturer and marketer of high-volume staple consumer goods. As a result of the sale, Dean Kasperzak and Kathleen Rarey left the company, which tested Kasperzak's earlier prediction that "if I left right now, this company could not disconnect from SOS." Due to the sale of the company, SOS and Calphalon marketing staff accelerated completion of a planned "impact" report.

In 1998 SOS received $400,000 in cash from Calphalon and $4.7 million from Taste of the Nation, which Calphalon co-sponsored. It also benefited from nationwide visibility, additional volunteers for local Taste of the Nation committees, and introductions to other corporate sponsors.

SOS used funds generated by Taste of the Nation to make several hundred grants, mostly in the $10,000 to $75,000 range. The local anti-hunger organizations that received these grants served more than 350 million meals in a year and ran programs to increase access to safe, nutritious and affordable food. For example, the Capital Area Community Food Bank in Washington, D.C., used its SOS grant to support an organic farm that provides fresh produce to low-income communities and to run Food and Skills, a ten-week nutrition education and lifeskills program. An informal evaluation found that 80 percent of program graduates reached the goals they had set for themselves. And while the organization values the grant it receives, Food Bank Executive Director Lynn Brantley believes SOS contributes something even more important. "SOS keeps the issue of hunger alive before the community," she says.

PART IV

Operational
Exchanges

8

HUMAN RESOURCES

*Ridgeview, Inc., and Newton-Conover
Public Schools*

In 1987, Ridgeview, Inc., a hosiery manufacturer based in rural North Carolina, agreed to an unusual request by a middle school guidance counselor to hold parent–teacher conferences on company premises—a place convenient for employee-parents. Twelve years later, this simple partnership had expanded into several new areas, benefiting the school, the company, employee-parents, and students.

For Ridgeview, this partnership is an important part of its strategy to increase productivity and improve its image as a family-friendly company. The program helps to attract new employees and retain existing ones.

The school system benefits from reduced truancy and improved relationships with families. The school's willingness to meet at a place convenient to parents and the company's sincere efforts to respond to employees' family needs send a strong message to parents about the importance of school involvement and the company's core values. The program has been adopted by several additional companies in the area.

Ridgeview, Inc., and Newton-Conover Public Schools

In 1987, business was good for Ridgeview, Inc., one of several hosiery manufacturers in the Catawba Valley of North Carolina. The family-owned company had recently added sport socks to its line. The new product quickly became the largest segment of the business. To help meet rising demand, the company had opened a new plant overseas and was gradually expanding its North Carolina operations.

Although the company was experiencing unprecedented growth, it faced several challenges. The unemployment rate for Catawba County was low, and that meant competition for labor was high. The recent opening of fiber optic cable plants in the area offered employees lucrative alternatives to hosiery. The number of workers who had been with the plant for twenty years or more was declining. The new workforce was younger and increasingly from families with two working parents. With new job opportunities available, they could easily jump ship. They were mostly women, and they had children—young children who went to school in the Newton-Conover public schools.

And so, when the local school system asked the company to participate in an experiment that would make it easier for parents to meet with school guidance counselors by bringing them to the work site, it seemed like a win-win proposition. "It would be easy enough to do. The only requirement was time," recalls Ridgeview's former Vice President Hugh Gaither. He saw the potential for this seemingly simple idea to help Ridgeview attract and retain employees. He knew it could help productivity: his own experience taught him that employees who were worried about their children could be distracted from their work, a point borne out by research.[1] He understood the value of employers helping employees balance work and family life and, with four children of his own in the local public schools, he knew the challenges first hand. It would be good for the children of his employees, good for the community, and good for Ridgeview. After discussing the idea with his cousin, Albert Gaither, who was president of the company, and Albert's daughter, Susan Gaither Jones, a vice president, he decided Ridgeview should give the program a try.

THE NEED

It was no coincidence that the school district had chosen Ridgeview to pilot a new program, later to be known as "PIECES" (Parents, Industry, Educators Cooperating for Educational Success).

Spearheaded by Newton-Conover middle school guidance counselor Susan Ballard, the program was intended to address a common problem in the largely blue-collar school district of 3,000 students, an hour north of Charlotte. North Carolina has the highest percentage of working mothers in the country, and Catawba County the third highest percentage in the state, 78 percent. Most of these parents work in factories—the area is known for its textile, furniture, and more recently, fiber optic cable plants. These jobs often pay by the piece, and it's hard for parents to take time off during the workday to attend meetings at the school, even though the schools are just a five-minute drive away. Some parents didn't like to visit their child's school, associating it with bad experiences they had as children. Still others thought of the conferences as an "us versus them" situation, with the school being the home turf of the other team.

Ballard knew parent involvement was important—studies correlate parent involvement in education to higher achievement for children. Middle school children are particularly vulnerable—it's at this age that parents often let their involvement slip, relying instead on their children for information. As chairman of the board of the Catawba County Council on Adolescence, Ballard knew that regular communication between the school and the parent can help both parties do a better job for the child, and can head off potentially harmful behavior before it happens.

Ballard was discussing this challenge with Larry Harris, the middle school principal, in the fall of 1987. Harris remembered reading about a practice in China, where the schools would go to the work site to hold parent conferences, and surmised that such a program could work well in Newton-Conover. To pilot the program would take the cooperation of a local business that understood the importance of parent conferences and would be willing to let employees take time off for the meetings.

THE MATCH

Ballard felt a family-owned business made sense because she believed there would be less red tape. Ridgeview Corporation came immediately to mind. The Gaither family had run the Ridgeview hosiery manufacturing business since it began in 1912 and had a history of supporting education. The president at the time, Albert Gaither, had served on the school board in the 1960s, and the company had an excellent record of responding to requests from the school for speakers, tours, and other support.

Acting on her hunch, Ballard called Hugh Gaither. After he discussed it with Edith Grimes, Ridgeview's director of human resources, he "was in total agreement," Ballard recalls.

THE TEST

Ballard and Grimes worked together to plan the initial visits. To help generate enthusiasm for the program, she arranged for the counselors to be photographed for the local newspaper. Edith Grimes promoted the program through Ridgeview's employee newsletter and made sure parents knew what to expect during the visit.

The company decided to allow the meetings to occur on company time. No employee would be docked for time spent at a meeting; workers paid by the piece would receive their average pay for the period they were off the line; and the time off would not count against credit earned toward the employee's bonus for perfect attendance.

Apprehensive, the counselors prepared for their first meetings—forty-seven parents were scheduled, several times the typical number of parent meetings held each week. The counselors planned agendas for the initial sessions. Counselors would introduce themselves, describe the program, and share the child's school record, which many parents didn't know they had a right to see.

Rather than resenting the intrusion into their work site, employees were "very kind, appreciative," according to Ballard. They brought pads to take notes, and several came in for their appointments on their day off. The meetings were held in the personnel office and two other offices to ensure privacy. One nervous mother who didn't want to meet in the personnel director's office felt music might make her more comfortable—the counselor offered her car, which had a radio. "We went to Ridgeview that day hoping to make those parents feel special," recalls Susan Ballard. "We left feeling special ourselves." By the second visit, the parents knew the counselors by name and were referring to the visitors as "my counselor."

GROWTH

Ridgeview, with its two-person human resources department, has sought other techniques to recruit and retain qualified workers.

In addition to hosting school guidance counselors, Ridgeview has implemented a pilot program to allow job sharing and flextime, sponsored lunchtime parenting seminars, and created an on-site day-care facility—all to help employees meet the needs of their families. These efforts appear to be paying off; although it has not done a formal study, Ridgeview has found that those employees who use the child-care facility have the highest rate of retention, a result consistent with more scientific research conducted by other employers providing similar benefits.[2]

To expand the future pool of qualified job applicants, the company engages in other human resource partnerships. It provides both youth and adult apprenticeships in conjunction with the North Carolina Department of Labor. Several employees teach at the Catawba Valley Community College Hosiery Technology Center, which trains potential workers on seaming and knitting machines. The center has been a good source of new employees, particularly among Hispanic and Hmong immigrants. To further meet these employees' needs, Ridgeview arranges with the community college for English as a Second Language classes to be offered at the plant and is teaching plant supervisors Spanish.

To prepare its workforce of the future, the company sponsors a variety of school-to-work activities, including a job shadowing program to introduce students to manufacturing, Junior Achievement, and career day.

Human Resource Partnerships

Human resource partnerships, in which a company *prepares, recruits, trains, or retains a high quality workforce in cooperation with a social sector organization,* have grown exponentially in recent years. Employers like Ridgeview appreciate the role of these institutions in developing and supporting the workforce, both current and future. At the same time, social sector organizations, like the Newton-Conover public schools, recognize the realities of economic life. They understand that parents are not free to come and go at their convenience. And they know that readying youth for the world of work is part of their responsibility to prepare young people to become good citizens.

Human resource partnerships enable social sector organizations to further their own missions by assisting businesses in recruiting, training, supporting, and retaining employees. These partnerships take many forms, including arrangements like the PIECES program that help employees balance work and family responsibilities; welfare-to-work programs that train and support individuals leaving public assistance; and school-to-work projects that prepare students for specific careers.

BALANCING WORK AND FAMILY

Beginning in the 1970s with the increased entry of women into the workforce and into senior management positions, businesses began to explore ways to assist parents with their family responsibilities. Arguing that child-care assistance would increase productivity, aid recruitment, help with retention, and reduce absenteeism, women's advocates called for companies to support child care. Early efforts focused on establishment of on-site child-care centers, but in practice they were expensive to operate and tended to serve mainly children of highly paid employees. Nonetheless, the number of employers offering on-site child care grew steadily, from just over 100 centers in 1978[3] to 8,000 in 1998.[4] Employers also support child care by subsidizing off-site care, donating funds to local day-care providers in return for slots for their employees, and by assisting employees in locating care.

These efforts often involve partnerships with nonprofit organizations, although the use of an intermediary organization to broker relationships is common. For example, since 1982, the American Business Collaboration for Quality Dependent Care, an alliance of major corporations initiated by IBM, has been expanding the supply and quality of child care in communities where its member companies operate. Working through a Boston-based consulting firm, Work/Family Directions (WFD), the collaboration assesses the needs of employees of participating companies, evaluates the local child-care market, allocates grant funds from the collaboration to fill gaps, and brokers deals between the companies and local child-care providers. In 1995, the collaboration announced a $100 million campaign sponsored by twenty-one major corporations to develop and strengthen school-age child care and elder care in sixty targeted communities through the year 2000. "We believe that supporting the diverse dependent-care needs of our employees is critical to our success as it enables our companies to attract and retain a productive, competitive, committed, and motivated workforce," according to the campaign's sponsors.[5]

Use of an intermediary has been critical to the success of the program. Early efforts by the companies to recruit local child-care providers were fruitless, and cultural differences stymied the building of good working relationships. "The provider community focuses on the dependent. They don't see the parent as the customer who pays their bills," according to Betty Southwick, a WFD consultant. At the same time, "businesses have no patience with the thinking process of providers. They ask, 'Where are the reports?' The provider's prime goal is to provide a quality place for children, not filing paperwork. There is a lack of understanding between these two different worlds."

As a result of WFD's efforts to bridge this gap, hundreds of successful cross-sector dependent care partnerships have been established in more than sixty communities. For example, Bank of America, IBM, Texas Instruments, and AT&T joined together in Dallas to fund the Visiting Nurses Association to arrange for safety audits, home repairs and transportation to help elderly parents of the companies' employees continue to live at home. The partnership responds to a concern that cuts across all levels of a company, according to Marie Reed, vice president and human resources manager for Bank of America in Texas.[6] According to one study, 20 to 30 percent of American workers care for older relatives, and the percentage is expected to grow.[7]

WELFARE-TO-WORK

When he signed landmark welfare reform legislation in August 1996, President Clinton challenged "every business person in America who has ever complained about the failure of the welfare system to try to hire somebody off welfare."[8] One response of the business community was the creation of the Welfare to Work Partnership, a national organization devoted to encouraging businesses to hire and retain welfare recipients and giving them the tools and networks to do so. Launched in early 1997 by founding companies United Airlines, United Parcel Service, Burger King, Sprint and Monsanto, the Partnership had enlisted over 10,000 large and small companies from all regions and business sectors by January, 1999.

Although companies joined partly out of a sense of civic responsibility, there was also more powerful business motivations. Hiring former welfare recipients can help businesses meet their hiring needs, especially in a tight labor market, and reduce payroll costs through tax credits or wage subsidies.[9]

Tapping this nontraditional labor source is easier said than done, however. One of the crucial elements in successful transitions is partnering with nonprofit organizations who provide specialized services such as employee screening, job readiness training, job placement, and development of job retention strategies.[10] Some organizations provide the services themselves, while others broker services with community-based agencies. Some provide just part of the package, for example, childcare, placements, transportation services, job coaching; others are "full service."

Organizations run the gamut from national groups like Goodwill Industries and the National Urban League, to small grassroots groups like Project Match in Chicago; some are community colleges, and others are targeted education and training programs, frequently government funded. One of the latter is Wildcat Service Corporation, a nonprofit organization in New York City that for over twenty years has helped welfare recipients move from lives of dependence to independence. In 1998 alone, Wildcat trained, placed, and moved over 750 people into full-time positions with full health care benefits, most with leading blue-chip investment and brokerage firms like Salomon Smith Barney. Wildcat's president and CEO, Amy Betanzos, attributed her organization's extraordinary success in recent years to a change in its thinking: "A few years ago, we began to recognize that we have two clients—welfare recipients and businesses. Training alone doesn't work. We need company- and industry-specific information. We need to know about a company's culture: its people, its turnover rates, its expectations."

While Salomon Smith Barney looks to Wildcats for its hiring needs, Sprint turns to Kansas City's Metropolitan Community College, where a six-week basic skills boot camp is the prerequisite for a full-time job at the company's new call center. The center, located in one of Kansas City's poorest neighborhoods, has a high retention rate of primarily former welfare recipients: the 77 percent retention rate is more than twice as high as the rate at a neighboring call center in the Kansas City suburbs staffed with no former welfare recipients. Hazel Barkley, the director of the call center, gives the credit to the "tough love" training at Metropolitan. Community colleges have played an important role in helping women and minorities leave public assistance for paid work, and assisting employers by providing job-specific skills training as well as job readiness courses. As of 1998, about half of the more than 1,000 community colleges in the United States offered welfare-to-work programming.[11]

The success of these partnerships is encouraging. Welfare to Work Partnership companies alone report an estimated 410,000 former recipients moving into jobs since the partnership began operations in 1997— primarily full-time positions with health benefits and high retention levels. The higher retention level among former welfare recipients than other entry-level employees is due partly to a quality relationship with a business-focused intermediary.[12] This success explains why in 1999 48 percent of companies were looking to community-based organizations for help in finding people to hire, up from 25 percent in February, 1998.

Going forward, these new human resource partnerships will be confronted with new challenges, particularly the reality that the more than two million people still on the welfare rolls are "the hardest to place." Company success at locating and nurturing nonprofit partners and nonprofit partner success in tailoring programs to the changing needs of the businesses they service, supplemented by new resources from the federal government, augers well for the next stage.

SCHOOL-TO-WORK

School-to-work programs are by far the most popular type of human resource partnership and the most common form of business-education partnership. They date back to the early 1900s with the development of cooperative learning programs that tied part-time jobs to vocational education.[13] In the 1980s, a series of reports, such as *The Forgotten Half: Non-College Youth in America* by the W. T. Grant Foundation Commission, highlighted the plight of youth whose education prepares them neither for work nor college.[14] These reports, coupled with policymakers' concerns about economic competitiveness and growing interest in European apprenticeship models, helped to spur bipartisan interest in school-to-work programs. As a result, many states passed school-to-work legislation and the federal School-to-Work Opportunities legislation was enacted in 1994 to provide funding for state and local school-to-work programs.[15] The tight labor market of the late 1990s stimulated growth in partnerships between high schools and businesses, increasing their number by 270 percent in just eighteen months.[16]

By 1997, the most common school-to-work activities were job shadowing programs, internships, and mentoring, with cooperative education and apprenticeships close behind.[17] According to a Department of Education study, 60 percent of companies with 1,000 or more employees engage in school-to-work partnerships, compared with 24 percent of small companies with under fifty employees. Companies in the health and communications industries are the most likely to be involved.[18] According to one study, most employers got involved with work-based learning programs in order to perform a community service, although the need to recruit a workforce was also commonly cited.[19]

Despite their proliferation, school-to-work programs have yet to become the norm for preparing youth for productive employment. This limited impact is perhaps due to the short-term nature of many programs that involve a one-time exposure to the work world. More intensive programs may still fail to include training, work experience, and academic learning in the right proportions.

To improve outcomes for both youth and business, school-to-work experts recommend that companies join industrywide coalitions, rather than pursuing programs on their own. Such arrangements reduce the burden on individual companies and offer more varied opportunities for students.

For example, Crown Auto World, a car dealership in Tulsa, Oklahoma, began in 1992 to recruit recent junior college and high school vo-tech graduates to address its dire shortage of skilled automotive technicians.[20] Two years later, Crown's owner, Henry Primeaux III, heard General Motors chairman Jack Smith give a keynote address about the potential of school-to-work programs. Primeaux was inspired to volunteer for GM's National Advisory Council for School-To-Work and to help bring GM's pilot apprenticeship program to Oklahoma. When the GM program expanded to include other car manufacturers, it became the Automotive Youth Educational System (AYES).

Students from the Tulsa Technology Center, serving students from forty local high schools, become eligible for AYES midway through their junior year, after they have completed automotive repair work at the vo-tech center. Those accepted interview with dealers and begin working full-time during the summer and part-time during their senior year.

Local schools have benefited from the program through improved student performance, but political struggles have developed between independent auto-shop owners on the one hand and dealers and manufacturers, who want an educational track developed for their own auto lines, on the other. (The school refused the dealers' and manufacturers' demands.)[21]

Crown Auto World has benefited from the program through increased productivity (students performing routine tasks free up technicians to do more complex work); opportunities to hire its graduating apprentices; improved customer satisfaction; and better employee morale, which has decreased turnover. As a small company, Crown could not have implemented a high quality program of this sort without the partnership with GM (which has put $5 million into the program) and the expertise of the well-established vo-tech program. The program has also received federal school-to-work funds and has been recognized by the automotive Industry Planning Council as the best of its kind in the nation.[22]

What Works

RIDGEVIEW: A CULTURE ENCOURAGING PARTICIPATION

A 1998 study by the Families and Work Institute found that the vast majority of employers offer family-friendly policies. Ninety percent allow workers time off for school events or to stay home with sick children, two-thirds permit flextime, and half allow employees to set aside wages for dependent-care expenses on a pretax basis. But although many companies profess to offer policies and programs to help families balance work and family needs, these pro-family policies may exist mainly on paper. One study found that almost 40 percent of human resource representatives surveyed said their companies didn't make "real and ongoing" efforts to tell employees of available work-family programs.[23]

Even if employees are aware of family-friendly benefits, making assistance available won't achieve its intended effect if the company discourages its use in subtle—or not so subtle—ways. Without the support of senior management, as well as line supervisors, employees may be reluctant to take advantage of opportunities provided by the company. This is particularly true for male employees in companies that expect women to take advantage of family-friendly policies but discourage men directly and indirectly from taking paternity leave or making flextime arrangements.

Ridgeview offers an excellent example of a company that conforms practice to policy. The range of supports for working parents at Ridgeview—from the day-care center to parenting seminars—sends a clear message about the company's commitment. It has also been willing to reevaluate company policy to be responsive to workers' needs. For example, when it became clear that the company's attendance bonus policy worked against employees with children, it changed the rules to allow parents more flexibility.

Offering benefits to employees at all levels, as Ridgeview does, rather than limiting support to a single class of workers, also makes sense. A program may be designed for entry-level workers (although ultimately the goal is to retain them and see them advance). But if benefits like child care or transportation or job coaching end upon promotion, employees may find themselves trapped on the bottom rung of the career ladder. Conversely, when benefits are too costly for anyone but professional workers, the company will not reap the full advantage of offering them. A 1996 study by Work/Family Directions found that corporate programs designed to support employees managing their work and family responsibilities often fail to address the needs of shift workers, who cannot afford to take advantage of unpaid leave or pay for on-site child care.[24]

A History of Involvement

In human resource and other cross-sector partnerships, the sincerity and care with which the company addresses social sector issues count. Social sector organizations will pursue those companies that they expect will provide a friendly reception. In this way, the companies that give the most get the most opportunities in return.

It was Ridgeview's and the Gaither family's history of support for the school that initially led counselor Sue Ballard to the company to pilot the PIECES program. The further goodwill developed in the relationship has led Ridgeview to support the school in other ways. "Our policy is if the school calls, we get that employee to the phone," says Human Resource Director Erskine White. The company actively participates in other activities with the school, like the job shadowing program for middle school students and participation in career day events. "We get involved in 90 percent of the things they ask us to get involved with," says White. These activities are helped along because Erskine White believes his job makes him an "ambassador to the school system." "I look at it the way we might work with a supplier of yarn—schools are going to supply us with workers. One of the things I sell to kids is that just about anything you want to do you can learn in the hosiery industry." In return, Ridgeview benefits from an outstanding reputation in the community and visibility among the students that may comprise its future workforce.

NEWTON-CONOVER PUBLIC SCHOOLS: A SUSTAINABLE PARTNERSHIP

In working with business, schools and other social sector organizations should tailor their requests to specific items or activities that the business can readily supply. These items and activities should be clearly tied to the organization's own programmatic objectives and be consistent with the business' own needs. In other words, there must be mutual benefit deriving from a matching of the needs and assets of the partners.

The PIECES program is a simple partnership intended to achieve clear programmatic objectives important to each party. It helps children succeed by increasing parental involvement. It increases employee loyalty at Ridgeview by helping employees balance their work and family responsibilities. And it creates a good public image for Ridgeview in the small rural community where the company is headquartered. Unlike more complex relationships found in the education arena, this simple partnership does not require intermediary organizations or a broad-based collaboration. In operation for more than a decade at a minimal cost, it has been easy for both parties to maintain. The company and the school understand the partnership in the same way and are committed to its multiple goals. Both parties have clear roles and responsibilities, and lines of communication between Ridgeview Human Resources Director Erskine White and Newton-Conover Middle School Guidance Counselor Susan Ballard are excellent.

OUTSIDE THE BOX

Too often, social sector organizations are unable to innovate, feeling constrained by tradition, culture, and resources. Unfortunately, this often means that simple solutions are out of reach. Over time, an inability to "think outside the box" leads to a kind of paralysis by tradition, preventing the organization from changing to adapt to a new context or circumstances.

Although there are many reasons to do so, schools rarely take their services outside the school walls. Parents may be unable to come to school because of transportation or scheduling problems, or may feel unwelcome or uncomfortable in the school, especially if they did not do well in school themselves. Adult education classes, parent meetings, and after-school tutoring programs, for example, all might be more accessible if they were held at community centers in other locations. Newton-Conover Public Schools' decision to take their counselors to Ridgeview broke with tradition. This seemingly simple act made it possible for parents to meet with school counselors at a convenient time and place.

OTHER GOOD PRACTICES

Businesses and social sector organizations pursuing human resource partnerships of any sort should consider several approaches common to many successful human resource partnerships:

Involve multiple businesses. Certain types of human resource partnerships—such as those intended to expand access to child care or provide job training—can be costly and out of reach of smaller companies. The involvement of several corporations with similar needs can create economies of scale. It may also provide greater benefits to the client—offering more job placements for trainees or more child-care choices for employees than might be available with an individual company. Of the Welfare to Work Partnership's 10,000 business partners, almost half have less than twenty-five employees, yet they receive the same information and have access to the same conferences, Web sites, and information on job-ready applicants as much larger companies.

Use intermediary organizations for connections and expertise. Particularly when multiple partners are involved, intermediary organizations can play an important role lending expertise to a program and managing diverse interests. In some cases, the social sector partner *is* an intermediary organization, such as Wildcat Service Corporation, which brings together businesses and prospective employees. In others, such as the American Business Collaboration and many school-to-work partnerships, the intermediary helps to bring the nonprofit or school together with business. In either case, intermediary organizations provide needed expertise, are able to apply lessons from a broader base of experience, can screen or prepare prospective employees or partners, and help translate between the two worlds. Although intermediary organizations generally charge fees that add to the cost, in the long run they can help create a smoother running, more successful program.

Buy, don't build. Unless the partnership involves a very large employer with a large number of geographically concentrated employees with similar needs, it may be more cost effective to buy assistance—such as slots in an existing child-care center or training at a local community college—than to create it.

Conduct a needs assessment. Companies should tailor services to employees' needs as determined by a formal needs assessment, rather than make "guestimates" based on the manager's own priorities. For example, many companies participating in the Welfare to Work Partnership found that, contrary to the assumptions of some experts, transportation outranked child care as the greatest need among individuals transitioning off public assistance. Often employees have a variety of interrelated needs—child care near public transportation, skill-specific training and English as a second language classes. Surveys can identify these needs and help employers determine what partners will best serve its workforce.

Don't expect less of employees with special needs. Employers may assume that hiring employees with special needs, whether they are people with disabilities, a history of public assistance, or a nontraditional education, will force them to lower their standards. Social sector organizations serving these populations, as well as experienced employers, argue that this is not the case. In fact, "one key to success cited by many companies is maintaining and enforcing high performance standards," according to the Welfare to Work Partnership.[25] Maintaining high standards is not the same as enforcing rigid job requirements, especially those unrelated to performance. Is a college degree really necessary? Could the job be done from 8:00 to 4:00, or is 9:00 to 5:00 essential? If an employer does have meaningful requirements that undermine the success of certain categories of employees, these should be communicated to intermediary organizations involved in preparing or assisting them. Child-care centers that close an hour before quitting time or a job skills program that communicates workplace norms inconsistent with those of the employer defeat their purposes.

Ridgeview and Newton-Conover Public Schools: The Impact

Twelve years after its inception, PIECES was still going strong. Employees at every level of the company participate, including Hugh Gaither, who became president and CEO. "In this fast-paced world, to go meet with a teacher at the school would take longer," says Gaither. "It is very helpful to have direct feedback." He is equally enthusiastic about the program's benefits to Ridgeview. "Our business is competitive. It's not high growth like Internet companies" or other high tech businesses, he explains. "We need to be very consistent and efficient about what we do or we won't be successful." The key, Gaither believes, is people. "Get a group of people who feel good about the company and you get better results over time. Our direct wages are simply not going to be as high as in certain other industries. We have to compensate by providing a good work environment and providing other benefits."

As for educational impacts, those involved in the program could see first hand its effects. Truancy no longer existed among children with parents in the program, and counselors built relationships with parents who formerly had little contact with the schools. Fathers, who typically left school matters to mothers, became involved for the first time. Pleased with the program, the school extended it to a second company, and then a third, when employees there heard about the program and asked their employer to support it.

A decade after its inception, neither the school nor the company had formally evaluated PIECES. Nonetheless, both regarded it as a success. The program helped Ridgeview receive *Working Mother* magazine's Golden Apple award as one of the 100 most family-friendly companies. PIECES was recognized by the *American School Board Journal* as one of the most creative programs in North America, and the program was featured in the Department of Education's "Employers, Families, and Education" report, earning Hugh Gaither an invitation to breakfast with U.S. Secretary of Education Richard Riley.[26]

Ridgeview went public in 1997, which according to Hugh Gaither made the company more cost conscious. Nonetheless, Ridgeview maintained PIECES and its other programs, confident that "what we're doing contributes favorably to financial results." The challenge of recruiting and retaining employees remains high in the Catawba Valley. Although the area saw significant immigration of Hispanic and Hmong, the unemployment rate remained at between 2 and 3 percent. Because of its steady growth—the company increased its local workforce by 100 employees in a decade, a 25 percent growth rate—recruitment and retention are critical to the company's success. Programs like PIECES "keep folks here," says Erskine White. "Because of the family-friendly policies we have in place, people tend to hang around."

9

❧

SOCIAL ENTERPRISE
Boeing and Pioneer Human Services

In 1966, Boeing helped Pioneer Human Services, a rehabilitation and train-ing organization, launch Pioneer Industries, a social enterprise intended to provide jobs and training for recovering substance abusers and ex-offenders. Boeing became a steady customer of Pioneer Industries, buying components used in the manufacturing of commercial aircraft. By engaging in social enterprise, Pioneer Human Services increased its revenues to $40 million annually and provided thousands of clients the chance for a productive future.

Although not all of Pioneer's other ventures have succeeded, its track record and businesslike approach convinced Boeing to invest the resources necessary to enable Pioneer Industries to take on an increasing volume of assignments. The partnership works for Boeing because the company is able to buy high quality supplies at a good price, while also contributing to the community where it is headquartered. It works for Pioneer because the nonprofit organi-zation can count on steady work and access to technical expertise from Boe-ing, which enables it to improve and expand its overall capacity.

Boeing and Pioneer Human Services

It's an ordinary light metal fabrication and finishing factory in the industrial section of south Seattle. At one end of the large hanger-like structure, a computer-controlled machine cuts a fiberglass-type material into a large irregular panel. At the other, a walk-in oven bakes a powdered finish onto metal. The whir and buzz of machinery makes ordinary conversation difficult.

Operating these sophisticated machines are men and women who are cheerful, serious, plain-clothed, and seemingly indistinguishable from other factory workers. Except most of them have had trouble with the law. Some are still under the jurisdiction of the Department of Corrections, out on work release. Many are fighting a daily battle against drugs or alcohol. And most know that this job, bending metal or punching a pattern onto its surface, is their chance to turn their lives around.

One of these employees is Joe Morales, who supervises the powder-finishing operation. Morales, like most of the people he works with, has had his share of trouble. At age 11, he went to live with his father, whose style of upbringing was "Disneyland" in comparison to his stricter mother. With Dad, he did whatever he wanted. Father and son smoked pot together. Morales was committing robbery at age 17, took up cocaine and heroin at age 20, and a few years later was convicted of selling drugs to an undercover agent.

At age 30 and fresh out of prison, Morales found a new career at Pioneer Industries, a unit of Pioneer Human Services, a rehabilitation and training organization. A father of a 2-year-old, and a stepfather to two other children, he wanted to make a clean start. He began as an intern on the powder coater and was promoted to trainer, then supervisor. "My life was a blank from 20 to 30," he says. "I'm starting to live again."

Ex-convicts and former drug abusers aren't at the top of most employers' list of most-desirable workers. But Pioneer isn't like most employers. "Our folks look just fine—it's their behavior that's the problem," according to Gary Mulhair, president of Pioneer Human Services from 1984 to 1998. "They break the rules."

The organization's founder knew what it meant to have a second chance. Jack Dalton, an alcoholic and disbarred attorney had spent time in the state prison for embezzling from his clients. "I had a few strikes against me. . . . Nobody would give me a job," he said in a 1966 newspaper interview.[1] With funding from friends, he created Pioneer Human Services.

Of the 300 people who work at the factory, 225 of them are former substance abusers, ex-cons, or both. To help them succeed, Pioneer offers employees benefits well beyond the norm. Health care, dental, vision, disability and life insurance, and mental health benefits begin the list; some employees receive low-cost drug- and alcohol-free housing and low-cost groceries; all are entitled to counseling, on-the-job training, classes in mathematics, communications, and career development, and other subjects. Even with these supports, not everyone makes it through the full eighteen-month training program. Annual turnover in the training program is more than 100 percent—about half due to success stories and half to dropouts.

And yet, with this workforce of people on their second, third, and last chances, Pioneer Human Services—a nonprofit organization whose mission is to "aid in the rehabilitation, training, care and employment of socially handicapped individuals"—grosses more than $40 million a year, most of it by delivering products and services valued on the open market.

SOCIAL ENTERPRISE

Pioneer Human Services is an example of a *social enterprise—a nonprofit or government entity that "operates like a business in how it acquires its resources.*[2] Also known as "community wealth enterprises,"[3] these resource-generating entities are neither purely philanthropic nor purely commercial, notes J. Gregory Dees, writing in the *Harvard Business Review*.[4] They serve two bottom lines: one defined by their social mission and one defined by their profit motive.

Bill Shore, in his book *Revolution of the Heart,* argues that "[g]overnment funds, charitable solicitations, and foundation grants all have one thing in common: they represent somebody else's money." He calls these funding sources "leftover wealth"—the funds that remain once others' needs are met and desires fulfilled. By relying on philanthropic and government sources, nonprofits "shift limited dollars from one place to another, dividing the philanthropic pie rather than taking steps to create a bigger pie."[5] According to Shore, "community-based nonprofit organizations must be reconceived and reinvented so they not only distribute wealth, but actively create the new wealth necessary to meet future needs."[6] Richard Steckel and his colleagues, writing in *Filthy Rich and Other Nonprofit Fantasies,* a how-to book on social enterprise, puts it more bluntly: "[T]his . . . is about changing your nonprofit organization from a poor, grant-dependent, sand-kicked-in-your-face operation into one that is muscular and self-reliant. It is about paying your own way with earned income ventures, and about using those ventures to improve the delivery of your mission."[7]

Pioneer Human Services, like other social entrepreneurs, "creates a bigger pie" and is "muscular and self-reliant" by providing goods and services to paying customers. It *generates* the wealth it uses to help people at risk by operating eight profitable businesses, which also offer employment opportunities to the ex-offenders and former drug abusers it seeks to help.

Offering for sale the work product of the hard to employ is not a new idea. Earlier relatives of social enterprises include sheltered workshops for people with disabilities, subsidized employment and on-the-job training programs for unemployed adults, and youth corps programs that engage at-risk young adults in "fee for service" conservation work. Most of these programs depended on grants and donations, with a minor portion of their budget funded by income-generating activities, and they were often underresourced. However, the idea of using market-based approaches to solve social problems took on a new life during the economic boom of the 1990s.[8] These new social enterprises are finding that by giving equal weight to both the social and financial bottom lines, they are better able to choose their own paths.

THE NEED

When Gary Mulhair took over Pioneer in 1984, the nonprofit earned only a quarter of its then $4 million budget from its enterprises; the rest came from government contracts and grants. But that was before threatened cuts in government social spending issued a wake-up call for nonprofits everywhere. Most were at a loss for how to make up for lost revenue. In 1977, the typical nonprofit held a quarter of its annual budget in reserves. Two decades later, the typical nonprofit ended the year with less than 1 percent of its budget in the bank.[9] By adopting business-oriented philosophies to guide its program and management decisions, Pioneer Human Services was able to reverse this ratio. In 1998, 75 percent was derived from Pioneer enterprises and 25 percent from government grants and contracts. Moreover, it has increased its revenues more than tenfold. It has been profitable every year since 1987, with surpluses exceeding $1 million each year since 1996.

Although much of the limited literature available on social enterprise focuses on the social sector organization, rarely can a social enterprise be launched without close relationships with businesses, which may be suppliers, customers, distributors, or partners in the venture. It is through its supplier-customer relationships that Pioneer Industries has forged its strong partnerships.

The Match

The Boeing Company helped Pioneer Human Services launch Pioneer Industries in 1966 and became a steadfast customer, accounting for between 55 and 70 percent of its annual sales. With revenues of $45 billion, Boeing is the world's largest commercial aircraft manufacturer, the largest NASA contractor, and the world's largest military aircraft manufacturer.[10] Almost half of the parts the company needs to produce commercial airplanes—1.2 billion parts per year—are purchased from 3,000 suppliers. A tiny fraction of these parts come from the less than 1 percent of suppliers who are not traditional manufacturers, but instead nonprofit organizations in business in order to provide jobs for the hard-to-employ.

In the 1950s, Boeing began its "sheltered workshop" program, contracting with a single nonprofit to make simple parts that are not related to the plane's ability to fly. Sheltered workshops traditionally employed people with disabilities who had difficulty securing jobs before the enactment of anti-discrimination laws. Usually subsidized with charitable and government funds, sheltered workshops typically provided supportive services to workers to help them learn job skills and succeed on the job.

No one currently involved with Boeing's workshop program was around when the first workshop began—"a person in our fabrication facility maybe had a relative or friend, or a personal interest in the program," believes Al Staples, the Boeing buyer who manages the workshops. Early on, Boeing regarded the workshops as "part of their responsibility to support the community—they help support several hundred people with direct labor jobs, to provide opportunities for people who might not have them," according to Staples.

In the mid-1960s, Boeing decided to expand its program. Jack Dalton "knew somebody who knew somebody at Boeing," according to Gary Mulhair. Dalton made a pitch for Boeing's business to provide jobs for the people he was helping make the transition from prison to productive lives. Boeing agreed and helped Dalton to start Pioneer Industries.

Boeing's early motives in establishing the workshop program were purely philanthropic. But today "we get good return," according to Staples. "Primarily, Boeing views the workshops as suppliers of quality parts. Therefore this is a business relationship," explains Mark Lindgren, senior procurement manager. "Sheltered workshops give Boeing an opportunity to reach out to the community while getting airplane components that meet the Boeing quality, cost and schedule requirements."

"Boeing works with subcontractors all day long. They're comfortable with that," says Mulhair. "We're not asking them to dress up like clowns and sell balloons at a fundraiser." By merging Boeing's philanthropic impulses with its operational needs, the potential for growth in the relationship is substantial. Mulhair calls this "operational philanthropy"—instead of donating dollars or goods, a company contracts with nonprofit organizations for things it needs, creating jobs for the hard-to-employ in the process. "It is deeper and richer than cause marketing," says Mulhair. "It is closer to the full engagement of the American enterprise."

The original workshops chosen by Boeing in 1966 were still participating more than three decades later, and others had been added. Collectively they produce 10 million parts a year. But consistent with the company tradition of keeping silent about its extensive philanthropic efforts (only recently did the company begin to publish reports of its community involvement), Boeing does not publicize the sheltered workshop program. Nor does it include its costs in the company's philanthropic total of $50 million in cash and in kind. It is not mentioned in Boeing's "Citizenship Report," which features a dozen other efforts ranging from its summer internship program to tuition reimbursement to Boeing employees, nor is it familiar to its community affairs staff. "That's because it is primarily a business relationship," explains a company spokesperson.

The workshop program is managed as part of Boeing's Commercial Airplane Group Material Division, which provides supplier contracting, management, and quality control for airplane parts. For the most part, workshop suppliers operate under the same system as any other maker of parts for Boeing, meeting the same quality standards and being held to the same production schedule. The major difference: Boeing treats the workshops as it does internal producers—providing the support, raw material, and tooling to make the parts, and inspecting the work according to Boeing quality standards.

This arrangement leads to a great deal of interaction between Boeing and Pioneer. On a daily basis, Pioneer Industries personnel spend time with Boeing's operating, shipping, quality assurance, finance, and purchasing staff. Pioneer managers speak the language, know the customer's needs, teaching "Boeing Blueprint" and "Boeing Tooling" classes to trainees. Through the years, Pioneer and Boeing have sustained their relationship with an uninterrupted series of contracts. Over time, the type of work has gone from relatively low-skilled tasks to those requiring higher skill levels—the kind of work rehabilitation programs often desire but rarely obtain for their clients. Says Gary Mulhair, "We look at Boeing as a customer. We meet their needs. We ask what we can do differently."

PIONEER HUMAN SERVICES STRATEGY

Several elements of Pioneer Human Services's strategy make it an excellent partner for Boeing:

No excuses. A workforce that is composed of no fewer than 75 percent ex-offenders and former substance abusers offers a world of potential excuses: The high turnover. The low level of skills employees bring to the program. Their poor track records, their past failures, their low education levels (trainees are required to meet only sixth-grade standards). The likelihood that they will relapse, returning to drugs or crime.

A partner that thinks of itself as a funder, a philanthropist, a doer of good deeds, might be ready to accept excuses. But because of the way both parties view the relationship, that kind of thinking is beyond either's imagination. Some of the supports needed to help employees succeed, like training and education, are included in Pioneer's contract with Boeing. Others are created by the revenues generated by Pioneer Industries and other profit centers that make up Pioneer Human Services.

Hiring and training. Pioneer Human Services does not naively believe everyone can benefit from its programs. At the day-long orientation, new recruits are graded on promptness, attitude, and ability to follow directions. Do they come back from breaks on time? Do they fall asleep during the session? Can they read at the sixth-grade level? Are they able to handle equipment? And, most important, are they "clean," with no evidence of drugs in their urine? Those who pass this test are asked to apply for a job at a starting salary of $6 an hour and sign a contract pledging that they will take academic classes offered through Pioneer Human Services. Trainees learn tasks on the factory floor, which is organized in "work centers"—such as high-pressure water cutting, milling, drills, and assembly. They also spend up to four paid hours in class each week, with an extra hour of tutoring if needed. Trainees can receive credit toward a manufacturing certificate for their course work at a local community college.

After ninety days, trainees receive full benefits. After six months, they get a twenty-five cents an hour raise, and after a year, another twenty-five cents an hour. Trainees can spend up to eighteen months in training, rotating from work center to work center. They're out if they get caught stealing or threatening co-workers on the floor. A "dirty UA" (urinalysis) sends the trainee to rehab for six months, at a cost to Pioneer of $7,000 plus disability pay. A second offense puts the trainee out of the program.

Employee assistance. Ahnetta Fields is there to help make sure employees are successful. One of two Employee Assistance Program counselors, Fields offers one-on-one advice and referrals to any employee who needs it, whatever the problem. Sometimes employees need housing, sometimes it's family problems, and sometimes legal issues, for example, men can owe child support from when they were in prison and have half of their wages garnished.

Fields is there for employees because she's been in their shoes. Twenty-six years ago, Fields was imprisoned at Purdy, the Washington State Penitentiary for Women. She was one of the first women to be allowed out on work release. Her personal experience in prison is an advantage dealing with employees who are ex-cons. "They have a lot of game playing—they can't do that with me," she says.

Quality. In the late 1980s, Gary Mulhair recognized that the ability to produce high-quality goods cost effectively was essential to expanding Pioneer's business with Boeing and other companies. With a workforce that is for the most part fresh out of prison, quality could be a challenge. Mulhair believed that quality was the key to providing greater value to Pioneer's partners, and to achieve it, he needed to focus on outputs, rather than inputs.

The high quality of Pioneer's training and employee assistance program and other services helps. The failure rate for random drug tests at Pioneer is less than 5 percent, lower than the industry average of from 5 to 8 percent. By listening to workers' suggestions, Pioneer cut its accident rates to an amount one-sixth what they had been a few years before. To reduce turnover, Pioneer increased its employment of individuals while they were still in prison, finding that these employees when released were more committed and had higher retention rates than those who began the program after their release. To provide for consistency and quality, staff developed written scripts that could be followed for the production of each part. Managers put a greater emphasis on communicating with customers to make sure their needs were met. And Pioneer installed a simple-to-use computerized data collection system that enabled Pioneer to improve inventory tracking while improving overall product quality.[11]

Pioneer's efforts culminated in the receipt of an international quality certification, the ISO-9002, issued for work quality and customer service measured against industry standards. Receipt of the designation made Pioneer the first nonprofit sheltered workshop and one of just seventy-five companies in Washington state qualified in this way.[12] Pioneer was also rewarded in another important way—through increased contracts from its customers. Heart Interface, a customer since 1988, consolidated its contracts and selected Pioneer to be the sole supplier for its sheet metal enclosures—strictly a business decision according to Heart Interface's director of manufacturing and operations.[13] Boeing, already Pioneer's biggest customer, increased its business with Pioneer, confident that Pioneer could meet the increased demand resulting from increased airplane orders.

BOEING'S ROLE

Boeing itself has played an important role in building Pioneer's capacity to serve its needs and, as a result, indirectly those of Pioneer's other customers. First, the reliability of Boeing contracts allows Pioneer to plan, to know that trainers' salaries will be paid and that jobs will be available for the steady stream of new recruits. It makes it possible for Pioneer to focus on the quality of its output rather than on constant development of new customers, and it has allowed Pioneer to capitalize equipment that it would not be able to afford on a three-month contract.

Second, Boeing staff are available to advise Pioneer, to help improve processes, and troubleshoot. This regular, often daily communication at many operating levels is essential for a strong partnership.

Finally, consistent with Boeing's practice of working with its suppliers, whether they are for-profit or nonprofit, it has worked with

Pioneer to modernize operations, thereby increasing its capacity to produce Boeing components. For example, Pioneer produces cargo bay liners—sheets of protective material similar to that used for bullet-proof
vests, cut to fit the parts of the plane that carry cargo. Originally Pioneer
used an old-fashioned method to produce the liners, similar to pinning a
dress pattern on fabric, then clipping around the edge. Pioneer employees would trace a template on the material, then using Exacto knives, scis-
sors, and punches, cut out the pieces. Trim on the edges would be glued
by hand and weighted down with bricks—all in all a labor-intensive,
rather inaccurate process. Boeing contracts enabled the nonprofit organization to buy a sophisticated, high-speed water-jet to cut out a shape
determined by a computer program. The machine increased Pioneer's
output five-fold and improved the quality of the component by as much
as 75 percent.

Because Boeing regards the sheltered workshops as business, not charity, it expects the nonprofit programs to meet regular production requirements. For this reason, it would not be likely to forge a long-term
relationship with a nonprofit that could not produce, no matter how
sympathetic its mission. No elements of cause marketing or public relations present themselves in this partnership. While the workshops "don't
always work as well as they're designed to," according to Staples, those that
have done well, like Pioneer, have taken on more responsibility—buying
their own supplies, becoming certified based on international quality
standards, or developing business processes. Although the relationship
began out of a desire to increase community involvement, the tie between
the two partners continues because Pioneer can produce a product that
Boeing needs at a competitive price and a high standard of quality.

OTHER SOCIAL ENTERPRISES

Independent Sector, a leading trade organization for nonprofits, estimates
that more than one million U.S. businesses are run by nonprofit organizations.[14] Although this figure includes hospitals and other nonprofit
organizations whose business and social missions are one and the same,
social service organizations have had success operating business partnerships that advance both their social mission and their need for revenue.

Juma Ventures. San Francisco's Juma Ventures owns two Ben & Jerry's
franchises: an ice cream concession at 3Com Park (where the Giants and

49ers play) and Ice Cream on Wheels, a catering service developed in partnership with another Ben & Jerry's franchise. A spin-off of Larkin Street Youth Center, which helps homeless youth get off the streets, Juma Ventures focuses on economic development, job creation, and on-the-job training for low-income young people. Three of Juma Ventures's four businesses are now profitable, making up half of the organization's revenue. The enterprises employ fifty-five young people.[15]

Juma began its first business by aggressively seeking a Ben & Jerry's "Partnershop" franchise and raising $250,000 to open it. A brainchild of a Ben & Jerry's board member, Partnershops were created in 1986 without a formal plan in place. Publicity surrounding the first Partnershop prompted other nonprofits to seek franchises and necessitated a more formal selection process. Ben & Jerry's receives more than 2,000 applications each year from groups and individuals seeking Partnershop arrangements, but accepts only one or two; only ten Partnershops have been funded, and two have gone under. The company waives its $25,000 franchise fee for its nonprofit Partnershops and provides expert advice and training. Otherwise, Partnershops operate like other franchises.

Minnesota Diversified Industries. Minnesota Diversified Industries (MDI) specializes in providing vocational training and employment experiences to people with disabilities. Convinced that the best way to build the self-esteem of his clients was to treat them like employees, in 1974 President John DuRand, a former construction executive, made a fundamental change in the way the nonprofit does business. In order to earn its own funding, MDI called on everyone, including clients, to take responsibility for the future of the organization. Within three years, the organization had turned its budget around, increasing earned income from 20 to 80 percent.[16]

Two decades later, MDI collected $46 million in annual revenues and was 99 percent self-sustaining. Among its ventures are contract manufacturing, distribution, and commercial packaging, with clients that include Honeywell, Zenith, the Pentagon, and the U.S. Postal Service. 3M has been a client for over two decades, using MDI Commercial Services group to beta test products before it invests in capital expenditures for large production facilities. MDI works for more than forty business units of 3M. 3M has supported MDI in other ways, for example, loaning MDI vans to transport employees with physical disabilities and placing a top-level executive on its board.[17]

GOALS OF SOCIAL ENTERPRISES

Although many nonprofit ventures have their roots in employment and training programs, others have different social and economic goals:

- The sale of Girl Scout cookies teaches girls economic skills while netting more than $200 million for the organization.[18]

- The Sacred Heart League, a religious organization, established Gregory Productions in 1994 to produce movies that reflect the values of the League and generate income to support its social causes. Gregory Productions's first movie, *The Spitfire Grill,* won the Sundance Audience Award and earned $4 million for the League.[19]

- National Geographic Ventures was founded in 1994 as a for-profit arm of the century-old magazine to manage its television, online and map-making businesses, which further the National Geographic Society's mission of "the increase and diffusion of geographic knowledge."[20]

- The Oakland, California, NAACP manages a gas station donated by Chevron Corporation that generates income for the organization and helps build the economic base of the African-American neighborhood.[21]

- The New York Association for New Americans (NYANA), established to resettle Jewish refugees, developed a relative assistance program, funded with grants and modest fees from Americans hoping to bring family members to the United States. Many clients took out low-interest loans to cover the fees. When NYANA determined it could do a better job collecting on these loans than its collection agency, it created a for-profit subsidiary to service these loans and those of other organizations.

Some social enterprises have no connection to the mission of the organization, except to provide an income stream. For example, Greater DC Cares, an organization that recruits, trains, and places volunteers, including many attorneys, established a temporary employment agency for lawyers. The Revelation Corporation pools the buying power of African-American churches, with profits going to capitalize a national housing fund.[22] Whether an organization should pursue related or unrelated business opportunities depends on many factors, including its culture, views of stakeholders, and the nature of its core activities.

Establishing a Social Enterprise

The experience of Pioneer Human Services and other nonprofit organizations offers lessons to others seeking to establish social enterprises.

CAUTION

First, although the success of Pioneer Industries and other enterprises may inspire nonprofits to try their hands at entrepreneurship, caution is warranted.[23] There is significant risk involved—up to 70 percent of *all* business start-ups fail in the first eight years.[24] Although many of Pioneer's ventures have been successful, not all have proven sustainable. For example, Pioneer had to shut down a successful program initiated in 1988 to monitor offenders under house arrest when the Department of Adult Detention decided a few years later to move to a new system using direct telephone contact rather than electronic monitoring.[25] More recently, Pioneer purchased commercial sewing equipment after conversations with a business looking for sewing subcontractors. When the customer changed its mind, Pioneer was forced to sell the equipment at a loss. Even successful enterprises usually take several years to become profitable, so there must be some means to sustain the enterprise until it can sustain itself. Pioneer's profitable St. Regis Hotel, a drug- and alcohol-free residence that serves Pioneer's clients as well as tourists visiting the Pike Place Market District, took two years and the replacement of several managers to develop a regular clientele. It took eighteen months and a change of managers to put the Mezzo Cafe, a cafeteria operated by Pioneer for Starbucks employees, in the black.

Organizations looking to social enterprise to respond to a financial crisis may find the effort has exacerbated, not abated, the problem. Initially, ventures usually require significant capital. Where regular businesses might look to equity investors or lenders, nonprofit ventures may have difficulty attracting this kind of funding. On the other hand, additional sources of start-up funding are available to nonprofits that are not available to other businesses. Pioneer recently obtained a $2.5 million program-related investment (PRI) loan from the Ford Foundation to acquire a new business. PRIs typically come in the form of a low-interest loan; some funders will convert these loans to grants if the recipients are unable to repay it.

When the business venture becomes known to the public, donors may come to believe the nonprofit no longer needs philanthropic funding. Juma Ventures's association with Ben & Jerry's convinced some donors that the nonprofit no longer needed philanthropic support. When the new business competes with other companies that had been donors, such as a catering business operated by a soup kitchen that receives surplus food from other caterers, the problem can be doubly dangerous. This may not be an issue for organizations like Pioneer and MDI that plan to rely almost exclusively on earned income. But for many nonprofits attempting business ventures to supplement, not supplant, other sources of funding, maintaining the support of funders is of great concern.

Finally, those enterprises attempting to meet a double bottom line will sometimes find the two goals in conflict with one another. For example, Juma Ventures's initial goal was to hire only at-risk youth. But to operate profitably, the businesses required some stable youth in the mix. Juma now hires about 50 percent stable and 50 percent at-risk youth. Similarly, the businesses might be more profitable if Juma emphasized in its marketing that it employs youth who might otherwise be on the street. But for those youth whom it hopes to help through its employment programs, such a message could be harmful.[26]

With the risk involved and slow payoff, other issues inevitably arise when nonprofits attempt for-profit ventures. Development of a successful venture will require hiring people skilled in the management of businesses. At least initially, it will demand significant oversight by key nonprofit staff, distracting them from the primary mission of the organization. When staff of the business venture are paid salaries competitive with the market but well above salaries of the nonprofit staff, resentment may occur. Changes in the orientation of all parts of the organization—from board to staff and even clients—may cause conflict. For example, MDI experienced 80 percent staff turnover in the first two years after the organization decided to earn its own way and to relate to those involved in the program as employees rather than clients.[27]

LEGAL ISSUES

Earned income may compromise the nonprofit's tax-exempt status unless care is taken to understand and comply with legal requirements governing nonprofit organizations. Income from "related" businesses is not taxable. A business is considered "unrelated" if it is regularly carried on by the organization and is not "substantially related" to the organization's work in furtherance of its charitable purpose (other than providing income to subsidize its charitable activities). For example, income from subscriptions to an educational organization's magazine covering school reform would be related, but proceeds from paid advertising would not. In this way, Pioneer and Juma Ventures are able to treat the profits from their businesses as related income, because the businesses are designed to employ their clients.

Nonprofit organizations can have unrelated business income and pay corporate income tax on any amount over $1,000. However, if the amount of unrelated business income becomes "substantial"—generally considered to be more than 15 or 20 percent of the organization's time and gross revenues—alternative organizational structures, such as for-profit subsidiaries, should be considered.

Structuring a business venture as a subsidiary does not insulate the nonprofit from legal issues. Minnesota Public Radio (MPR) created a for-profit mail-order business, including the popular Wireless and Signals catalogs. When the new business refused to disclose its CEO's salary and MPR employees claimed they were asked to work for the business on MPR time, the Minnesota attorney general launched an investigation. The attorney general ultimately did not fault the nonprofit organizations for any illegal or improper activity but did stipulate that the group should take steps to clarify its compensation policies. When the company was sold, MPR was able to add $90 million to its permanent endowment of $19 million and invest more than $15 million in another for-profit subsidiary. But MPR group again came under criticism, this time from the National Charities Information Bureau, a watchdog group, because $7.3 million was paid to MPR officers as a result of the sale.[28]

Nonprofit status can be helpful in launching business ventures. "Our strategies have involved aggressively developing ways to take advantage of our nonprofit status," according to Gary Mulhair of Pioneer Human Services, which paid only $3,847 in taxes on the $1,131,225 million it earned in 1996. These advantages, which Mulhair values at about $1.5 million a year, include the ability to raise money through tax-exempt bonds, avoiding both worker's compensation taxes (through self-insurance) and FICA taxes (as a training program), access to discounts available to nonprofit organizations, the ability to receive deductible donations of products, and exemptions from sales tax and other state and local taxes. These savings help to offset the higher operating costs associated with the employment support and training of the clients served by Pioneer Human Services. By reserving 75 percent of positions for its clients, Pioneer Industries was able to ensure that the enterprise will be seen as related to its nonprofit mission.

Ventures of this sort are controversial precisely because nonprofit status is thought to give these ventures an unfair advantage over for-profit businesses. A 1984 report by the Small Business Administration charged that "[t]he increasing phenomenon of nonprofit organizations engaged in commercial activities in competition with for-profit small businesses cannot be ignored." It argued that the "traditional justifications for granting nonprofits tax-exempt status have been stretched beyond recognition."[29]

Nonprofit status can be a liability as well as an asset in business transactions, as Juma Ventures found when it attempted to secure a lease for its first Ben & Jerry's Partnershop from landlords who believed a company run by a nonprofit was a bad risk.[30] It can be equally difficult to secure traditional forms of financing for ventures and to attract customers whose biases cause them to expect substandard quality from nonprofit providers. This has been Pioneer's experience. "Most businesses don't think that a nonprofit is going to be a competitive supplier," says Mulhair. "The way you overcome it is an opportunity to perform." The double bottom line places increased burdens on the nonprofit business, which may experience higher turnover, higher training costs, and higher administrative costs as a result.

PLANNING

Pioneer Human Services and other entrepreneurial nonprofits have found ways to help the rewards of engaging in social enterprises outweigh the risks. The key is in proper planning.

Identify a social entrepreneur. The process begins with a "social entrepreneur"—a nonprofit manager who believes in the project and has the "requisite skills and passion required of an entrepreneur," according to Jed Emerson, director of the Roberts Foundation, which funds social entrepreneurs in the San Francisco Bay area.[31] This individual "[m]ust be given the time and responsibility to implement the necessary changes, and the power to make them happen," writes Richard Steckel.[32] The social entrepreneur must therefore be both *senior* enough to be an effective champion, able to command resources and communicate directly with the highest levels of the organization, *inspired* about the project, *able* to bring it about, and *available,* in order to devote the substantial time that will be required for a successful venture.

Create a planning team. The social entrepreneur should lead a team of staff and board members. Steckel recommends that the team be composed of two key staff, two key board members, and a business person who is not a board member.[33] Although this composition is sensible, we believe the right team composition depends on the individual organization and type of venture. Involving at least some senior staff, board members, and individuals with business expertise is advisable, as is keeping the team small. Involving too many staff will surely undermine the organization's day-to-day operations and can lead to long, unproductive meetings; involving too few will shortchange the project by limiting available expertise and human resources.

Involve stakeholders. The success of the venture will depend on internal support. A board that has not been kept apprised of the planning could easily throw a wrench in the venture later in the process. Unhappy staff left out of the design team could sabotage the project if not kept involved in some way. To prevent internal problems from undermining the enterprise, the planning team should communicate regularly with all parts of the organization, from board to junior staff, seeking their input and taking their concerns seriously. Staff concerns about a venture could expose a fatal flaw, and should be taken seriously. While it may be tempting to move quickly without slowing down to engage those not directly involved in the venture, in the long run, this kind of communication is important to the success of the nonprofit and its enterprises.

The board should not be overlooked as an important part of the planning. Not only should the board approve capital expenditures and other aspects of the venture, including how much risk the organization should take, but board members may themselves have business connections and skills that can prove helpful. When Greater DC Cares began planning for its temporary employment agency for lawyers, a board committee chaired by the CEO led the planning effort—convening focus groups of friendly business leaders and assessing a variety of business alternatives. Law firm donors were willing to give the service a try, and the volunteer base, which included over 1,000 attorneys, provided a second source of business and of potential recruits.[34]

Stakeholders are, of course, more likely to be supportive if the venture is clearly related to the mission of the organization. The Sacred Heart League's board turned down a proposal to expand its direct-mail operations to serve other organizations because it would distract the organization from its primary goal. But the movie project, Gregory Productions, gained the board's support and was enthusiastically received by donors as well—they had been informed for many years of the league's interest in media projects, and 25,000 donors were surveyed before the venture was launched to see if they would support use of their funds for this purpose.[35]

It is important to temper expectations—overpromising in order to win the support of skeptical stakeholders should be avoided. Being able to state clearly the purpose and goals of the venture is good practice. As early as possible, the nonprofit organization should define the reasons behind the venture and its goals. Is the enterprise simply intended to make profits that will fund the organization's work? Or does it have a dual mission, for example, to employ clients or make products and services available that further the organization's mission?

Stakeholders should understand the long-term nature of enterprise development. "The process of establishing a start-up small business can average three to five years in the traditional, for-profit context," according to Jed Emerson. "In the nonprofit environment . . . it will take at least that long and possibly longer."[36]

Acquire business expertise. It is essential that the nonprofit have, or more commonly, acquire business expertise appropriate to the venture at the earliest possible stage. Pioneer Human Services's presidents have all come from the business world; Gary Mulhair attended the Graduate School of Business Administration at the University of Washington and came to Pioneer as a business consultant. When more specialized expertise is needed, Pioneer gets it. For example, upon obtaining its PRI loan from the Ford Foundation, Pioneer Human Services hired an investment banking firm to identify a business that met its criteria—a business with a lot of entry-level jobs.

Conduct a self-assessment. The planning team should use a self-assessment process to examine the organization's needs, its assets, and the organization's capacity, culture, and context as it relates to a social enterprise. This process will enable the organization to define its goals for the venture and understand how these goals relate to the organization's social mission. Chapter 10 provides greater detail about this process.

Develop options. Based on the organization's self-assessment, the team should identify several different enterprise options to research. Depending on the organization's decisionmaking style and the resources available to consider the options, the amount of effort that is expended fleshing out these possibilities may be limited (a description of the business, a preliminary assessment of the market, and an informed guestimate of needed resources). Alternatively, it can approach the first draft of a business plan. The options should be presented to senior management, which should in turn recommend a preferred option or options to the board for approval.

Choose a legal form. Depending on the type of business involved, an organization may be able to treat income from the business as "related" income and pay no tax, or as "unrelated business income," subject to tax. As noted earlier, if the income is expected to be substantial, or if the business needs greater flexibility (for example, in employee compensation or access to additional forms of capital) than the tax code offers nonprofits, the organization should explore creating a for-profit subsidiary. Earnings from the subsidiary may be paid to the parent organization in the form of dividends, rent, interest, or royalties. The parent can avoid tax liability as long as the subsidiary is not considered a "controlled" corporation (one in which the parent owns more than half of the stock, by vote or value). The law in this area may change as the field of social enterprise grows. Social entrepreneurs are advised to work with a lawyer familiar with these issues to avoid unexpected or unnecessary tax liability.

Write a business plan. Once a decision has been made to pursue a specific business enterprise, the organization should develop a business plan. Writing a business plan forces the organization to confront important issues: Is there really a market for the good or service? What resources are necessary to start the enterprise and where will we get them from? Do we have the expertise to manage production or service delivery? How much control should the staff and board have over the enterprise?

It is at this point that the composition of the planning team should be revisited. However much work has already gone into the enterprise development, a great deal more will be needed. It may be time for staff to move onto other projects, with new staff hired who have the kind of expertise needed to carry out the plan. It may be time to bring in consultants to help develop the plan, although we caution against turning over the project to outsiders who don't know the organization and its social mission well, and who will not have long-term responsibility for the success of the project. A good role for consultants is to offer needed financial, legal, or industry-specific expertise, or guide the staff in developing the plan.

Many resources are widely available to guide the group in writing the business plan—software, how-to books, and other guides. The business plan should be approved by senior management and the board, and be used as the basis of important decisions concerning the enterprise going forward.

Obtain financing. The last step in planning the venture, before staff can be hired and start-up operations can begin in earnest, is to obtain financing for the enterprise. Depending on the legal form of the enterprise (for-profit or nonprofit), different sources of funding may be available. For-profit subsidiaries may be capitalized by the nonprofit parent, by equity investors, through private or bank loans, or business partners. A nonprofit enterprise (whether or not it is a separate subsidiary) has access to funds from the nonprofit's own reserves, donations, grants, private or bank loans, or business partners. It may also be financed with program-related investments or PRIs—usually low- or no-interest loans offered by foundations to support income-producing ventures that accord with their own goals.

What Works

PIONEER HUMAN SERVICES: PUT GOALS IN BALANCE

With good planning and a careful balancing of goals, "sound business practice can help drive the realization of the organization's social mission," according to Jed Emerson.[37] But that is not always the case. As discussed earlier, social enterprises can strain the organization by diverting energy and resources away from core functions or requiring compromises that make stakeholders uncomfortable.

With two decades of experience, Pioneer is able to manage its double bottom line successfully. The interrelationship between the organization's goal of giving its clients a "chance for change" and giving its customers what they want is almost seamless. Manufacturing a quality product in a cost-effective manner has led to steady work and more jobs for clients. The ex-offenders it employs receive support that helps them succeed on the job. And what Pioneer has learned through its business operations has improved its social services.

While making no secret of its social sector mission, the organization does not currently expect its customers to buy its products for any reason other than quality, service, and cost. Mulhair believes that like Boeing, businesses may again one day be attracted to Pioneer as a supplier initially based on philanthropic motives. But over time, it expects to keep them as customers by working at the relationship and delivering value. It has done so in the past by acting as a business—adopting the kind off planning, R&D, market research, and good management necessary to turn a profit.

BOEING: SUPPORTING THE COMMUNITY THROUGH ENTERPRISE

Boeing's commitment to sheltered workshops benefits the Seattle community significantly and provides a model for other companies, including those unable to make major dollar gifts. Buying goods or services, engaging in joint ventures, or investing in social enterprises allows a business to support causes it cares about at little or no extra cost to the company. The potential for social sector support through this kind of "operational philanthropy," as Gary Mulhair calls it, is vast. Every time a company buys a product or service, sells a franchise, or invests its reserve funds, it has a theoretical opportunity to help a cause by engaging in operational philanthropy. Although this will often remain a theoretical possibility until substantially more nonprofits establish social enterprises, a positive attitude of business toward these efforts will help nonprofits over the hump of finding a market for their goods and services.

BUILD A SUPPLIER-CUSTOMER PARTNERSHIP

Rosabeth Moss Kanter describes "value-chain partnerships," such as supplier-customer relationships, as the strongest kinds of business alliances, resulting in strong commitments, the development of joint activities in many functions, overlapping operations, and substantial change within both organizations.[38] Other analysts agree with the power of such partnerships: "In the last few years, customers have been rejecting traditional transaction-based vendor relationships at a dizzying pace.... [C]ustomers are working today with a third fewer suppliers than they did ten years ago."[39]

Boeing has been an important part of Pioneer Industries's success story by working with the nontraditional vendor in a manner resembling the high-value partnerships described by Kanter. Boeing provides Pioneer with four critical things, according to Mulhair. First, it provides technical expertise, which has helped Pioneer become ISO certified and to branch out into new lines of work. Second, it has allowed Pioneer to fund purchases of new equipment through an operating contract rather than paying for it outright or borrowing money. Third, by providing steady work, Boeing saves Pioneer the cost of marketing its services more widely. This predictability has made it possible for Pioneer to operate its training program knowing it will have jobs to offer and funds to pay trainers. Fourth, Boeing has insisted on quality, holding Pioneer to the same standards it has for other suppliers. It has ensured that contracts grow only when Pioneer is able to demonstrate the capacity to meet them, ensuring that good intentions don't inadvertently sabotage the product. As a result, Boeing obtains higher quality parts, on schedule, at a price that is comparable to other suppliers.

Boeing and Pioneer Human Services: The Impact

Pioneer Industries attributes much of its success, even its very existence, to more than three decades of support from Boeing. The company's steady business and technical advice helped Pioneer achieve a high level of quality and improve its profitability. And that enables Pioneer to give more than 225 people a year the chance to turn their lives around. Although not everyone makes it, most stick with it and go on to become productive citizens. Evidence suggests that the program significantly reduces recidivism rates; one study found that over a six-year period the rate of recidivism for women offenders who had participated in the program was 11 percent, half the overall rate for women offenders. A related study found that 100 percent of women participants released in the previous two years were still employed in the community.

Profits from Pioneer Industries may be used to expand its capacity or to subsidize other programs of Pioneer Human Services. These programs include a 154-bed residential facility for the chemically dependent and mentally ill; a thirty-bed residential drug and alcohol treatment center for youth; twelve properties with 385 alcohol and drug-free residential units; and outpatient counseling, mental health, and drug and alcohol treatment programs. Other Pioneer enterprises include a wholesale food buying service that supplies 7.2 million pounds of low-cost food annually to 400 food banks and nonprofit groups; food service, facility maintenance, and laundry services; and a real estate management business. Most recently, in 1998 Pioneer purchased a full-service mail production house with a PRI loan from the Ford Foundation. By supporting its work largely through enterprise, Pioneer Human Services can forego philanthropic and government grants—which therefore go to other organizations, expanding the resources available to help people in the Seattle area.

To further expand its services, Pioneer surveyed CEOs and senior marketing managers in the Seattle area to determine if they are receptive to "operational philanthropy." Early returns showed that "they haven't thought about it before," according to Mulhair. He is not discouraged by this lack of awareness because he sees efforts to promote operational philanthropy as a long-term process. "It's like what the environmental movement went through years ago," says Mulhair. "Now it makes sense to buy green."

PART V

Setting Up a Partnership

10

――――――― ❧ ―――――――

PARTNERSHIP ANALYSIS

WHAT CAN WE LEARN FROM THESE PARTNERSHIPS? The partnerships we have described represented different types of exchanges. Some
were relatively longstanding, others of recent vintage. They involved
companies ranging from Fortune 100 giants to small, family-owned
manufacturers. The social sector organizations involved included start-
ups and one of the nation's oldest international charities. They included
national and local organizations, and both a large membership nonprofit
organization and a small public sector institution.

Yet despite their differences, these alliances tended to follow similar
paths. And when compared to the partnership development processes
recommended by social sector and business analysts, we find many similarities. From this information, we have constructed a step-by-step
process to guide business and social sector organizations seeking cross-
sector relationships. The challenges facing cross-sector partnerships differ from those typical of each sector. Many common pitfalls of social sector partnerships, such as turf battles and competition for resources, don't
apply in a cross-sector context. Similarly, some of the typical challenges
of business alliances, such as the threat of acquisition and concerns about

sharing proprietary information with a potential competitor, should not arise when the partner is a social sector organization.

Instead, other obstacles loom large in cross-sector partnerships. These include:

- *Different language.* Communication may be difficult between entities that have their own jargon.

- *Different culture.* The stereotypical business with its "time is money" orientation will clash head-on with a slower moving, consensus-oriented, and resource-poor nonprofit.

- *Different status.* Because of their greater resources, businesses may receive or expect greater deference than their nonprofit partners.

- *Different world views.* Nonprofits may consider business to be "part of the problem" and view a business partner only as a check writer; a business may believe social sector organizations foster dependency and fail to solve the problems they were created to address.

- *Different bottom lines.* Because each sector measures success differently, cross-sector partners may clash over goals for the alliance.

If the parties talk about their differences and work to appreciate the others' needs and style, meaningful cross-sector partnerships can develop and flourish. The accompanying outline summarizes the steps in the development of a cross-sector partnership. Following this process will help organizations address their differences and form strong, mutually beneficial alliances.

Who Should Seek a Partnership?

Before an organization plans a partnership, it should examine its management, financial strength, and program or product. Partnerships work best if they meet specific needs of an otherwise healthy organization. They are not a panacea—a way to save a failing nonprofit or create a new image for a disreputable company. Business literature in particular cautions against alliances between the strong and weak. Joel Bleeke and David Ernst found that these kinds of business partnerships succeed just a third of the time, largely because "the 'weak link' becomes a drag" on

Stages of Cross-Sector Partnership Development

1. **Self assess:** *Consider an organization's needs and assets and identify factors that will encourage or inhibit partnerships in order to analyze whether or not to pursue a cross-sector alliance.*
   A. Identify your needs
   B. Catalog leverageable assets
   C. Examine your organizational culture
   D. Build capacity
   E. Consider the context
   F. Analyze

2. **Identify:** *Seek out and contact a prospective partner that will meet the organization's needs.*
   A. Consider cause/company fit
   B. Scan for potential partners
   C. Narrow the field
   D. Contact prospective partners
   E. Make a pitch

3. **Connect:** *Engage in a shared process of exploration about what the alliance will look like, how it will run, and what results it will produce.*
   A. Assess potential for impact
   B. Determine compatibility
   C. Consider culture
   D. Acknowledge chemistry (or lack of it)
   E. Take time

4. **Test:** *Plan, carry out, and evaluate an exchange to learn whether the partners can work together effectively for mutual gain.*
   A. Plan together
   B. Write an agreement
   C. Build support for the partnership
   D. Try it out
   E. Check in

5. **Grow:** *Extend a relationship beyond an initial exchange by resolving differences and planning additional activities.*

the venture: "When one partner is weak, managing the alliance seems to be too great a distraction from improvements needed in other parts of the business. When unbalanced partnerships do succeed, it is usually because the strong partner brings the capability that is crucial to the venture."[1] The ability of one partner to carry the other in a cross-sector partnership seems even less likely, given the different capacities of the parties.

A healthy organization ripe for partnership should exhibit the following qualities:

- *Financial strength.* Although the experiences of BankBoston and Denny's demonstrate that even under severe financial pressure companies can be good partners, nothing guarantees long-term financial health. Had things turned out differently for these companies, their partners might have been left suddenly without needed support. No matter how valuable a cross-sector partnership may be to a company, it is going to be less important than making payroll, servicing debt, and fulfilling contractual obligations. On the other side, nonprofit organizations sometimes pursue corporate partnerships because they are having trouble raising money from other sources. Indeed, most nonprofits would describe themselves as financially needy. The important questions are: What has been their track record for raising money? How diversified is their funding base? How do they manage their budget process, and what does their balance sheet look like? Corporate partners should be wary of nonprofit partners that may have trouble living up to commitments because other sources of funding are not forthcoming.

- *Management capacity.* Partnerships take work. They draw on the time and psychic energy of senior managers, and require staff at other levels to carry out exchanges and maintain regular communication. Partnerships invariably put unanticipated pressures on an organization. Strong organizations require leadership, functioning systems, and the ability to plan, monitor, and evaluate. A poorly managed nonprofit will not only have difficulty attracting corporate partners; it will almost surely lose its partners if it cannot fulfill its responsibilities. Such a nonprofit will have trouble ensuring that the partnership does not detract from its social mission. At the same time, a poorly managed company will have difficulty maximizing the advantages offered by a social sector partnership. Nonprofits should be wary if private sector organizations lurch into cross-sector partnerships inconsistent with their history and culture.

- *Program/product quality.* A strong social sector program should be a prerequisite for most cross-sector partnerships. A weak program creates risks for corporate partners, regardless of the type of transaction involved. A marketing partnership, of course, could suffer from bad publicity relating to program problems. Poor quality in an operational partnership could lead to a quick contract termination, as in any customer-supplier relationship. Even in a partnership with purely philanthropic ends, a corporate funder may conclude its resources would yield a greater impact directed elsewhere. Similarly, a corporation whose products or services are substandard will make a poorer partner than one with higher quality offerings. Even where it is not explicit, partnerships may imply endorsement of a company and its products or services. Social sector organizations would be wise to steer clear of businesses that may reflect badly on them.

Most of the organizations we studied exhibited strength in all three categories. Where weaknesses existed and were exposed, they did jeopardize existing and future partnerships. Later in this chapter, we discuss in greater depth how to evaluate prospective partners and touch on financial, management, and program strength again. But before seeking partners, organizations should be attentive to building their own strong systems in all three areas.

Building Cross-Sector Partnerships: The Five Stages of Partnership Formation

SELF-ASSESS

Consider an organization's needs and assets and identify factors that will encourage or inhibit partnerships in order to analyze whether or not to pursue a cross-sector alliance.

Consider your needs. Although cross-sector partnerships can be an innovative and effective strategy for both social sector and business organizations, they are not right for every need or every organization. The rising popularity of cause-related marketing, strategic philanthropy, and corporate volunteering may lead organizations to believe they should follow or be left behind, but such partnering may not be the best way to meet their needs.

Every partnership should begin with a self-assessment. What are my organization's current and future needs? And is partnership the best way to meet them? Table 10.1 summarizes the nonprofit needs that were addressed through the corporate partnerships that were discussed in earlier chapters. Other needs of social sector organizations that can be met through partnerships include access to influential individuals (such as elected officials and corporate leaders), "social marketing" opportunities (to change the behavior of the public; e.g., to encourage recycling or decreased drug use), and training for staff.

Often, businesses choose social sector partnerships to improve their images as good corporate citizens, but partnerships can address other corporate needs as well. Table 10.2 summarizes the corporate needs that were addressed through the partnerships discussed in the preceding chapters. In addition, corporations may find that social sector partners can provide access to influential individuals (such as elected officials and community leaders), training for employees, and access to customers.

Catalog leverageable assets. Exchanges involve an exchange of value. Organizations should begin relationships understanding their own needs. But they also must be aware of their assets, what they offer prospective partners. Some assets are obvious; others are less so. Businesses may offer the following assets:

- *A strong philanthropic tradition* can be leveraged through a marketing campaign. It provides nonprofits with a comfort level that the company is serious about the social mission as well as the financial bottom line. BankBoston's leading position as a good citizen has given the company credibility to advertise its cross-sector partnerships and to be well positioned to become an initial investor in interesting new social ventures.

- *Skilled employees may be willing to volunteer for nonprofits.* The construction skills of Home Depot employees made them valued contributors to KaBOOM!, Habitat for Humanity, and other nonprofits. UPS and United Airlines made senior executives in operations and human resources available for up to one year to support the activities of the Welfare to Work Partnership.

- *Products and services can be available as in-kind donations.* American Airlines used its excess capacity to help AmeriCorps by donating frequent flier tickets to corps members. A company can leverage the assets of one nonprofit partner to help another, as BankBoston did when it gave to City Year corps members tickets to a concert series it sponsored. The high-tech and pharmaceutical fields are leading givers of products.

TABLE 10.1 *Nonprofit Needs That Were Addressed through Corporate Partnerships*

Organization	Need
KaBOOM!	• Building supplies • Volunteers • Introductions to prospective funders • Pro bono services • Funding
American Library Association	• Equipment • Technical expertise • Benefits for members • Positioning in high-tech field
Save the Children	• Organizational visibility • Access to prospective donors • Access to volunteer fundraisers • Funding for new program
City Year	• Volunteers • Introductions to other social sector partners • In-kind services for members • Funding for new ventures and existing program
Share Our Strength	• Organizational visibility • Public awareness of hunger issue • Funding for grantmaking program
Newton-Conover Public Schools	• Access to parents • Job exposure for students
Pioneer Human Services	• Training opportunities and jobs for clients • Business expertise

- *Facilities* may be used as training sites, locations for dinners and fundraising events, even staff picnics. For example, the law firm Hale and Dorr allowed its nonprofit partner Jumpstart to use its posh offices for a celebratory luncheon and policy roundtable intended to honor its corps members and attract new donors, board members, and supporters to the nonprofit.

TABLE 10.2 *Business Needs That Were Addressed through Social Sector Partnerships*

Business	Need
Home Depot	• Stronger community relationships • Team-building opportunities for employees
Microsoft	• Good public relations • Better employee morale • Knowledge about public access computing • Enlarged base of potential advocates • Acceptance of product as industry standard
Denny's	• Better employee morale • Improved relationships with franchisees • New customers • A better public image
BankBoston	• Greater employee loyalty • Good public relations • Reinforced image as early investor • Improved quality of life in community
Calphalon	• Increased sales • Increased attention from retailers • Implied endorsements by influentials • Differentiation from competitors
Ridgeview	• Employee recruitment and retention • Continued leadership role in community
Boeing	• High-quality component parts • Improved quality of life in community

- *Purchasing volume* can be leveraged to assist nonprofit partners. When Timberland renegotiated its long-distance phone service, MCI agreed to provide Timberland's key nonprofit partner, City Year, the same volume discount.

- *Connections to other companies, funders, or social sector organizations* may be valuable to nonprofit organizations. Burger King introduced the Welfare to Work Partnership to its advertising agency, Ammirati Puris Lintas, which created a public service announcement campaign for the nonprofit on a pro bono basis. A corporation's influence with policymakers and others allows the nonprofit access it might not otherwise have. For example, former Procter & Gamble CEO Brad Butler testified numerous times before congressional committees about the importance of early childhood education.

- *Marketing opportunities* can help raise the visibility of nonprofit partners or causes. Calphalon shared space at housewares trade shows with its partner SOS. Characters or other properties can be licensed at no charge to nonprofit organizations who may use them in promotions. For example, licensors of more than two dozen popular children's characters from Barney to Scooby Doo donated the use of the characters to the Josephson Institute for an entertaining but educational video called "Character Counts." Celebrity endorsers may also be willing to assist nonprofit partners of the companies that hire them. For example, the Harlem Globetrotters, which are sponsored by Denny's, performed for children served by Save the Children local partners.

- *The ability to honor and recognize* volunteers, staff, clients, and community partners is always needed by social sector organizations. BankBoston holds an annual breakfast to recognize Quincy School teachers, which allows the school community to start the year on a high note.

- *Customers* can serve as a fundraising base, as when Denny's collected spare change for Save the Children from customers at the cash register.

Early in the planning process, a business should establish a cash and product donation budget for the partnership. But these other forms of assistance may be of substantial value to social sector partners and may be leveraged by the company at very little cost.

Social sector organizations also have assets that can be used to meet the needs of corporate partners and generate resources for them. These include:

- *A well-known name, a compelling cause, an attractive logo, and a good reputation,* which make up the social sector organization "brand," can be an essential ingredient of a marketing exchange. Save the Children, with name recognition of over 75 percent, leveraged its brand through licensing.

- *The ability to demonstrate impact* may also be an asset. In some cases, impact is easily perceived—a Habitat for Humanity house or KaBOOM! playground is tangible, immediate evidence that the organization yields results. Other types of social sector organizations can demonstrate impact through evaluations or testimonials from clients.

- *A well-known, charismatic leader or spokesperson* may be attractive to corporate partners. America's Promise has used its popular chairman, General Colin Powell, to attract business and social sector partners alike. Although less well known, Share Our Strength founder Bill Shore has proven a strong asset for the nonprofit, especially after appearing in American Express Charge Against Hunger television advertising. Shore's low-key, sincere approach helped lend credibility to this and other campaigns, even though the nonprofit was not a household name.

- *Connections to influential individuals are also beneficial.* For example, Save the Children was able to secure an invitation for Denny's to the Summit for America's Future, attended by all the living presidents.

- *The ability to provide a good, service, or expertise needed by a business* is another asset. Save the Children's ties, Pioneer Human Services's manufacturing capacity, and City Year's ability to plan service projects for BankBoston and other corporations are some of the contributions nonprofits make to their business partners.

- *Volunteer opportunities* can motivate and inspire corporate employees. All of the organizations we studied provided volunteer opportunities that were well integrated into the core program of the organization.

- *Events* like Share Our Strength's Taste of the Nation provide useful exposure and help build a company's image.

- *Facilities or equipment* may also be marketable. When AmeriCorps hosted a conference on afterschool programs, instead of renting a hotel banquet room, it paid the Latin American Youth Center a fee to hold the opening dinner at their facility located in an old church. Other nonprofit organizations can offer meeting space, sites for retreats, or child care facilities for special use after hours.

- *An extensive distribution system* can be useful to the business partner. The American Library Association has connections to 57,000 librarians and other library personnel across the country, and the Welfare to Work Partnership has access to companies employing over 20 million people.

- *Ability to provide recognition or awards* is attractive to businesses. KaBOOM! signed a deal with Walgreens to build playgrounds in the nine communities with the most purchases of designated products in Walgreens stores. The Points of Light Foundation sponsors annual awards to individuals and organizations for outstanding volunteer service.

Examine your organizational culture. Many of the successful partnerships we looked at, and others that were recommended to us, involve companies that made social involvement part of their culture. Home Depot, Timberland, and Ben & Jerry's are examples of companies that integrate their community involvement into their core culture and values. Some companies do not necessarily define themselves principally in these terms. Nonetheless, they have been able to form strong social sector partnerships. The key is finding a good fit with a nonprofit organization.

To find a suitable partner, it is helpful to take a close and thoughtful look at one's own organization early in the process. An employee survey will reveal a lot about the company's culture as it relates to social sector involvement. The views and beliefs of employees should be considered carefully in the planning of a partnership. Even if the company does not intend to involve employees as volunteers, their attitudes toward the company will be shaped in part by its identification with a cause, for better or worse. If the cause is not supported by employees, the company could experience lower morale and higher turnover.

Like businesses, social sector organizations should also assess their internal culture. Do staff and board members have positive attitudes toward business? Would a person with a business background feel comfortable working in the organization? How quickly does the group make decisions? Although it is the subject of some debate, we believe that an organization lacking a business-friendly culture can take steps to become more compatible with prospective partners. Step up the pace of decisionmaking. Add businesspeople to the board and staff, if possible. Invest in the kind of management training common to for-profit organizations. Invite business speakers to keynote conferences, make business publications available to staff, and reward innovation. In addition to familiarizing staff with the world of business, these actions can surface prospective partners, improve the operation of the organization, and create a culture that can work effectively with the corporate world.

Build capacity. Early in the process, a business will need to appoint responsible staff and develop a structure for managing a cross-sector relationship. There is not necessarily a need to create a new position or department. Relationship managers in this book resided in several different departments—marketing, procurement, corporate contributions, community affairs, public relations, human resources, and the office of the CEO. Staff should be assigned based on the likely activities of the partnership—an alliance designed to create a new identity for a company might be housed in the office of the CEO; one aimed at attracting workers could be managed through the human resources office.

Knowledge of or affinity for social sector issues should also be considered. When Denny's CEO Ron Petty needed a point person to develop a philanthropic program, he chose a staff person who seemed to have a passion for children's issues. An employee survey or a more informal internal fact-finding process is a good way to find individuals within the company who have an interest in the social sector and who might serve on a committee to oversee the project or act as informal leaders within their divisions.

Certain capacities of nonprofit organizations are useful in the creation of corporate partnerships. Public relations capacity makes it possible for the organization to publicize the corporation's support and build its own visibility, making itself more attractive to business partners. Relationship managers ensure that the business's needs are considered at all appropriate opportunities. The organizations we studied that manage multiple partnerships have dedicated staff assigned to each company.

Social sector organizations considering business partnerships should also prepare staff and board. Some of the nonprofits we studied had built corporate interaction into their designs from the earliest days; others had to spend time laying the groundwork to help internal stakeholders understand the relationship of corporate involvement to the organization's mission. This might take place over many months or even years, but such investment is essential. Studies have found that nonprofit board involvement and support are critical to the success of social enterprises; notes one report, "If the board is actively and positively involved, it can lead the way, ask probing questions, and raise needed capital. . . . If the board is resistant or obstructionist, it can make the organization retreat from opportunities and even surrender or collapse under market pressures."[2] Before entering into a significant partnership, nonprofit organizations should seek the endorsement of the board, which will more likely be forthcoming if the concept is discussed *before* a deal is on the table.

We have observed that the social sector organizations that are highly successful at attracting and maintaining corporate partners are excellent communicators. They have professional-looking materials that are attractive and contemporary, but not slick or expensive looking. They explain what they do in layman's terms, avoiding convoluted jargon. When good communicators speak to the public, they share a powerful vision, describing in clear, compelling language the impact of their program.

Bold but measurable objectives show that a plan is realistic. Measurable objectives may be tangible (building 100 new playgrounds) or intangible (cutting the dropout rate by 50 percent). Ideally, they involve numbers—one out of ten local people know the number for the city-wide hotline; there is a 20 percent increase in the number of successful placements. Demonstrating results often means paying greater attention to collecting data and finding ways to measure outcomes. The trend is for funders of all types to demand greater accountability. Of course, not everything that counts can be counted, and not everything that is countable counts. But having empirical data that show that the inspiring anecdote is not an isolated occurrence will strengthen the case.

Consider the context. In same-sector alliances, context plays an important role in encouraging the formation of partnerships. Social sector organizations partner with one another when resources are declining or the political or financial climate favors collaboration. Businesses seek alliances in response to competitive pressures, or when the market creates a need to move quickly.

Monitoring the climate is essential in these alliances. Just as certain environments favor alliances, others make it difficult for them to flourish. In fact, one study by the Conference Board suggests that dramatic, unanticipated change in the market environment is overwhelmingly the reason that alliances fail.[3]

Context is equally critical in cross-sector alliances. Barbara Gray, in *Collaborating*, suggests that cross-sector alliances occur in response to economic change in a region or when solutions are needed to balance interests.[4] Cross-sector partnerships are also warranted when public concern is raised about an issue relevant to both sectors (such as education or child labor) or when there is a shift in the supply of human resources (such as an increase in the number of working mothers or decline in the education or skill level in a community). Although it is rarely a good idea to pursue a partnership solely because context warrants it, without a view toward specific needs and assets, it is folly to pursue such relationships when the environment is inhospitable.

IDENTIFY

***Seek out and contact a prospective partner that will meet the organization's needs.*[5]**

Understanding an organization's needs and assets, as well as its culture, capacity, and context, are prerequisites for identifying prospective partners. These factors should guide decisions about whom to pursue and frame a "value proposition" that compellingly explains "what's in it for you." The key, then, is to find a partner that might respond to that value proposition; whose assets respond to your organization's needs; and whose culture, capacity, and context are compatible with yours.

Consider cause/company fit. Before searching for an organizational partner, think about the fit between cause and company. As discussed earlier, businesses should look for a cause that will make sense to the public, but not one that is obviously self-serving. In our case studies, there were many good cause–company fits: a family restaurant and a children's charity; a cookware company and the cause of hunger; a builder of playgrounds and a building supply company.

In her study of advertising campaigns with social dimensions, Minette Drumwright identified three types of affinity that seem to contribute to the success of marketing partnerships: relationship to the core business, affinity for the cause among key constituents, and the active support of the cause community. "Dissonance resulted when there was no relationship and sales people and retailers did not develop an affinity for

A Word about Deal Brokers

Deal brokers can be intermediary organizations, consultants, PR firms, professional fundraisers, facilitators, or any other professional who purports to be able to help develop cross-sector partnerships. Few of the organizations we studied used outside experts to develop their partnerships. Those that did have experience with deal brokers had mixed results. Nonetheless, we believe the involvement of deal brokers can contribute to the development of healthy partnerships if certain conditions are met.

First, and most important, the intermediary should view its role as building the knowledge and capacity of its client to be a good partner, not to own or manage the partnership. Planning and matchmaking are common ways that deal brokers are used in partnering. Sarason and Lorentz[7] describe an effective matchmaker as one who knows the territory, has the ability to scan the environment for possibilities and the imagination to create them, perceives assets, and builds on strength. Good deal brokers are able to see opportunities for connections between people and organizations that appear to be separate. They have influence and power, but are selfless.

Like a good matchmaker, an intermediary is committed to making the match, not the commission. A case in point: One of the nonprofits we studied worked with a public relations firm, which developed a lucrative deal for the organization with one of its corporate clients. The initial exchange was considered successful by both partners. But because the intermediary had positioned itself between the two partners, in fact, insisting that all communications go through the firm, the two were unable to establish a true partnership. Not until the business and nonprofit mutually agreed to bypass the firm were they able to work toward a relationship that could create greater value for them both. Unlike this firm, outside consultants committed to building partnerships should encourage direct communication between the organizations, coach them, make introductions, help them to structure effective exchanges, but not act as the connective tissue.

Second, outside experts should be just that—experts. They should fill gaps in the organizations' knowledge base. We caution against using outside agents to pitch a deal, beyond an initial query or introduction. It is the organization itself that should establish its credibility, not the outside consultant. A consultant's expertise in structuring cause-related marketing or sponsorship arrangements may help an organization up a steep learning curve. But no expert will know either party's needs better than the organization itself, or be able to reach into the depth of the organization to describe assets that could be used in an innovative way to advance the partnership.

Third, in certain circumstances, deal brokers may play a useful role as facilitator. When there is a history of mistrust or conflict, when there are more than two organizations involved in an alliance, when one or both parties has difficulty thinking out of the box (but is willing to try), or when high stakes are involved, a facilitator with expertise building partnerships may be well worth the cost.

Fourth, deal brokers may serve as translators. They should understand both worlds well enough to be able to explain the actions of each partner to the other, to translate the jargon, and coach each in how best to present itself.

Fifth, there will be experts involved in many exchanges who should not be allowed to take over the dealmaking. Lawyers, accountants, and public relations agencies fit this bill. Their role is to provide expertise, contribute pieces to the whole, but they should not be allowed to control the relationship.

In sum, we appreciate the important role that outside experts can play in building a partnership. But we issue a strong caution that consultants and firms of various sorts *cannot do the hard work for you.* They may coach you, scan for you, spot issues, or introduce. But ultimately, you will do the hard work of building the relationship.

the cause," she writes. "When there was too close a relationship, managers pointed to cynical reactions from consumers about the company's motive, who perceived it to be opportunistic or exploitative."[6]

In many types of exchanges, particularly those intended to increase employee loyalty, it is important to involve internal constituents actively with the cause. But if employees don't support it—or perceive their activities to supplant other efforts they care about—the company is unlikely to be able to sustain a partnership. Companies we studied were careful to see that new programs did not supplant local efforts. Denny's did not attempt to end the locally driven "community cheer" program; Home Depot and BankBoston created ways for employees to initiate volunteer projects for their colleagues; Microsoft maintained its generous matching gifts plan as one of its major giving efforts.

The support of internal constituents is important because they serve as "evangelists" among external constituents. If retailers or salespeople lack an affinity for the cause, they may become a "source of resistance that can sabotage the campaign."[8] Support of those active in the cause is as important as corporate employee support. Writes Drumwright: "Antagonism or skepticism can doom a campaign. Interaction and association with the cause community lends credibility and expertise to the company's efforts."[9]

Drumwright's findings are consistent with our observations about the partnerships we studied, regardless of their marketing goals. Those partnerships with strong marketing objectives (remember, philanthropic and operational partnerships can have marketing goals) tended to pair social sector organizations with related industries, but not those who would make the company appear self-serving. Even Microsoft, which had the closest tie between company and cause (software and public access computing) and is the only company we studied to draw public criticism of its efforts, was generally viewed favorably because it focused on low-income communities and avoided giving in a way that would appear completely self-serving. In cases where there was no obvious tie (youth service and banking), the manner of giving (serving as an initial investor) and the consistency with the bank's internal values (teamwork, initiative, integrity, diversity) eliminated any dissonance that might have occurred.

From the point of view of the social sector organization, the particular industry of the prospective partner appears to be less important than its record of corporate responsibility, particularly as it relates to the cause. Most of the nonprofit organizations we studied used a limited number of criteria to screen corporate partners—Save the Children avoided companies that do harm to children; City Year avoided tobacco and alcohol companies and corporations doing business in apartheid South Africa. But beyond this base level of screening, social sector organizations looked much more carefully at the people involved and the care with which they approached the cause. Even if the company had a less than perfect record of social responsibility, the social sector organizations we studied were willing to take a chance if they perceived the partnership was part of a sincere effort to improve. The social sector organizations understood that their business partners had business goals. But if doing good was not part of the calculation, social sector organizations took a pass.

Scan for potential partners. When ideas about cause–company fit are sufficiently well developed, research about potential partners can begin in earnest. As Microsoft did in its planning process, the search might start by surveying employees about their relationships with nonprofit organizations. Such organizations might include the company's grant recipients, organizations where employees volunteer, nonprofit institutions on whose boards employees serve, or social sector groups that have proved to be good sources of new hires. Are there any organizations in this pool that have been particularly responsive to the needs of the corporation? Or that work on a cause that is particularly attractive to the company? Such organizations deserve further research.

If the company has no internal expertise about the social sector, joining a coalition or network is a good way for a business to become familiar with a large number of related organizations working on a specific issue or in a specific community. Participating in such networks helps staff learn the language of the social sector and get a taste of its issues and culture. Attending national or regional conferences offered by leadership groups in the field is also helpful.

Reading about organizations, while no substitute for talking to knowledgeable people, can provide companies with helpful information about the social sector. Compared with business, the social sector receives comparatively little coverage in the press, which contributes to a lack of awareness about the work of nonprofit organizations.[10] We recommend that businesses seeking nonprofit partners use the Internet and searchable databases, and that they seek out "umbrella groups"—coalitions or trade associations whose members include large numbers of related organizations—to learn more about a field of interest.

Like business managers preparing for cross-sector alliances, social sector leaders will want to become familiar with the world of their prospective partners. Knowing how business works and speaking the language is important. Reading business publications on a regular basis helps—City Year, Share Our Strength, and Save the Children staff do. Employees of the organization itself may have business ties, as may board members, donors, and volunteers, as well as vendors, landlords, accountants, attorneys, and other professionals. Like motivated job hunters, social sector managers without business experience would be wise to interview their connections to gain advice about working with the business sector and to identify potential partners.

General information about a wide range of companies is easy to find, via the Internet, annual reports, Foundation Center libraries, directories of corporate giving histories and priorities, the business press, and the news media. Social sector organizations seeking specific types of exchanges also may read related trade publications.[11]

Narrow the field. Once potential partners have been identified, a preliminary assessment of the match between needs and assets should be conducted. Examples of this type of synergy include the pairing of a group that organizes one-time, high-impact volunteer projects with a company that can contribute needed supplies and volunteers and is looking for ways to build teamwork and community relationships (KaBOOM! and Home Depot) or a partnership between a company wanting to improve its employee morale and image as a corporate citizen and a well-known nonprofit looking to grow its program (Denny's and Save the Children). Without a matching of needs and assets—for both cause and company—strong partnerships are unlikely to emerge.

Another dimension of organizational fit involves the pairing of national organizations with national partners, regional with regional, and local with local. Most national or multinational corporations support local programs in the communities where they operate. In this sense, they act as local companies. Examples include BankBoston's support of City Year and the reason it declined to become a national partner when City Year expanded beyond the New England region, Boeing's interest in sheltered workshops in the Seattle area, and Ridgeview's support of the local schools in Newton-Conover. There appears to be a growing demand for national nonprofits with local chapters or affiliates who can engage employees at key sites. In addition to trade associations or national nonprofits with local chapters, corporations may consider "issue consolidators" like Share Our Strength in the hunger area or Children's Miracle Network, an international nonprofit that raises funds for children's hospitals.

Finally, organizations initiating alliances will want to examine prospective partners based on self-defined threshold criteria relating to the social sector mission or business needs. Both business and social sector organizations should consider a prospective partner's reputation and ethics. A business may want to look at the effectiveness of a social sector organization, based on its ability to achieve social goals; and a social sector organization may consider a business's market position vis-à-vis competitors. Criteria may also include image—companies seeking a "cutting edge" image for their products will want to pair with social innovators; those whose business reflects tradition and security will look to longstanding mainstream nonprofits.

A prospective partner's experience with partnerships should also be considered. An organization with multiple partners will likely have systems in place to meet partners' needs and a more sophisticated approach to working across sectors than those new to partnering. On the other hand, these organizations may also have their attention divided in many different ways that make it hard for a new partnership to become visible. It was for this reason that Denny's declined to pursue a relationship with Children's Miracle Network, which it greatly admired, in favor of Save the Children, which had no major U.S. corporate partner.

Finally, before proceeding too far, a sort of "due diligence" search should be conducted. A review of Internet information, financial statements, annual reports, press clips, nonprofit 1099 forms filed with the IRS, court filings, information on file with the Council of Better Business Bureaus* or the National Charities Information Bureau, membership in trade associations that adhere to standards, and quality certifications (for example, the accreditation of child care organizations by the National Association for the Education of Young Children or selection as an AmeriCorps sponsor) can provide useful information about the organization or company. Interviewing the organization's other partners and colleagues also provides useful information. But relying solely on these sources is a little like entering marriage with a "mail-order bride" one hasn't yet met. Face-to-face meetings will provide far more insight into the match.

Contact prospective partners. Identifying a contact person who can make an introduction will help the initiator get a return phone call. The partnerships we studied that were initiated by the social sector partner involved a personal contact. Darell Hammond of KaBOOM! had met Home Depot's Suzanne Apple when they spoke on a panel at a housing conference; City Year founders scoured their acquaintance network to identify people who could introduce them to targeted companies; sous chef Monique Barbeau met Calphalon's Dean Kasperzak on a plane. A

---

* Information about specific charities can be obtained through the Philanthropic Advisory Service of the Council of Better Business Bureaus.

business volunteer with the organization, an acquaintance of a board member, or the friend of a friend could help the organization penetrate a business. Due to the volume of requests received by many businesses, cold calls should be a last resort for social sector organizations. Even businesses, which tend to have an easier time reaching out to nonprofits than vice versa, may find cold calls don't work with "in demand" nonprofits, as Denny's early experience calling national children's organizations demonstrates.

Use your contact to get to the right person within the organization. A marketing proposal should be presented to marketing executives; a proposal that will provide useful help to employees might be best reviewed by human resources. Pitching to the wrong person can lead to an early refusal.

Make a pitch. If a contact determines there is interest and a potential fit between the organizations, it's appropriate to set up a meeting to make a pitch. Because so much of a good relationship between institutions is based on relationships between people, early face-to-face meetings make sense. Vickie Tassan of NationsBank* tells a story about her encounter with a representative of a large, national community-based organization. After meeting him at a conference, she agreed to discuss how his organization and NationsBank might work together for the "greater good of the community":

> He arrived twenty minutes late for the appointment—mostly because he forgot to ask for directions. I asked him to tell me about the organization—who had been past corporate supporters, what types of corporations supported his group, strengths and weaknesses, board involvement and composition. As executive director [ED] of the organization, it should have been a no brainer. He was unprepared. Instead of being able to talk specifics, he kept saying NationsBank needed to support him because what they did was so important to the community. . . . The coup de grace was when I mentioned that our program dollars are set for the upcoming calendar year in August. Meaning that there was no large unassigned pot of funds to help this ED fund a new program. Well, that piece of information did not sit well with the ED. He must have been really teed-off because he committed the fatal error of telling me that I had to give his group money because the "[Community Reinvestment Act] says you have to."[12]

---

* NationsBank has since become Bank of America as a result of a merger.

The Community Reinvestment Act is a piece of federal legislation that requires banks to extend credit in all parts of the community they service, including low- and moderate-income areas. "But just so you know, CRA does not say I have to give a community organization money!" says Tassan.

Tassan's anecdote carries some obvious lessons for social sector organizations. Be prompt. Be courteous. Arrogance is never attractive. But you don't need to beg. You have assets that you are offering the business you are approaching. Do not assume the prospective funder knows about your good work or is committed to your cause. Be prepared to present your organization in a way that will give a prospective funder confidence that the corporation's money will be well spent. Develop and share professional materials—they should offer specifics about why your cause is important, how you do business, who supports you, how you are governed, and what results you have achieved. Never assume that just because you work for a compelling cause you will attract corporate support. A social sector initiator should be prepared to demonstrate its effectiveness in achieving its own mission with both anecdotal "human face" examples and hard numbers, stressing impact rather than inputs as much as possible. For example, talk about how many children increased their reading levels, not just how many tutors you fielded last year, and include a story about a specific child who made particularly remarkable progress because of your program.

A business initiator should provide an overview of the company, its mission or values statement, and why it is interested in the cause: "Our research shows that education is the number one concern of our employees." "As a provider of health care, we realize the role community groups play in educating the public about healthy living, which is important to achieving our mission of building healthy communities." A common mistake of business initiators is failing to recognize that social sector organizations have objectives of their own. Companies should share their business and philanthropic objectives early on, but they should also solicit information from potential partners about their own needs and goals and plan to be attentive to them.

A common error we found among individuals new to partnering is to pitch a detailed exchange that assumes the needs of the other party. "It's like going out on your first date and spending the whole evening talking about marriage," explains Rackham and his coauthors. "Usually it's better . . . not to go to a customer with a fully developed concept of partnership."[13] Yes, the successful initiators we studied had done their homework prior to contacting a prospective partner and had some idea what types of assistance they would appreciate. But they did not present a fully formed design for the partnership. "The company always knows better what they need," says Judith Kidd, who has worked at both Bank-Boston and City Year, and then became dean at Harvard and director of its student volunteer organization. She notes that City Year's founders "didn't pitch what benefits BankBoston would achieve." Instead, the partners "dreamed up ideas together."

CONNECT

Engage in a shared process of exploration about what the alliance will look like, how it will run, and what results it will produce.

Once a prospective partner has heard your pitch and signaled an interest, it is time to begin a joint exploration of the partnership's potential. This process should look at likely impact, compatibility, culture, and chemistry. It should also allow for sufficient time for the parties to get to know one other to make sure the match makes sense.

Assess potential for impact. Without potential for impact, there is no point proceeding. Rackham and his coauthors consider this the most important selection criteria, but concede it is "something of a Catch-22. You don't know if there is sufficient justification for partnership until you have enough of a partnership to explore the question."[14] It can only be answered through freewheeling discussions in which executives from both organizations are candid about their hopes for the partnership, their goals, and vision. We don't recommend going through a formal strategic planning process until after the test phase, but in early discussions there must be a purpose in view; otherwise, when the infatuation ends and the hard work begins, the parties may find they have invested a lot for little gain.

Determine compatibility. Assuming that early meetings demonstrate compatible needs and assets and that the executives involved want to proceed, partners will need to go deeper into the organizations before they make a major commitment. Rosabeth Moss Kanter, using the metaphor of marriage for partnership development, describes this phase of partnership building as "meeting the family":

The rapport between chief executives and a handful of company lead-
ers needs to be supplemented by the approval, formal or informal, of
other people in the companies and of other stakeholders.[15]

We agree. This stage in the relationship has all the complexity of planning a wedding, including high hopes and blindness to potential problems.

Experts advise seeing a prospective partner in its "native habitat" in order to understand more completely the partner's important qualities.[16] Most of the partnerships we examined involved travel by each party to the other's headquarters and included "site visits" by the company to see the social sector program in action.

Deeper engagement between the staffs provides helpful clues about the relationship. Do both partners understand the goals of the partnership the same way? Is the prospective partner's reputation consistent with reality? And do they share your world view?

As in global business alliances, stereotyping "polarizes the partners, setting up us-versus-them dynamics that undermine the desire to collaborate," according to Kanter.[17] Nevertheless, stereotypes abound, and they are easy to identify: the company that pollutes in low-income communities rather than middle-class neighborhoods because the residents are less likely to protest; the corporation that shuts down a plant with little notice, leaving a ghost town with high unemployment in its wake; the business that keeps women out of top positions; the company that negotiates property tax breaks that undermine funding for schools. Such negative attitudes of social sector organizations toward business can leave companies feeling that their resources aren't being used effectively. Business, of course, has its own stereotypes for nonprofit organizations: Poorly managed; advocates for big government with little appreciation that corporate profits result in more jobs; overemphasize credentialed professionals while stifling the engagement of volunteers and others with years of experience but no degrees; unable to solve problems that have plagued communities for decades, but resistant to new ideas. These biases can leave social sector organizations frustrated that their partners don't appreciate the challenges they face. When that translates into political action, partners may find themselves on opposite sides of an issue.

In the partnerships we studied, there was strong synergy between nonprofit and business staff with regard to their philosophies of social change. KaBOOM! founder Darell Hammond and Home Depot's Suzanne Apple subscribed to an "asset-based" theory of community organizing and even read the same authors. BankBoston's Ira Jackson and City Year's founders shared the vision that City Year would provide the model for large-scale national service. Microsoft and the American Libraries Association believed that public libraries should offer universal public access to the Internet. Save the Children and Denny's shared a view that the best way to help children is to help families help themselves. Having a compatible philosophy regarding the social mission of the partnership allowed the partners to focus on other issues and put the organizations on firm ground. This type of compatibility usually surfaces through conversations, not a review of materials.[18]

The way the social mission relates to the business and its operations also contributes to the success or failure of the partnership. Ridgeview's decision to allow Newton-Conover school guidance counselors to meet with parents at the factory was rooted in the family values of the founders of the company, which had been integrated into the values of the business. In contrast, consider Sunbeam, a company whose CEO eliminated the company's philanthropy budget, stating that "the purest form of charity is to make the most money you can for shareholders and let them give to whatever charities they want."[19] When Sunbeam pursued the American Medical Association for a cause-related marketing partnership, the nonprofit organization would have been wise to explore the values of the company before signing an agreement.

Consider culture. Face-to-face meetings and in-depth conversations will also reveal whether the partners' cultures are sufficiently similar for a strong partnership. Cultural conflict arises in same-sector alliances and need not be fatal to the partnership. For example, when Mazda's bankers asked Ford Motor Company to turn around the failing company, in which Ford had a minority interest, Ford executives struggled to make American management techniques fit Japanese culture. Executives participated in Japanese traditions like golf outings and visits to a Shinto shrine to wish for the company to become globally competitive.

But Ford discovered that several other time-honored Japanese traditions were contributing to Mazda's poor health. Mazda's supplier structure included hundreds of companies dedicated almost solely to producing parts for Mazda cars, and expecting "parent-like support and loyalty" in return. In order to cut costs by buying a portion of parts from cheaper sources overseas, but not offend Japanese managers and suppliers, the Ford-Mazda team "spent long hours explaining why this relationship needed to change and helping suppliers draw up strategies for cutting costs." Mazda, in the tradition of other large Japanese companies, held shares of stock in its major suppliers, customers, and banks to cement relationships. Ford ordered the unproductive stock sold. Labor costs were another high-cost item, but layoffs were taboo in Japan and could destroy carefully cultivated trust. So Ford "persuaded labor unions to take a substantial cut in their bonuses, with the promise that the old levels would be restored once the company returned to the black." By clearly explaining their objectives, working toward similar goals, and understanding the key cultural taboos that cannot be broached, Ford put Mazda on the road to health—and restored employee bonuses, as promised.[20]

Not surprisingly, cultural difference is one of the most often cited problems in cross-sector partnerships and the second most common reason for alliance failure.[21] The following aspects of culture may be present in both for-profit and not-for-profit organizations:

- *Decisionmaking style.* Are many people involved in every decision or is authority vested in a few people at the top? Are decisions final when made, or open for later examination? Is an extensive amount of data needed for a decision, or are managers encouraged to rely on their experience and instincts?

- *Approach to problemsolving.* Does the organization use a team-based approach, or is a single manager or division responsible for resolving problems? Is there a focus on people or systems? Is trial and error part of the culture, or does the organization engage in extensive, detailed planning?

- *Work style.* What are the hours and pace of work? Is staff rewarded for working the most hours, for quick results, or for productivity, creativity, or team orientation? Is risk taking and innovation encouraged, or is consistency and longevity rewarded?

- *Communication.* Is the culture open or secretive? Is communication encouraged across hierarchical levels or must it flow in a formal process through established channels? Are meetings formal, with agendas, overheads, and PowerPoint presentations, or informal and flexible?

- *Ethics.* How does the organization balance ethics and expediency? Is integrity a prized value, even if it costs the organization, or does management take a "don't look, don't tell" approach?

- *Employee development.* Is there a commitment to the professional development of employees, with many senior managers promoted from the ranks, or is there an up and out philosophy—a tradition of bringing in new talent to expand the organization's perspectives?

- *Formality.* Is there a casual dress code in operation or are suits and stockings the norm? Does the managerial hierarchy permeate all interactions or does the organization encourage informal interaction and equality? Do managers have open doors, or are appointments necessary?

- *Mission-driven.* Have employees internalized the organization's mission, beliefs, values? Are there myths and rituals within the organization that help define its character?

In the best case, an organization would find partners that share the most important elements of its culture. When Hale and Dorr sought nonprofit partners, it looked for entrepreneurial organizations that it felt would match its own style. However, successful partnerships can be developed where there is a cultural mismatch, although these relationships are harder to manage and sustain.

Microsoft and the American Library Association provide a good example of a culture clash and how to resolve it. After months of planning and crafting solutions to dozens of challenges, computer equipment and software had arrived at the Libraries Online pilot sites. Eager to hold the press conference, Microsoft was baffled by library staff's reluctance to open the computers to public use until the librarians became familiar with the new technology. This standoff was rooted in library tradition and resulted in a fundamental culture clash. "Librarians are control freaks—they don't want to put anything out to the public until they know it themselves," says then Public Library Association Director George Needham. Microsoft wanted to make the computers available to the public immediately, thinking the librarians and the public could learn together. "A 14-year-old user might know something they don't," explained Needham. "They wouldn't look like the information master— it was very threatening." The librarians wanted to keep the computers in the back for two weeks. "It drove Microsoft up the wall," he recalls.

In the case of a culture clash like this, the first rule is to talk about it. What may seem to be stubbornness or lack of urgency may simply be normal operating procedure to the partner. Understanding the partner's point of view can help an organization come up with possible compromises—ways to accomplish the same thing in a different way. In the case of Microsoft and the library community, the culture clash was addressed through discussions to get to the root of the cause, and then negotiation. Ultimately the librarians' resistance dissipated, according to Needham. "They know they can't know everything."

Some issues may be simple—a nonprofit with a casual dress code may change its look when meeting with corporate partners. But some elements of culture are not easily addressed and may be important to a long-term relationship. A company that is risk averse will not be happy with a partner that is eager to gamble, just as a nonprofit used to building internal consensus slowly may find it difficult to work with a company dedicated to fast-paced innovation. In these cases, an organization should make a decision about how much they are willing to adapt their normal practices. Of course, cultural differences may not surface until later in the relationship. But like an engaged couple that has undergone prenuptial counseling, cross-sector partners that have discussed their history, values, missions, and decisionmaking and problemsolving approaches before they needed to be exercised may find themselves better able to bridge differences after the wedding.

Acknowledge chemistry (or lack of it). A major factor cited by many of the organizations we studied regarding their decision to pursue a relationship was chemistry between the leaders. Kanter observes that business deals "often turn on rapport between chief executives. And the feelings between them that clinch or negate a relationship transcend business to include personal and social interests."[22] In the cases we studied, the personal connection between the senior staff involved helped the partnership take hold. The people liked working together. They felt an immediate chemistry, they shared their partner's world view. They wanted to make the relationship work, at least in part because of that personal connection.

"People give to people," observes Home Depot's Suzanne Apple. We share this observation with several cautions. Rackham and his coauthors call personal relationships "The Fool's Gold of Selection Criteria." While they argue that intimacy—closeness, sharing, and mutual trust between people in the partnering organizations—is a key ingredient of successful partnerships, it can be given too much weight.[23] In fact, unlike trust, respect, and common values, chemistry is not required in good partnerships. In addition, chemistry plays a far bigger role in the courtship or planning phase than it does over the long haul. Second, as it does in other contexts, chemistry may in fact blind the parties to problems in the relationship until it is too late. And finally, dependence on chemistry, because it occurs between people rather than institutions, may make the relationship vulnerable if specific individuals leave the organization.

Take time. Finally, a critical factor in the formation of successful partnerships (like successful friendships) is time to get to know the prospective partner. Organizational consultant William Bergquist and his coauthors call this problem "the Danger of Whirlwind Courtships." They write: "Partnerships often fail in part because insufficient time is devoted to matching the reasons for forming the partnership with the intentions, competencies, and perspectives the other partners bring to the relationship."[24] Although in many of the alliances we studied the partners were eager to move ahead together, they began with a single modest project, deferring a more substantial commitment until they had completed an exchange together. We call this the "test" phase.

TEST

Plan, carry out, and evaluate an exchange to learn whether the partners can work together effectively for mutual gain.

Plan together. Kanter describes the test phase, again using a metaphor of marriage: the "romance of courtship quickly gives way to day-to-day reality as partners begin to live together."[25] As the partners go about "setting up housekeeping" like newlyweds, they may be tempted to engage in extensive planning at this stage. But few of the organizations we studied used their first exchange to develop a long-range plan. Like newlyweds that move in together, organizations working together for the first time will learn a lot from the process, which can inform future strategic plans. Extensive planning done before you "move in together" and learn each other's ways may be time wasted.

That doesn't mean no planning is needed. In their discussion of potential impact, partners will have shared their ideas for possible exchanges. Some of these will have mutual appeal. It is important that the partners work together to develop a shared vision—it is through this process, rather than by one organization selling the other on a predetermined idea, that a true partnership is developed.

We recommend that partners focus their planning on a single exchange with short-term results. The manageability of a single exchange allows partners to have an early success without undue strain. The experiences of the pilot effort create greater buy-in and yield useful lessons for future exchanges.[26]

Like organizing a wedding, determining the details about the exchange will surface additional issues relating to culture, values, and resources. Analysts of cross-sector alliances also recommend that teams from each organization, rather than single individuals, plan the exchange. Working this way allows for greater buy-in among different departments or levels of an organization and brings both creativity and structure to the relationship. Involving multiple people in its genesis makes the relationship less dependent on a single individual over the long term. Team-to-team negotiation also allows for a broader range of experience to be brought to the relationship.

Write an agreement. The most important elements of the agreement are the agreed upon goals. These should include goals important to the social sector organization as well as business goals. They should be created with a view toward how success will be measured.

Failure to communicate goals can present serious challenges to a relationship. For example, when a major manufacturer of children's products decided to launch an education program, it found a willing nonprofit partner, which used the company's funds to create a top-quality model program. The nonprofit was pleased to present its excellent results to its major funder and prepared information documenting favorable educational outcomes. But the company had *assumed* the program results would be positive. What it wanted to know was *how many people knew that the company was responsible* for making the program possible. How many impressions? The nonprofit had no idea. In this case, the partnership continued, but only by the nonprofit agreeing to replace the program director with a person the company had identified.

The challenge of the double bottom line seems to come up most often in marketing partnerships, but may in other contexts as well. Social sector organizations measure their effectiveness not in dollars and cents but by lives changed and social goals achieved. These effects may be hard to measure. And they may conflict with the needs of business organizations that value the visibility of the effort over the achievement of social goals. At the same time, social sector partners accustomed to government or foundation grants may assume that social goals are the only goals, even when attention to the needs of the business partner would not undermine social objectives and would enable a longer-term, more rewarding alliance to take hold.

Problems can be avoided if the agreement focuses on the concrete—the *exchange* not the underlying *partnership*—just as friends might negotiate the details of a future outing, not the future course of their relationship. The negotiation and agreement should address:

- *Goals.* The strategic rationale for the alliance.

- *Objectives.* Milestones that can be identified.

- *Responsibilities.* Expectations for both parties.

- *Decisionmaking.* The governance structure.

- *Structure.* The lines of communication and accountability.

- *Financials.* Contributions of both parties.

- *Legal forms.* The structure of the arrangement.

- *Measures.* How success or failure will be determined.

- *Exchange.* Specific items defining the planned exchange.

The agreement should be in writing whenever possible—even in the most trusting partnerships we studied, the parties signed written agreements, sometimes in the form of grant proposals, others as memoranda of agreement, and still others as formal contracts drawn up by lawyers. It is worth noting that while lawyers and other professionals may be involved in formalizing a partnership exchange, they should not drive it. As Kanter reminds us, "Third-party professionals . . . play their most important roles at this point in the process. But if they dominate, the relationship can become too depersonalized and lose the leaders' vision."[27] In none of the strong partnerships we studied did lawyers play a major role in negotiations.

Build support for the partnership. Before launching the partnership, an effort should be made to build support among key stakeholders—staff, board members, and others. If the organization followed an inclusive process in initiating the partnership to begin with, this will be an easy job. If not, extra effort should be made to brief internal opinion leaders and gain their approval.

A conscious effort to communicate the goals and activities of the partnership, along with information about the partner, should occur as soon as the deal is signed, if not before. The businesses and social sector organizations we studied used a variety of techniques to inform employees about its partnerships, most commonly including employee newsletters, memoranda from the CEO, and E-mail and intranet communications.

It is important that organizations not oversell the deal in their attempts to build support for the partnership. "If partners fall prey to unjustified optimism, disappointment is bound to follow," caution Yves Doz and Gary Hamel. Such circumstances often lead to early termination of a partnership. Doz and Hamel recommend care in communicating possibilities, and ensuring some overlap between those who negotiate and those who implement the deal.[28]

Try it out. The next step, of course, is to carry out the deal. Hold the event, run the promotion, offer the training. Individuals who are central to the partnership at all levels should witness the pilot first hand, if possible by visiting the site, participating in the event, or volunteering.

Check in. And then, assess results. Did both parties view the exchange as successful? How do they judge success? If an evaluation of the exchange was conducted, it can provide useful lessons that will help the partners construct future exchanges. Even if no evaluation information is available, the partners should share their own assessments and the data on which it is based.

Evaluation received short shrift in almost every relationship we studied. Most of the parties noted that they were in the process of planning for an evaluation, or trying to determine outcomes based on information they had available. A little foresight will make this kind of assessment easier, and more accurate. We encourage partners to agree upon measures of success and to establish baseline data in advance of an exchange: What was the business' average monthly turnover before the volunteer program was introduced? What was the sales volume during a similar period before the cause-related marketing campaign was initiated? What percentage of community members recognized the nonprofit's name before it became associated with a major company in the area?

Although baseline information should be collected as early as possible, a partnership's first exchanges should be evaluated mainly to improve future exchanges, rather than judge the overall efficacy of the alliance. Studying impacts too soon may cause an organization to conclude failure prematurely, before a partnership has had a chance to mature. We therefore return to the subject of evaluation in chapter 11.

Inevitably, new partners discover operational and cultural differences when they attempt their first exchanges. Like newlyweds, how the partners handle their differences determines whether they will enjoy a long and fruitful relationship or a short-term alliance.[29]

GROW

Extend a relationship beyond an initial exchange by resolving differences and planning additional activities.

Not every partnership will reach the "grow" phase. The completion of an exchange is a time for a graceful exit if the experience was less than ideal. Those that do reach the "grow" phase are positioned to become "New Value Partnerships"—relationships that offer fertile ground for mutually beneficial exchanges to occur over an extended period of time. Because it is time consuming and expensive to develop new partnerships, there are incentives to work at growing existing ones. At this point in the relationship, partners should undertake longer-term planning.[30]

Inevitably, partners change as a result of a partnership, although the amount of change varied greatly in the cases we studied depending on the depth of the relationship and its goals. Together, strong partners not only learn from one another, they develop a third new culture, language, and systems that define the alliance. And as partners come to understand each other's needs, they find ways to add new value to the relationship. They become the best friend who knows what you like, is there for you when you're down, and helps you dream up new possibilities. The next chapter describes the qualities that define these New Value Partnerships.

11

⁂

NEW VALUE PARTNERSHIPS

ALL OF THE RELATIONSHIPS profiled in chapters 3 through 9 provide good models of exchanges, from strategic philanthropy to social enterprise. Some, however, became stronger partnerships than others. Microsoft and the American Library Association, for example, are no longer engaged in a partnership. Neither organization had been looking for a long-term relationship. What they found was a short-term partnership that met their goals. Microsoft, having sought out ALA because of its knowledge and credibility, found that once the Libraries Online program had been accepted within the library community, it no longer needed such a partner to have an impact. In contrast, City Year and BankBoston partnered for more than a decade, with the relationship continuing even after the bank announced its merger with Fleet Financial Group.

City Year and BankBoston, and most of the other alliances in this book, are New Value Partnerships—long-term, high-yielding alliances between businesses and social sector organizations. The strength of these alliances allowed most of them to continue despite major changes and challenges—including the acquisition of Calphalon by Newell, the departure of Denny's top executive, and the transition of Ridgeview from a family business to a public corporation. New Value Partnerships are

213

characterized by several elements. We have created the acronym COM-MON to describe these elements:

Communication

Opportunity

Mutuality

Multiple levels

Open-endedness

New value

We derived this list by examining the partnerships described in this book as well as others we knew, and by reviewing the literature from both the business and social sector. The literature yielded interesting lessons in language—what a social sector book might call "asset mapping" a business writer might describe as "identifying core competencies." Nonetheless, there is substantial consistency in the literature, regardless of the field that originated it. These lessons are easily applied to cross-sector partnerships. Here we lay out the COMMON elements of New Value Partnerships.

Communication

Communication is a key to sustaining any meaningful relationship. Without regular, substantive interaction, partners cannot build trust, clarify goals, generate ideas, keep informed about problems, or participate in joint problemsolving. In fact, all of the other elements of New Value Partnerships require good communication. Formal communications—such as written agreements, letters of acknowledgment, and required reports—should be handled conscientiously and are of course important to the development and maintenance of any cross-sector partnership. But in the long run, less formal interactions are far more important to deepening a relationship.

JOINT PLANNING

Face-to-face communication is particularly important during the planning phase of a relationship. We strongly recommend joint planning meetings involving both senior-level and line staff to develop goals and objectives, discuss the progress of ongoing projects or the success and shortcomings of completed exchanges, and define new ones. A back-and-forth process, in which one partner formulates a plan and the other reacts and revises, may have appeal to some. It is often easier to carry out, given busy schedules, and it is simpler to come up with a proposal that specifically addresses your needs without worrying about the other party's. But as noted in chapter 4, Microsoft and the American Library Association used this kind of process, and found it time consuming and frustrating. It can also anger individuals who see a partner's revision as "rejecting" important points of their proposal.

Although it may not seem that way at first, joint sessions that allow both partners to air their hopes, concerns, and ideas are far more productive and expeditious. Joint planning sessions allow for interaction that is essential to problemsolving and avoiding conflicts. They allow individuals to explain what they like about another's idea or why it won't work. Many more ideas can be aired and opportunities surfaced in an exchange like this. And importantly, the personal interaction—particularly if social time is included—leads to stronger personal relationships that are also useful to the long-term sustainability of a partnership.

Ongoing Communication

The form and frequency of communication depends on the exchanges involved, but in all cases, good communication must be:

- *Candid.* Organizations need to be assured that their partners will keep them informed of new developments, good or bad—as Save the Children and City Year did when adverse press was expected, and KaBOOM! did when operational challenges surfaced. "It doesn't work if it isn't an entirely honest and trusting relationship," says Home Depot's Suzanne Apple. "Don't tell me the sales pitch. I can deal with reality." Partners must be prepared to be direct about whether their own needs are being met, so changes can happen. The companies that Pioneer Human Services works with "aren't bashful about beating us up if we're not doing a good job," according to Gary Mulhair. "Boeing tells us on a weekly basis how we're doing." This kind of feedback, routine in business, may seem uncomfortable in ordinary cross-sector relationships. But it is essential to New Value Partnerships.

- *Regular.* The relationship managers we spoke with are in regular contact with their counterparts, in some cases several times a week, in others less often, depending on the types of exchanges and the intensity of the relationship. In this era of new technology there is no excuse for "Out of sight, out of mind." Whether by phone, mail, fax, E-mail, or face-to-face, ongoing communication is an important part of a New Value Partnership.

- *Reciprocal.* Communication must move quickly beyond the "sales" phase, where one party works to convince the other of the exchange's value. A two-way flow of information and full engagement of both partners will allow for adjustments to be made mid-course, surface opportunities to create new value, and keep the partnership in view of both organizations.

INTERNAL COMMUNICATION

In addition to interorganizational communication, it is important to share information about the partnership with staff and board members who are not directly involved. Knowing about a social sector partnership can be inspirational to corporate employees and increase their loyalty to the company. Keeping social sector organization stakeholders (board, staff, funders, etc.) informed about the relationship and its benefits will decrease the chance that they will generate resistance to corporate involvement. For both business and social sector organizations, internal promotion of the partnership will also increase the odds of identifying additional opportunities to create value through the partnership.

Many but not all of the companies we studied promoted their cross-sector partnerships in employee newsletters, company intranets, and memoranda from the CEO. Regular communication of this sort appears to be particularly important in the case of partnerships designed to build employee morale, even if employee volunteering was not the aim. Site visits by staff to the program or interaction with its beneficiaries is particularly effective. For this reason, Hale and Dorr invited two of its non-profit partners to identify student participants in their programs who could intern at the firm during the summer. City Year's serve-a-thon and its well-structured visitors program allow for the nonprofit to give thousands of visitors the "City Year experience" each year.

These kinds of interactions also help social sector organizations spread knowledge about their corporate partnerships throughout their organization. Social sector staff are often kept informed about corporate partnerships in informal ways, through staff meetings and by involving staff on an as-needed basis. Nonprofit organizations typically keep their boards apprised about corporate partnerships in much the same way they update them about other resource prospects.

INTIMACY

As partners come to know one another better, they experience greater intimacy, which Rackham and his coauthors describe as a "level of organizational closeness that is often exciting and dramatic":

> *The focus of partnering is never what's in it for me? It's what's the value we're creating together? This is a different perspective than selling. . . . It is this shift toward broad business value that provides the competitive advantage of partnering.*[1]

This kind of closeness, like a strong friendship, "makes the impact of partnering identifiable and possible, and in doing so provides the 'lock-in'—the ever-increasing returns to insiders and the thickening barriers to outsiders—of partnering relationships."[2]

Opportunity

Just as new partnerships must have some possibility for impact, long-term relationships must continually generate new opportunities to create value or they will be hard to sustain. Writes Rosabeth Moss Kanter:

> *Like all living systems, relationships are complex. While they are simpler to manage when they are narrow in scope and the partners remain at arm's length, relationships like these yield fewer long-term benefits. . . . Many benefits . . . derive from flexibility and being open to new possibilities. Alliances benefit from established multiple, independent centers of competence and innovation.*[3]

Yes, a good partnership can be sustained for years with a single, ongoing exchange, just as two friends may rely on a longstanding weekly tennis date to bind them together. But to create new value, individuals in both organizations must be attuned to new possibilities that advance the strategic goals defined by the partners.

ENGAGING TOGETHER

In many strong alliances, partners will explore ideas for additional exchanges together, thereby ensuring that both parties feel invested in projects and are able to articulate their own needs and assets. This was the experience of the Learning First Alliance, the coalition of major education associations described in the preface. The Alliance's pilot project was to develop joint action papers in reading and mathematics and to convene a summit of the leadership of all twelve member organizations. But as the individuals involved in the group began to communicate more frequently and trust one another more, additional projects were added. In addition, because of their participation in the Alliance, the organizations saw additional opportunities to work together on efforts outside its scope.

The key to creating new value is to seek new possibilities actively and not confine the relationship to a single type of exchange. Consider Share Our Strength's relationship with Calphalon. It began with a single event—the Bloomingdale's kickoff for the *Home Food* cookbook. Buoyed by the success of the event, Calphalon agreed to sponsor SOS's awards dinner at its annual conference. From there, SOS asked Calphalon to sponsor its Taste of the Nation food and wine event series and agreed to reduce the price in the initial years to make it affordable for the company. Then, to raise the funds, Calphalon created a cause-related marketing program, licensing the names "Taste of the Nation" and "Share Our Strength" to use on pieces of cookware. To add value, the partners developed the Chef's Alliance to participate in retailer-sponsored events featuring SOS and Calphalon cookware.

This partnership was not an "it's June, time to write the check for the annual dinner" relationship. Rather, the exchanges changed over time because new opportunities evolved as the organizations strived to create new value together. Of course, the risk in this kind of expansive thinking is that the possibilities will outstrip the resources available to support them. The SOS-Calphalon Chef's Alliance proved costly to manage and created tension between the partners regarding who should pay for additional staff needed at SOS to support the project. Because of the partners' strong commitment to each other, issues were resolved and the project was able to go forward with both organizations learning from the experience.

Despite this risk, partners seeking new opportunities to create value from their alliance should not confine their relationship to a single exchange or they will stifle its growth and deprive themselves of a greater return on their investment. Internal communication will help surface additional possibilities. For example, staff in the restaurant marketing division of American Express promoted the effectiveness of their sponsorship of SOS's Taste of the Nation to other parts of the company. According to Karen Aidem, former vice president for AmEx, the restaurant marketing division's enthusiasm prompted the student card division to explore a program with SOS based in college bookstores. American Express's sponsorship of Writer's Harvest (an anthology of stories donated by noted authors generating funds to fight hunger) grew out of those discussions. Later, when Aidem participated in a group generating ideas to increase use of the American Express card:

> [O]ne of the ideas that hit the top of our list was donating a portion of every transaction to a cause in the Thanksgiving through Christmas season. And as we thought through causes, we already had the connection to Share Our Strength through two of our business lines, and they had clearly shown themselves to be a worthy partner—very aboveboard, in-line with our corporation's business needs. I think it had a lot to do with the fact that they had a track record and had proven themselves before.

WILLINGNESS TO CHANGE

Implicitly, the ability to be open to opportunities means both partners must be willing to change in order to preserve the partnership and create new value. Like good friendships and marriages, one should never enter the partnership with a view toward changing the other. Nonetheless, it is hard to imagine a good relationship that does not have a larger influence on both partners.

The literature of both the for-profit and nonprofit sector stresses change as an inevitable and desirable characteristic of a successful partnership. Some change will be one-sided, as one partner learns from the other and assimilates this learning into its own organization. If exchanges have been wildly successful, it will almost certainly create another sort of change for the partners, possibly opening up new opportunities from other potential collaborators or allowing the original partnership to expand to a new level. Partners may add new capacities, develop joint systems, or reorganize their priorities. Without ever planning it, the partners learn from one another, adapt to one another, and change together to take advantage of new opportunities.

Mutuality

Martin Blank, an expert in coordinating education and social services, describes collaboration as "shared vision, shared power, shared resources, shared responsibility, and shared accountability." Yves Doz and Gary Hamel, who come from the business perspective, stress that every alliance has two dimensions: "one is concerned with what the partners can achieve together, the second with what the partners can gain for themselves." They liken it to baking and then sharing a pie—each partner contributing different ingredients or skills, and each receiving a slice when it's done.[4] In the cross-sector context, we call this "mutuality."

In New Value Partnerships, both organizations take responsibility for the success of the relationship. They contribute more or less equally to defining the goals of the partnership, controlling its direction, contributing resources, and enjoying its benefits. This kind of equality doesn't mean equal in form—one party may offer funds while the other organizes and staffs a project; one may receive volunteer assistance while the other benefits from more motivated employees. What is important is that neither party feels that it is being exploited and that both believe they are contributing and are vested in a successful outcome.

VISION AND GOALS

Shared vision and goals, which result from joint planning, are fundamental to a strong partnership. Goals are formed as a by-product of the interactive efforts of the parties to define their needs. Therefore, goals may relate to specific interests of either party—to strengthen the social sector organization's programs or to further the corporate partner's business interests. But they must be understood and agreed upon by both partners and committed to paper. Each partner must own the goals, regardless of who proposed them, because both are responsible for achieving them.

RESPONSIBILITY

"When one partner is weak or lazy or won't make an effort to explore what the two can do together, things can come apart," writes Kenichi Ohmae in "The Global Logic of Strategic Alliances." Like Kanter, he likens business partnerships to marriage: "If a wife goes out and becomes the family's breadwinner *and* does all the housework *and* raises the children *and* runs the errands *and* cooks the meals, sooner or later she will rebel."[5] As would the husband.

In cross-sector partnerships, an imbalance like this can occur when one partner, in a quest to create new value for itself, loads the other up with requests. Or it can occur when one partner fails to carry out agreed upon responsibilities, jeopardizing a return on the other's investment of time or money. A relationship may be more important to one partner than the other. Any of these circumstances will make it impossible to sustain a New Value Partnership.

EQUALITY

Equality of the partners is recommended by students of both social sector and business alliances, and its importance does not diminish when cross-sector partnerships are formed. Having a junior and senior partner in the relationship shifts the balance of power and responsibility. It makes one party accountable to the other, but not necessarily vice versa. It skews communications if the "junior partner" feels the need to "manage up," withholding negative information and reporting only good news. This in turn can undermine trust. Ultimately, one partner may become resentful of the other, leading to the demise of the relationship.

The history of cross-sector relationships, however, makes true equality elusive. Corporations and nonprofit organizations in the past have interacted as donor and recipient, philanthropist and charity. Bill Shore calls it the "'Blanche DuBois Syndrome' because like the character in *A Streetcar Named Desire,* nonprofits find themselves at the mercy of the kindness of strangers."[6] Many nonprofit managers have internalized this view of their sector—donors should give because the cause is worthy.

The idea of a donor asking for something in return is anathema to some nonprofit organizations, as it is to some corporate donors. It upsets the basic premise of their belief systems, although in reality, traditional donors do receive benefits from the nonprofits they support—dinners, entertainment, recognition, and of course, good feelings.

Even for those who accept this new paradigm, the notion of equality within the context of philanthropy may be difficult to create in practice. Often, it's easy for business partners to carry out their end of the bargain—they can write a check while social sector partners struggle to balance their social mission with the needs of the business. "They say 'jump,' I say 'how high,'" joked a manager at one of the nonprofits we studied. In reality, the partners in this relationship worked together as equals. The relationship manager at the nonprofit was willing to be attentive to the needs of the partner—an important part of the "shared resources, shared responsibility" in the equation. But the old paradigm is close to the surface, ready to break through if any disequilibrium occurs.

RESPECT

Respect is an important part of mutuality. Beyond showing basic courtesy, partners must show respect for each other's expertise. Recall the American Library Association's experience with the fast food company—rather than relying on the ALA expert staff, the company intended to write the children's reading material that would carry ALA's logo. A company that doesn't respect the knowledge of its nonprofit partner ought to look elsewhere or go it alone. At the same time, a nonprofit that is asked to sell its name without any control over how it will be used ought to think hard about a partnership with a company that shows so little regard for the nonprofit's expertise. In the partnerships we studied, most of the parties had a great deal of respect for each other and showed it by deferring to the other party's expertise, treating one another with courtesy, and trusting each other's good intentions.

TRUST

A common theme in the partnerships we studied and in the literature we reviewed was the importance of trust. According to Rackham, whose team interviewed hundreds of business executives involved in alliances, the "simple idea of trust turned out to be the most compelling topic, on the minds of the vast majority of people we spoke with. Over 80 percent of those we interviewed pointed to trust as the most important precondition of partnering."[7] Some level of trust must be present when the partnership is formed. But it should continue to grow through communication and consistently honorable behavior.

Each partner should share information about its own goals and vulnerabilities. Sharing proprietary information with a partner indicates good faith. But how the partner uses that information is even more indicative of whether trust is well placed. Similarly, an organization should check with its partner before pursuing a relationship with one of its competitors, as City Year did in checking with BankBoston before it contacted its then competitor Fleet Financial to ask it to sponsor a team. Telling the truth, including disclosing self-interest, confronting disagreements, and following through on commitments, are other essential ways to enhance trust. Ultimately, as in a committed personal relationship, your partner's interest becomes as important to you as your own.

Multiple Levels

New Value Partnerships require multiple levels of engagement—ties between executives, between relationship managers, and at operational levels. Our use of friendship as a metaphor for partnership breaks down a bit here, unless one thinks about a relationship between two families— moms, dads, and kids all interacting in ways that make sense given their ages and interests. We think of "multiple levels" in relationships as bringing structural integrity to the partnership, something stressed in both the business and social sector literature.

THE CHAMPION

For a partnership to thrive, each organization involved must "own" it— consider it part of their extended family, nurture it, treat it with regard. For an organization to take ownership, there usually is a champion within the organization who feels passionate about it who drives it forward. Notes David House, formerly with American Express:

You need somebody . . . who's not only a zealot for the cause, but who has the wherewithal to keep a level head about the business issues. We had that, especially for the first few years, with a woman named Natalia Cherney. She . . . right from the get-go felt so strongly about this idea that she would literally not let any door close in her face. She was at the director level of our organization, which is lower-middle management . . . , and she would literally take it right to the chairman.

The champion may be a middle manager, but is often a senior executive who is able to see the strategic potential of the relationship and who enjoys both a high level of credibility with the organization and an ability to navigate the many levels and divisions of an organization. Bank-Boston's Ira Jackson and Calphalon's Dean Kasperzak are examples of business "champions"; Save the Children's Charles MacCormack, Darell Hammond of KaBOOM!, and Sue Ballard of the Newton-Conover Public Schools are social sector champions. These individuals were not only committed to their partner organizations, they almost all formed strong relationships with their counterparts as individuals.

EXECUTIVE AND BOARD INVOLVEMENT

Executive involvement is critical in certain cases, such as an identity-building relationship intended to define a company. Ron Petty's was critical to the Denny's/Save the Children partnership. Major, image-defining, mission-centered relationships should be endorsed by the CEO, and senior executives should signal support by attending events, mentioning the partnership in employee communications, and other ways.

Rosabeth Moss Kanter found that "successful collaborative relationships nearly always depend on the creation and maintenance of a comfortable personal relationship between the senior executives."[8] We agree. Even where senior executives had a minimal or no operational role, their support was important to partners as an indication that the relationship would be part of the organization's overall strategy and that it was valued by the organization as a whole, not just a small group of staff.

Executive involvement doesn't necessarily mean the CEO. Although Bill Gates himself made decisions relating to Microsoft's Libraries Online program, he had no direct contact with the American Library Association except for appearances at press events. In seven years of working with American Express, Share Our Strength founder Bill Shore never met the CEO of the company, although Shore appeared in American Express television commercials and his organization received more than $21 million from the Charge Against Hunger campaign.

Board involvement and support is important for nonprofit organizations. Because of the role they play in setting the strategic direction for the organization, boards of directors must approve of the organization's decision to seek partners and certainly must be consulted about significant or controversial relationships. A board that hasn't been consulted, or that actually opposes an alliance, can make it impossible for a partnership to go beyond an initial exchange.

While boards of nonprofit organizations, CEOs, and other top-level executives may need to bless the partnership, they don't necessarily need to interact directly with the partners. Rather, the important relationships frequently are formed at the division level—the directors of business units who make strategic decisions for the part of the organization that is most relevant to the partnership, such as marketing, procurement, or human resources.

RELATIONSHIP MANAGERS

To make the relationship operational, staff must be assigned to manage it. In the cases we examined, the staff responsible for the day-to-day management of the partnership were located in the unit of the company responsible for the exchange: Denny's initially staffed its relationship with Save the Children out of the office of the CEO because the main goal of the partnership, according to CEO Ron Petty, was to build an "image for the corporation of giving back to the community" extending to all facets of the company from human resources to public relations. But when the relationship took on a marketing focus, the marketing unit took over responsibility. Microsoft managed its philanthropic partnership with the American Library Association out of its community affairs staff, and ALA delegated responsibility to the Public Library Association division because public libraries were the focus of the project. In every case, regardless of the business goals, the form of the exchange determined the staffing structure for the corporation.

In most cases, the relationship manager was high enough in the company hierarchy to have good access to top managers. Curt Weeden, in *Corporate Social Investing*, recommends that companies "[a]ssign day-to-day management responsibility for corporate social investing to a position that is no more than one executive away from the CEO or COO." This positioning enables the individual to be able to "(a) collect the information needed to make good decisions, (b) interact with other senior executives in the company, and (c) command attention and respect from those inside and outside the business."[9] Although we don't believe this is necessary in every case (Boeing's relationship manager Al Staples was a buyer in its Materiel Division), it is probably most important in identity-defining partnerships like Denny's and Home Depot. We've also seen partnerships work well with lower-level managers in charge if senior-level executives are also highly engaged.

OPERATIONS

In addition to relationship managers, other staff become involved in partnerships on an as-needed basis, when opportunities arise or problems need to be addressed. When Share Our Strength worked with Calphalon on a Chef's Alliance event, SOS staff and volunteers were in contact with Calphalon staff many times a day. When Denny's participated in Save the Children's training for its afterschool program providers in Los Angeles, program staff at the nonprofit worked directly with Denny's trainers on multiculturalism. This kind of direct interaction, undertaken with the full knowledge and approval of the relationship managers, allows for more streamlined communication and probably for a better result than an effort that involves several layers of management.

New Value Partnerships often have multiple centers of interaction. For example, although BankBoston appointed both a program liaison and a financial liaison to work with City Year, many other bank employees also work directly with the nonprofit. The bank's director of corporate contributions serves on City Year's Boston advisory board. The bank's volunteer program staff coordinate the bank's participation in events like City Year's serve-a-thon. City Year's Boston director, corporate development staff, education specialist, serve-a-thon coordinator, and BankBoston team leader all interact with bank staff. Both organizations have clearly articulated roles and responsibilities—a cross-organization management structure that has proven highly effective for both organizations.

TURNOVER

Creating a structure that extends beyond a single relationship is important given the likelihood that staff changes will occur. In the seven cases we studied, all but one experienced turnover of a person significantly involved in the partnership either at the executive or operational level. In every case but one, the partnership survived the personnel change.

Although many factors contributed to the sustainability of these alliances, the fact that engagement and support occurred at many levels was identified as a key reason the partnerships survived. Although there is no question that personal relationships between individuals can further a partnership and ensure amicable resolution of conflicts, and indeed, make it more personally rewarding for the people involved, a partnership sustained solely on that basis is extremely vulnerable. A multi-leveled alliance with a clear structure in place helps ensure the partnership is integrated at the strategic level (involving the executives and board members), as well as the tactical level (involving middle managers or professionals who plan exchanges and link the organizations in other ways).

Open-Endedness

Exchanges often have limitations, ending dates, or timelines. "Purchases made during the last quarter of the year 2000 will benefit the cause." "We will complete four major volunteer projects during this calendar year." "Training will be conducted monthly for a period of eighteen months." These are exchanges. But a partnership, the relationship between the organizations engaged in the exchanges, should not have an end date. It may lapse, as when friends drift apart, when an exchange is completed— at the conclusion of Libraries Online, Microsoft and ALA did not continue to seek new opportunities together. Sometimes external events change the context for the partnership (such as a merger or acquisition), or the shifting priorities of one of the partners prevent the partnership from continuing. But if the partners see possibilities for new value arising from their continued association, they need not go their separate ways at the completion of an exchange.

CONTINUOUS LEARNING

Having a commitment to the relationship, rather than the exchange, creates a mindset within the organizations to make decisions that affect the long-term. In an exchange-focused, time-limited relationship, organizations may paper over difficulties or create short-term fixes. If, for example, a volunteer project was poorly organized, the company might be silent and not pitch in to help. The incentive in a short-term arrangement can be to let things go, even to avoid conflict by not saying anything. But as in a long-term friendship, the incentives in New Value Partnerships are to help make it right, communicate concerns in a constructive manner, and ensure that both partners learn from the experience.

This commitment to continuous learning is essential for a partnership to generate benefits for both parties on an ongoing basis. By being willing to make adjustments, the partners are able to adapt to new contexts, incorporate the lessons of previous exchanges, and apply learning from all sources to improve future exchanges. As a result, each subsequent exchange potentially yields greater benefits for the partners.

CYCLES

There is often a cyclical nature to an open-ended relationship, as exchanges are planned, executed, and completed. Yves Doz and Gary Hamel, in *Alliance Advantage,* identify the stages of a successful learning cycle as: (1) successful learning from an initial experience; (2) positive reevaluation, including willingness to increase scope and commitments, and to make adjustments to improve efficiency; and (3) constructive adjustments, which heighten value creation expectations and result in greater and more irreversible commitments.[10] The cycle repeats itself after every exchange, each time resulting in greater value for the partners.

For nonprofit organizations relying on resources generated through cross-sector partnerships, down periods of adjustments between exchanges may present a challenge. When American Express ended the Charge Against Hunger after four years, Share Our Strength experienced a significant drop in revenues. The end of the campaign was anticipated—advertising campaigns generally lose their effectiveness after several years. AmEx continued to be a major partner of the nonprofit as a sponsor of Taste of the Nation; nonetheless, the end of this lucrative exchange could have put SOS at great financial risk. However, by continually seeking new partners and diversifying its income streams, it has continued to thrive. This is a lesson for all nonprofit organizations seeking New Value Partnerships: Regardless of the strength of the relationship, interdependence shouldn't mean dependence. Preparing for the natural cycle of a long-term alliance is essential for the health of the organization and the sustainability of the partnership.

New Value

Ultimately, a partnership must create new value for both partners if it is to continue. Even if opportunities continually arise, if they don't advance the mission of both organizations, the partnership cannot be sustained.

EVALUATION

The organizations we examined universally believed they derived new value from the partnerships. However, as we noted earlier, few had conducted formal evaluations. Most relied on the observations of individuals, as Home Depot did. Notes Suzanne Apple: "There are enough people who have seen the benefit with their own eyes." Echoes Calphalon's Peter Barnhardt: "There's enough of a buzz that you say 'maybe this is working.'" Data supported individual observations in some cases: Calphalon used focus groups and tracked sales of its SOS co-branded pans; American Express used employee surveys to gauge Charge Against Hunger's impact on its employees' views of the company as a corporate citizen, and focus groups and charge volume figures to measure consumer reaction. Many partners were planning to do an evaluation in the future.

The demonstration of impact is important for many reasons. For Share Our Strength and Calphalon, hard numbers and scientifically valid data became much more important when a corporation that did not have experience with cause-related marketing purchased the company. Because of the resources expended in most relationships, whether in cash or in kind, boards of directors and senior managers may want to see that benefits are exceeding costs. As helpful as they are, inspiring anecdotes and testimonials may not be sufficiently convincing. And when a key official involved in the relationship leaves the company, the partnership may be jeopardized if empirical data are not available to support it.

We define evaluation as the assessment of impact on declared objectives in order to improve future activities and demonstrate the value of the partnership to internal and external stakeholders. In general, we recommend that partners evaluate individual exchanges, not the partnership as a whole. Such studies are more manageable and provide useful data that can inform both the design of future exchanges and the conduct of the partnership.

It is important that any empirical study incorporate information on both the economic and noneconomic objectives of an exchange. If an exchange is intended to increase employee loyalty as well as stimulate sales, studying the latter and not the former will almost certainly result in the partnership being undervalued by the company. These "softer" impacts can be quantified, provided that baseline data are available or can be collected before the exchange begins—turnover, absenteeism, and employee satisfaction surveys all measure employee loyalty, for example. Employee loyalty can be linked to the economic bottom line by determining the cost of replacing employees, lost productivity due to absenteeism, or the value of customer referrals by employees.[11]

For the social sector partner, the value of the relationship may also be measurable. If the partnership simply generates funds for the organization, to measure the impact may require that the organization be able to determine its unit cost; for example, Big Brothers/Big Sisters, one of Save the Children's nonprofit partners, estimates that it costs $1,000 to match and monitor each Big/Little mentoring relationship. Outcome is far more difficult for most social sector organizations to measure. What impact does the mentoring relationship have on the child? On the mentor? On the community?

Of the organizations we studied, Pioneer Human Services had the most sophisticated evaluation system, tracking everything from product cost and quality to recidivism and employment rates of women who came through its work-release program. Pioneer sets outcome-based goals and maintains rigid control over day-to-day performance through extensive computer-based reports and audits. As a nonprofit provider of social services, Pioneer is subject to external standards imposed by government agencies or other organizations, like the American Corrections Association. Pioneer typically sets even higher standards for itself, evaluates its progress using internal auditors and a state-of-the-art management information system, and then works to apply the successful practices of each program to other programs.[12] This method of continuous improvement enables Pioneer to consistently exceed its own goals and has earned it numerous awards, ranging from Governor Booth Gardner's Safety Award to President George Bush's 30th Point of Light.

When the business's contribution to the partnership is not in cash but in-kind—goods, services, expertise, or volunteers—social sector organizations should attempt to quantify their value. Again, gauging impact will be more difficult. Did donated computers increase the number of clients served each month by decreasing time staff spent performing administrative tasks? What effect did that have on the clients? Did the management training offered by the company provide useful information to nonprofit leaders? Did the nonprofit leaders act differently as a result and what impact did that have on the organization? Did flyers about the cause distributed by the corporation increase awareness of the issue? Did the number of donors, clients, or volunteers increase as a result?

In the development of AmeriCorps, we were determined to be able to measure the impact of the program on communities and to quantify the impact nationally. That proved a challenging task. The nonprofit organizations that fielded AmeriCorps members for the most part had no systems in place to collect this information, and by scientific standards, it was nearly impossible to quantify impact rather than input. We developed forms that helped grantees count how many trees were planted, children tutored, meals served, and so on. But to determine the impact of those trees on the spirit of a low-income neighborhood or its air quality, the impact of tutoring on children's academic achievement or the improved health of children who were immunized was much harder. Several programs commissioned economists to conduct a cost-benefit evaluation which found that every dollar spend on AmeriCorps programs returned as much as $2.60.[13] This information proved very useful in sustaining AmeriCorps as a national program and for grantees to attract their own funders. And by shifting their thinking from "input thinking" (How many volunteers did we field? How many hours did they serve?) to "outcome thinking" (What impact did they have?), we believe that we increased the impact of the programs and made them more attractive to corporate funders.

VALUING A PARTNER'S RESULTS

In cross-sector partnerships, both partners should be interested in the others' results. The social sector partner should be concerned with whether the corporation increased its sales or built morale or increased the quality of its product as a result of the partnership because this information will enable it to serve the company better in the future. Knowing such outcomes will also help the organization build its own capital—future partners will be interested in its track record as a partner. Some companies are reluctant to share this kind of information even with its nonprofit partners. Special Olympics worked with Procter & Gamble for almost two decades, and yet the company never shared the result of the exchanges with the nonprofit. But we would argue it is important for the company to entrust its partners with information that will increase the effectiveness of similar exchanges in the future.

Businesses should be interested in their social sector partners' results as well. Those outcomes relating to the social mission of the organization can help the business derive value from the relationship. As the nonprofit becomes more effective, corporate employees and other stakeholders should derive satisfaction from these good works, thus increasing their loyalty to the company. Public awareness of the nonprofit's positive results will be beneficial for a corporate partners' image and will help drive a cause-marketing program.

Nonprofit organizations should share with the business evidence of both the nonprofit's overall effectiveness and any specific results that can be traced to the involvement of the corporation. In traditional philanthropic relationships, nonprofits typically provide funders with reports of how their donations were used. In less formal partnerships or business-oriented arrangements, this step is sometimes omitted. But failure to communicate results is shortsighted. Nonprofits experienced at corporate partnerships know how to reinforce these relationships effectively. Share Our Strength provides funders with copies of the letters it receives from local grantees, along with press clips and other information documenting impact. Special Olympics encourages friends of the organization to express their support to stores participating in its Procter & Gamble promotion. City Year collects stories of corps members whose lives were deeply affected by their year of service and asks its community partners that host teams to report on their impact. In cross-sector partnerships, the reinforcement of the business by the social sector organizations is an important ingredient, regardless of the type of exchange.

Celebrate

Finally, a lesson that comes through clearly in the social sector literature, but rarely in business commentary, offers what we believe to be a useful piece of advice: Celebrate, reward, and publicize. There may be natural opportunities to celebrate. When the first AmeriCorps members were sworn in at the White House, corporate supporters were invited to share in the event. Ira Jackson presented diplomas to the corps members sponsored by BankBoston at City Year's graduation. When Calphalon was ready to make its first donation to SOS from its cause-related marketing campaign, it did so at a Taste of the Nation dinner. KaBOOM! playground builders are encouraged to plan an annual birthday party for the playground.

Rewards may come in the form of special awards—Save the Children awarded Denny's CEO Ron Petty its distinguished service award; Denny's Lend-A-Hand awards recognize employees who make the greatest contribution to Save the Children. The American Library Association made Bill and Melinda Gates honorary members of the Association, and the Welfare to Work Partnership honors the business that has done the most to advance the cause with its Willard D. Marriott award, honoring the trailblazing efforts of one of its directors.

Publicizing the results of the partnership internally is also important. Share Our Strength shares news coverage and letters of appreciation with its entire staff, including those not directly involved with the project, recognizing that it is the team as a whole that makes it happen. KaBOOM! publishes a regular newsletter for its community and corporate partners, offering tips to making playground building more effective, highlighting the contributions of its partners, and sharing stories of the children who have a safe place to play thanks to KaBOOM! and its partners. Denny's employee newsletter devotes significant coverage to its Save the Children partnership, including the ways that individual employees or restaurants have raised money for the nonprofit. The Welfare to Work Partnership touts a different business partner's achievement each week in its blast fax.

As for external publicity, in addition to traditional press releases and media coverage of special events, many of the organizations we studied found ways to assist their partners in obtaining favorable notice. BankBoston's Ira Jackson has spoken about City Year in front of influential audiences: Renaissance Weekend attendees, Associated Grantmakers of Massachusetts, senior officials in the Bush White House, and the Senate Committee on Labor and Human Resources. The American Library Association featured an interview with Bill Gates on its Web site, and when Gary Mulhair was president of Pioneer Human Services, he spoke extensively about "operational philanthropy," giving significant public attention to Boeing's leadership role in the field.

Conclusion

The New Value Partnerships we studied that possess most of the COM-MON elements listed here have proven resilient, surviving financial crises, staff turnover, public relations challenges, and programmatic set-backs. Because the partners are already familiar with each other and need not spend time learning each other's culture and needs, each subsequent exchange is less costly than the initial exchange. As a result, these partnerships will provide a greater return on investment over time. Like good friendships, New Value Partnerships may have more intense periods and downtimes. But the richness of the relationship will make it a valuable asset to each partner as it faces new challenges and opportunities.

12

🙦

CONCLUSION

IN AUGUST, 1998, the *Chronicle of Philanthropy* ran a feature story on Res-Care, an organization whose mission is "to insure that all human beings have the chance to realize their full potential, no matter what the obstacle, no matter what the challenge. We care. We serve. With compassion, with skill, with effectiveness, with results . . . and with respect." Based in Louisville, Kentucky, Res-Care provides residential care for people with mental disabilities, troubled children, and others with special needs. Among other programs, the organization has a contract to manage the nonprofit Georgia Center for Youth, a program for children referred by public schools.[1]

A few months earlier, National Public Radio's *Talk of the Nation Science Friday* featured an interview with David Muchnick, founder of Big City Forest, a small business in the south Bronx. Using wood from shipping pallets and crates (which local companies would otherwise have had to pay to have hauled away), Big City Forest manufactured wood flooring, home furnishings, and office furniture featured in design magazines. The company began turning a profit in 1997. By using wood that would otherwise have been discarded, Big City Forest kept more than 9,000 tons of wood from landfills from 1994 to 1997 and saved local companies over $2 million in waste disposal costs.[2]

Reflections and Recommendations

These kinds of stories might seem commonplace, except for the fact that Res-Care is a publicly traded, $300 million business and Big City Forest is a subsidiary of the nonprofit Bronx 2000, a community development organization. The lines that once defined precise roles for the for-profit and not-for-profit sectors have blurred, and threaten to break down all together. Nonprofits are engaging in the marketplace, charging fees, producing commercial products, and adopting market-savvy approaches from the business sector. Businesses, on the other hand, are entering the social services field in record numbers, meeting consumer demand for a range of services once offered only by charitable groups or the government. The highly competitive and extensively regulated health care field was one of the first to push the limits on the distinction between the for-profit and not-for-profit worlds. Today, the dependent care, community recreation, education, social services, and job training fields are close behind.

The "morphing" of the sectors has some advocates calling for revision of the tax laws governing nonprofit organizations and has both sides arguing that they are being subjected to unfair competition. But beyond the legal issues is the deeper question of what really defines the sectors. "If money is being designated for services to help people, that's where it should go—not to shareholders, not to corporate executives," says a manager in a nonprofit residential services organization that the *Chronicle of Philanthropy* asked to comment on Res-Care. She argues that nonprofits provide superior care because of the personal connection, access to donations and volunteers, and a community orientation.[3] A business's concern for profitability could cause it to turn away those most in need. However, for-profit managers contend that their attention to the bottom line creates incentives for them to provide excellent customer service and to keep costs down.

We don't propose a solution to this debate. The old stereotypes characterized by the extremes—the ruthless business exploiting its workers in pursuit of the almighty dollar, and the do-good nonprofit with heart above head—don't apply. We worry equally about losing our nation's competitive edge as we do sacrificing those whom an economic boom leaves below the poverty line. We are not suggesting that businesses put aside their drive for profits to pursue a social mission. In fact, the former co-chair of Businesses for Social Responsibility, former CEO of Stride Rite Arnold Hiatt, believes the "first act of social responsibility is to make money"; and at least one study has found that people judge corporate citizenship based first on whether companies stand behind their products and produce high quality goods, with donations and volunteering ranking significantly lower.[4] Nor do we advocate that nonprofits adopt a hardheaded approach that looks only at the bottom line. To do so risks both their tax-exempt status and legitimacy, and leaves those hardest to serve with nowhere to turn. Nonetheless, as the sectors converge, we want each to add to its capabilities and best qualities of the other. Therefore, what we do suggest is that increasingly, the business and social sector have a common interest in working together and much to learn from one another.

What can the social sector learn from business? To borrow a list from David Osborne and Ted Gaebler's seminal book *Reinventing Government*, the social sector can learn to be:

- *Competitive.* Creating incentives for higher performance.

- *Customer-driven.* Meeting the needs of clients, not the bureaucracy.

- *Results-oriented.* Focusing on outcomes, not inputs.

- *Enterprising.* Generating revenues, not just spending them.

- *Market-oriented.* Leveraging change rather than controlling it.[5]

At the same time, as Peter Drucker points out in his 1989 *Harvard Business Review* article, business can learn from the social sector how to be:

- *Mission-driven.* Making decisions based on mission rather than money.

- *Board-led.* Holding the CEO accountable to the board.

- *Attractive employers.* Motivating staff (and volunteers) to be more productive and committed.[6]

In addition to Drucker's list, businesses can learn from nonprofit organizations how to be attentive to diverse stakeholders—being responsive to the interests of employees, board members, clients, and communities.[7]

Cross-sector partnerships create opportunities for the sectors to learn from one another while meeting the needs of individual businesses and social sector organizations. Of course, thriving businesses and effective social sector organizations are good for the community and the public at large. But beyond the benefits generated for individual organizations, these partnerships stimulate a public good: a sense of shared responsibility among organizations for our common destiny.

Perhaps the growth in cross-sector partnerships derives from an evolving understanding of the way in which the social health of families, communities, regions, and the country affects business, and the way our economic status affects social health. It is well accepted among business leaders that the quality of educational and cultural organizations affects the ability of employers to attract and retain employees. The sustained low unemployment rate of the mid- and late-1990s underscored for many the important role played by organizations that prepare youth and adults for the world of work. Less often articulated is the value of civic participation and social cohesiveness to the health of the business sector. Similarly, while most social sector organizations appreciate the importance of private sector jobs for their clients, only recently have they begun to explore other ways business can support social causes.

In working more closely together, organizations need not, and should not, abandon their central missions. Over-commercialization of non-profit organizations could undermine their legitimacy, discourage donors and volunteers, and cause them to neglect those who are hardest, and costliest, to serve. Businesses that put social change ahead of profits risk losing shareholders and customers, and ultimately, threaten their own survival. The key is for business and social sector organizations alike to strike the right balance as they move in these new directions.

Although we are mindful of the pitfalls, we view the interconnectedness of the business and social sectors as a positive new direction that creates limitless opportunities for our country. To appreciate the potential of cross-sector partnerships, compare the philanthropic and marketing budgets of almost any Fortune 500 company. IBM, one of the most generous corporations in the country, made contributions totalling approximately $100 million in cash and product in 1996,[8] but spent almost twice that amount on advertising alone.[9] Add to that the purchasing volume, investment dollars, excess capacity and surplus inventory, training funds, and other resources that could be utilized in cross-sector partnerships and one begins to appreciate the possibilities available. As the cases in this book demonstrate, these resources can potentially serve two purposes: the business's bottom line and the social sector's need for resources to achieve its mission. To do this well takes work. It also demands faith, imagination, and will.

We are not arguing against doing good for good's sake. Traditional corporate philanthropy should continue and grow as a percentage of revenue. At the same time, social sector organizations should remember that the effectiveness with which they pursue their social missions is their strongest sales tool and should ensure it remains the number one concern of all affiliated with them. But even where selfless good work is a business's prime motivation for social sector involvement, the development of a strong partnership will make it all the more effective.

Governments, civic leaders, and ordinary citizens can all encourage partnerships between business and social sector organizations. The government, which we have in some cases treated as part of the social sector, can pursue business partnerships as we did at AmeriCorps. However, in its role as regulator, government at the city, state, and federal levels is also responsible for policies that can inhibit or encourage cross-sector partnerships. For example, laws limiting nonprofit "unrelated business income"[10] have been construed to allow a nonprofit organization to license its name to a business without incurring taxes on the revenues, but not to help market the product. In a true partnership, these legal limitations create a barrier between the partners that limits opportunities for both, and therefore the public, to benefit.

Similarly, state laws that require nonprofit organizations to register if they plan to solicit funds in the state have been interpreted by state attorneys general to cover cause-related marketing campaigns. As a result, a nonprofit partner may put itself at risk when a business offers to make a donation to the organization for each item sold, unless the organization goes through the expensive and cumbersome process of registering in any state in which the advertisements might appear. On the business side, legislation has been proposed that would require shareholder involvement in corporate philanthropic decisions;[11] such legislation would likely create additional administrative barriers to corporate giving and significantly limit corporations' ability to engage in strategic partnerships with nonprofit organizations.

Instead of taking a narrow regulatory view, government and civic leaders should think about ways they can stimulate connectedness among organizations of different sectors. When convening key organizations concerned with a specific social or economic issue, community leaders should include both business and social sector leaders. They should help divergent organizations find common ground and explore ways they can contribute to the common good. And by rewarding and recognizing cross-sector partnerships, they will validate the practice and inspire others to explore its many possibilities.

Ordinary citizens also hold great power in influencing whether cross-sector partnerships fade as a fad or continue their steady growth. Citizens, in their role as consumers, may choose products with cause-related ties or that were manufactured by social enterprises. They may look at the record of a business' support for social sector causes they care about in making purchasing decisions or deciding to invest in a publicly traded company. They may communicate their support to both the business and social sector partners if they approve of a transaction—by sending a letter or E-mail to the company president or engaging a salesperson or store manager in a discussion about the cause. And in their role as civically engaged citizens and voters, they can support policies that encourage partnerships and oppose those that inhibit them. These efforts will help create a context that not only supports new involvement in cross-sector partnerships, but makes existing partnerships more valuable.

Challenges

To take advantage of the many benefits of cross-sector partnerships, business and social sector organizations in general will need to widen their view and reexamine not what they do but how they do it.

THE CORPORATE AGENDA

For business, we see three challenges.

Be about something larger. In *Built to Last,* James Collins and Jerry Porras studied eighteen "visionary" companies along with comparison businesses.[12] They found that what set the visionary businesses apart was not charismatic leadership or a great idea, but the ability to "preserve the core" while at the same time stimulating change. These companies had several things in common: they set "Big Hairy Audacious Goals" to stimulate progress, they "Try a Lot of Stuff and Keep What Works," and they had "Cult-like Cultures" and "Home-Grown Management." They were "clock builders, not time tellers," meaning that their founders built outstanding organizations that could yield a continual stream of great products and services, rather than let the products and services define the company.[13] And at the core of these visionary companies, they found an ideology that went beyond making profits. The authors point out:

> *Profitability is a necessary condition for existence and means to more important ends, but it is not the end in itself for many of the visionary companies. Profit is like oxygen, food, water, and blood for the body; they are not the* point *of life, but without them, there is no life.*[14]

This ideology is made up of both core values, "the organization's essential and enduring tenets," and purpose, "the organization's fundamental reasons for existence beyond just making money"[15]—such as, "to alleviate pain and disease" (Johnson & Johnson)[16] or "to use our imagination to bring happiness to millions" (Disney).[17]

Having a mission that goes beyond making profits opens up possibilities for natural partnerships with social sector organizations. LensCrafters' corporate mission, "We will be the best at helping the world see," brings meaning to the company's core business of selling prescription eyeglasses. But it also connects the company's community service program, "Give the Gift of Sight," to its core purpose. In partnership with Lions Clubs International and other local charities, the company will provide free vision care for one million needy people over a five-year period. In 1995, when the company made an acquisition that increased its store count by 10 percent, and was then acquired itself, the Gift of Sight program helped establish a connection among employees, new and old, and helped employees put their own anxiety about the change in perspective. "When you help someone who is truly in need, you realize your own problems aren't so big," according to LensCrafters CEO David M. Browne. Recognizing its value, the new corporate parent not only continued the Gift of Sight program, but agreed to sponsor a new Vision Van. This show of commitment "helped reassure associates that the new owners were committed to our Vision. It helped us worry less and focus more on the job to be done," writes Browne.[18]

Nurture and sustain social sector partners. The sincerity—or lack of it—demonstrated by a business in supporting a cause is often evident to its partners, employees, and the public at large. The strength of a social sector partner, and its ability to help a business meet its needs, is derived from its effectiveness in achieving its social mission. But even when a business has good intentions, by falling into patterns common to philanthropic funders it may create challenges for its nonprofit partners.

Christine Letts, William Ryan, and Allen Grossman, writing in the *Harvard Business Review,* compare how philanthropy and venture capital investments differ.[19] Venture capitalists invest based on the strength of the organization, but foundations make grants based on the efficacy of a single program—creating incentives for nonprofits to neglect such core functions as financial systems, human resource development, quality control and planning. Furthermore, venture capitalists offer noncash assistance, particularly expertise, whereas foundations spend more time screening out applications than overseeing their investments. Finally, venture capitalists spend five to seven years with a start-up, compared to foundations who make one-year grants better than 90 percent of the time.

Letts and her colleagues conclude that foundations ought to act more like venture capitalists. In most cases we agree. Too often, corporate funders, like foundations, restrict their support to certain programmatic purposes, not appreciating that nonprofit organizations are often forced to scrimp on key administrative and other supports because of the need to minimize these costs at the request of funders. What business would accept dollars from investors who insisted that the funds be only for a specific, preordained purpose? Corporate funders usually offer short-term grants, forcing their partners to deal with uncertainty of funding and expend energy every year to secure new support. They may be attracted to new start-ups, but eschew providing second stage funding that would allow successful pilots to expand. And they may provide dollars, but neglect other important ways they could support a partner. If they had a better understanding of the nonprofit's needs they might look beyond the involvement of a single corporate department in order to engage customers and distributors, provide marketing assistance, or offer in-kind services such as legal or accounting services.

Rosabeth Moss Kanter concurs that corporations can play an important role in producing sustainable social change, while at the same time stimulating their own business development. The key: to approach the social sector "not as an object of charity but as an opportunity for learning and business development, supported by R&D and operating funds rather than philanthropy."[20] This approach requires building strong partnerships with investment by both parties, a commitment to change, rootedness in the community, and links to other organizations—from both the business and social sector. Perhaps most important, Kanter stresses the need for a "long-term commitment to sustain and replicate the solution."[21] Unexpected problems and opportunities can derail best-laid plans. Investments in the social sector, she concludes, require patient capital.

Show and tell. We don't necessarily advocate issuing self-serving press releases about good works. There are other ways a business can share information about its social sector involvement both within the business and with the public. Internal communication channels can highlight the work of the social sector partner and encourage employee involvement. Key employees or business partners (such as distributors or suppliers) may be invited to tour the social sector program. Social sector partners may be invited to participate in company functions, such as trainings or social events. These are all ways not just of cementing the partnership by building relationships and understanding between the staffs, but also of helping internal stakeholders become more knowledgeable about the social sector partner. For external audiences, businesses may be able to underscore their own association with the cause by highlighting the non-profit partner's contributions or inviting others to support it. Speeches, op-eds, press events, social marketing, community forums, and other efforts aimed to draw attention to the good work of a partner present opportunities for a company to subtly draw attention to its support without directly patting itself on the back.

THE NONPROFIT AGENDA

We see different challenges for social sector organizations:

Involve others meaningfully in what you do. Direct engagement in the social mission of the organization can inspire volunteers to stretch their capacity to help, and help them derive a greater sense of meaning from the experience. Because business organizations are made up of individuals, the ability of a social sector organization to enable its partners to participate in its social mission—as volunteers, on its board, or even as observers—creates a stronger connection with its partners. City Year's visitors program and serve-a-thon, KaBOOM! playground builds, and Save the Children's child sponsorship system all provide opportunities for business partners to put a face on the people they are helping and to see its impact.

Savvy nonprofits also find ways for business partners to contribute things other than money. SOS, City Year, and KaBOOM! all offer seats on their boards to key corporate partners, and most of the social sector organizations we studied were open to forms of assistance like volunteers, product donations, and management or marketing expertise. In providing advice to their nonprofit partners, the business people we interviewed became more invested in the success of the organizations. Finally, experienced social sector organizations learn how to "share the glory" with their partners—inviting them to join in accepting awards, speak to the press, or brief influential people.

Specialize, but don't compartmentalize. A high degree of cooperation is needed among different functions of the organization in order to be most effective. Program staff should share stories, results, and needs. Public affairs staff should to seek out opportunities for communication, help refine messages and create attractive, compelling materials. Executive staff and board members should ensure integration of functions, consistency of message, and program quality. Without this kind of coordination, opportunities will be lost.

Consider the experience of a grassroots nonprofit organization we know whose volunteer recruitment coordinator, community outreach specialist, and development director all operated autonomously. When the community outreach specialist spoke to corporate audiences about the cause, she didn't ask for volunteer recruits or donations; the volunteer coordinator preached the cause and signed up volunteers but didn't solicit other kinds of contributions; and the development director asked for money but not volunteer help. No one thought to use these opportunities to generate names for the organization's mailing list. And when donated clothing and household goods were not needed, they were turned away by the program staff, even though these kinds of offerings, when graciously accepted, sometimes inspired donors to contribute volunteer time or cash in the future. When this organization started coordinating across departments, it was able to almost double its budget and inform thousands of additional people about its services. In order to make use of donated goods that were not needed by clients, the organization contracted with a thrift shop, which agreed to provide gift certificates for the nonprofit's clients in exchange for the donated goods.

Be a visionary organization. The description of a visionary institution found in *Built to Last* is not limited to business organizations. As Collins and Porras discovered, both business and social sector organizations *face the need to transcend dependence on any single leader or great idea. Both depend on a timeless set of core values and an enduring purpose beyond just making money. Both need to change in response to a changing world, while simultaneously preserving their core values and purpose. Both need mechanisms to encourage forward progress, be they BHAGs [Big Hairy Audacious Goals], experimentation and entrepreneurship, or continuous self-improvement. Both need to create consistent alignment to preserve their core values and purpose and to stimulate progress.*[22]

In short, social sector organizations can be visionary institutions, able to prosper over many decades and weather many changes of leadership.

Finally, a reminder for both business and social sector organizations: Although we have tried to lay out the stages of partnership development and the elements of New Value Partnerships, the nature of relationships demands flexibility and responsiveness to the unique circumstances and style of the partners. The people who made the partnerships we studied work drew on their own reserves of common sense and experience in relationships of other sorts to craft successful alliances. It turns out that they tended to follow similar patterns, which are instructive to those seeking partnerships. But ultimately, these relationships are organic—individualistic and ever changing.

We have used the metaphor of friendship (and sometimes marriage) throughout this book to enable readers to draw on familiar experiences that help explain the development of institutional relationships. Now we encourage readers to think about their own experiences—friendships that have lasted, those that have withered and died, and even those that ended explosively—for answers when situations arise that aren't covered by the plan.

An Invitation

We invite you to step across the line, to make connections across the sectors. Within each sector, greater potential for increased efficiency exists between organizations than within them. We believe this is also true across sectors. We see this demonstrated in small ways when the back of a cereal box that would otherwise be printed with empty content can be used to help educate children about safety; when a company makes it easy for customers to make donations to a nonprofit partner, improving its own image as it easily generates revenues for a cause; when a community organization eager to provide preventive health services can do so conveniently at the work site; when a manufacturer can eliminate surplus inventory by donating it to a nonprofit that will get it in the hands of people who need, but cannot afford, the items; when corporate employees find greater meaning in their work because of the company's tie to the community; when a company can build teamwork sending employees to spend a day renovating a preschool instead of relaxing at a corporate picnic.

Our history and our society have erected barriers that keep the business and social sectors from communicating informally and interacting professionally. Let us eliminate these barriers. Consider the sheer volume of organizations not yet participating. And then imagine the potential of cross-sector relationships to advance the interests of the institutions that make up our communities and our country.

In the end, their common interest is for the common good.

❧

NOTES

Preface

1. Lester M. Salamon, *Holding the Center: America's Nonprofit Sector at a Crossroads* (New York: Nathan Cummings Foundation, 1997), 18.
2. "Overview and Executive Summary: The State of the Independent Sector," Independent Sector Research, <http://www.indepsec.org/programs/research/almanac_overview.html> (5 October 1998).
3. Nancy Rubin, Melinda Hudson, Mark Feldman, and Chuck Supple took a leadership role in developing private sector partnerships for AmeriCorps.
4. General Accounting Office, *National Service Programs-AmeriCorps*USA—Early Program Resource and Benefit Information report* HEHS-95-222, 29 August 1995.

Chapter 1

1. In 1987, the average nonprofit received about a quarter of its revenues from public funds. Calculated based on data from Independent Sector Web site [on line]. Available: <http://www.indepsec.org/programs/research/table4_2.html> (1 October 1998).
2. From 1980 to 1986, federal spending on social services decreased 40 percent in inflation-adjusted dollars. Alan J. Abramson and Lester M. Salamon, *The Nonprofit Sector and the New Federal Budget* (Washington, D.C.: Urban Institute Press, 1986).

3. American Association of Fund Raising Counsel Trust for Philanthropy, *Giving USA, 1998* (New York: American Association of Fund Raising Counsel Trust for Philanthropy, 1998), 155.

4. KPMG Peat Marwick, *Organizations Serving the Public: Transformation to the 21st Century* (New York: KPMG Peat Marwick, January 1997), 57.

5. Ibid., 31.

6. Ibid., 41.

7. American Association of Fund Raising Counsel Trust for Philanthropy, *Giving USA, 1998.*

8. Alison H. Watson and Jay W. Lorsch, "The United Way in America: Governance in the Nonprofit Sector (A)," Case 9-494-032 (Boston: Harvard Business School, 1993).

9. KPMG Peat Marwick, *Organizations Serving the Public,* 49.

10. Neil Rackham, Lawrence Friedman, and Richard Ruff, *Getting Partnering Right: How Market Leaders Are Creating Long-Term Competitive Advantage* (New York: McGraw-Hill, 1996), 36.

11. Ibid., 47.

12. Joel Bleeke and David Ernst, "Is Your Strategic Alliance Really a Sale?" *Harvard Business Review: Strategic Alliances* 73, no. 1 (1995): 13–22.

13. Rosabeth Moss Kanter, "Collaborative Advantage: The Art of Alliances," *Harvard Business Review: Strategic Alliances* 72, no. 4 (1994): 34–46. For an in-depth treatment of alliances, see Rosabeth Moss Kanter, *World Class: Thriving Locally in the Global Economy* (New York: Simon & Schuster, 1995).

14. Andersen Consulting, "Partnership Choices and Challenges: A Framework for Success" (presentation materials at the Drucker Foundation Management and Leadership Conference, San Francisco, 1 November 1996).

15. Bleeke and Ernst, "Is Your Strategic Alliance Really a Sale?" 13–22.

16. Seymour Sarason and Elizabeth Lorentz, *Crossing Boundaries: Collaboration, Coordination and the Redefinition of Resources* (San Francisco: Jossey-Bass, 1998), x.

17. Atelia Melaville and Martin Blank, *Together We Can: A Guide for Crafting a Pro-family System of Education and Human Services* (Washington, D.C.: U.S. Department of Education, 1993), 9.

18. An excellent illustration of this point is found in the transcript of a hearing by the House Committee on Economic and Educational Opportunity, Subcommittee on Oversight and Investigations, *Simulation Hearing on Obtaining Federal and State Assistance,* 104th Cong., 1st sess., 27 March 1995. This hearing was organized by the Institute for Educational Leadership, a leading expert on social sector collaboration.

19. Linda Zukowski, "Connecting with Corporate Funders," *Grassroots Fundraising* 17, no. 1 (1998): 6.

20. KPMG Peat Marwick, *Organizations Serving the Public,* 61.

21. Sharon Kagan et al., *Collaboration: Cornerstone of an Early Childhood System* (New Haven: Bush Center in Child Development and Social Policy, Yale University, 1992).

22. See, for example, Kagan et al., *Collaboration*; Melaville and Blank, *Together We Can*; and Chris R. Warren, ed., *How to Compete and Cooperate at the Same Time: A Guide for Nonprofits Working Together in This Dog Eat Dog Day and Age* (Santa Fe: Adolfo Street Publications, 1997).

23. Focus group conducted by Peter D. Hart Research Associates, Inc. for the Ford Foundation and Share Our Strength, 23 June 1998.

24. National Association of Partners in Education, *Integrating Telecommunications Technology into Education: The 21st Century Challenge for Partners Navigating the Four Cs of Change* (Alexandria, Va.: National Association of Partners in Education, 1996), 87.

Chapter 2

1. A more complete, if cumbersome, definition of marketing partnerships, adapted from the *Dictionary of Marketing Terms,* 2d edition, edited by Peter D. Bennett and published by the American Marketing Association, © 1995, reads: "The partnership of a business and social sector organization in planning or executing the conception, pricing, promotion or distribution of goods and services to create exchanges that satisfy consumer, franchisee or distributor needs and wants."

2. Operational partnerships may also involve a business supplying a nonprofit with goods or services. These partnerships closely resemble vendor-customer alliances within the business sector.

3. Craig Smith, "The New Corporate Philanthropy," *Harvard Business Review* 72, no. 3 (1994): 105–116.

4. American Association of Fund Raising Counsel Trust for Philanthropy, *Giving USA, 1999,* Executive Summary (New York: American Association of Fund Raising Counsel Trust for Philanthropy, 1999).

5. Ibid., 4.

6. American Association of Fund Raising Counsel Trust for Philanthropy, *Giving USA, 1998,* 22.

7. Ibid.

8. By law, businesses may give up to 10 percent of their pretax profits annually. Curt Weeden, a former Johnson & Johnson vice president, advocates that companies give a minimum of 2.5 percent of pretax profits. See Weeden, *Corporate Social Investing* (San Francisco: Berrett-Koehler Publishers, Inc., 1998).

9. Myra Alperson, *Corporate Giving Strategies That Add Business Value,* report no. 1126-95-RR (New York: The Conference Board, 1995).

10. Cathleen Wild, *Corporate Volunteer Programs: Benefits to Business,* report no. 1029 (New York: The Conference Board, 1993), 13.

11. Ibid.

12. David Lewin, *Community Involvement, Employee Morale, and Business Performance,* IBM Worldwide Social Responsibility Conference, 1991, as cited in Wild, *Corporate Volunteer Programs,* 20.

13. Sarah J. Stebbins, "The Influence of Community Service Volunteer Work on Perceptions of Job Satisfaction and Organizational Commitment among Oregon Employees of Pacific Bell Northwest" (Unpublished Ph.D. diss., University of Michigan, 1989) as cited in Wild, *Corporate Volunteer Programs,* 21.

14. Wild, *Corporate Volunteer Programs,* 22.

15. The number of corporate volunteer councils increased from 600 in 1985 to 1,048 in 1992. See Wild, *Corporate Volunteer Programs,* 9.

16. Kelly Prelipp Lojk, "Corporate Gifts Rise 31 Percent, Report Says," *Philanthropy Journal* (9 February 1998).

17. Lesa Ukman, *IEG's Complete Guide to Sponsorship: Everything You Need to Know about Sports, Arts, Event, Entertainment and Cause Marketing* (Chicago: IEG Inc., 1998).

18. Ben Cohen and Jerry Greenburg, *Double Dip: Lead with Your Values and Make Money Too* (New York: Simon & Schuster, 1998).

19. "Marketing Deals May Reap $1-Billion," *The Chronicle of Philanthropy* XI, no. 9 (1999): 40.

20. For more informaion on social marketing, see Philip Kotler and Eduardo Roberto, *Social Marketing* (New York: The Free Press, 1989).

21. Minette E. Drumwright, "Company Advertising with a Social Dimension: The Role of Noneconomic Criteria," *Journal of Marketing* 60 (October 1996): 13.

22. "See Donor Survey on Charity Business Marketing," *Insight on Philanthropy* 3 (Council of Better Business Bureau's Philanthropic Advisory Service, 1991): 5.

23. See Arthur M. Smith, "Understanding and Building the Nonprofit Brand," in *Marketing the Nonprofit: The Challenge of Fundraising in a Consumer Culture,* ed. Margaret M. Maxwell (San Francisco: Jossey-Bass, 1997), 5–26.

24. Drumwright, "Company Advertising with a Social Dimension."

25. Ibid., 11.

26. Ibid.

27. Cone/Roper, "Cause-Related Marketing Trends Report," sponsored by Cone Communications Inc. and Roper/Starch Worldwide, Inc., Boston, Mass., 1997.

28. Drumwright, "Company Advertising with a Social Dimension," 12.

29. Ibid., 16.

30. Ibid., 20.

31. Ibid., 15.

32. Alan R. Andreasen, "Profits for Nonprofits: Find a Corporate Partner," *Harvard Business Review* 74, no. 6 (1996): 47–59.

33. Drumwright, "Company Advertising with a Social Dimension," 3.

34. "About Goodwill Industries" [on line]. Available: <http://www.goodwill.org> (5 October 1998).

35. Jennifer Moore, "A Corporate Challenge for Charities," *The Chronicle of Philanthropy* X, no. 20 (1998).

36. Ibid.

Chapter 3

1. Ashley's account is reported in: Darell Hammond, "A Playground for Ashley," *Guideposts*, July 1996, 32–33; and Laura Blumenfeld, "A Little Girl's Promised Land," *Washington Post*, 21 October 1995, A01.

2. John McKnight, *The Careless Society: Communities and its Counterfeits* (Reading, Mass.: Perseus Books, 1996).

3. Lynn Smith, "A Community Effort," *Los Angeles Times*, 24 April 1997, home edition.

4. Hammond organized the project as a consultant to Youth Service America, one of a handful of national nonprofit organizations that supports young social entrepreneurs.

5. Shepard Barbash, "The Guys in Orange," *Stratos* 1, no. 1 (1997): 73–78.

6. "Did You Know? Home Depot Fact Sheet," <http://www.homedepot.com> (15 September 1998).

7. Barbash, "The Guys in Orange," 73–78.

8. Ibid.

9. "The Home Depot 1996 Social Responsibility Report," <http://www.home-depot.com> (15 September 1998).

10. *The Playground Bully-tin*, KaBOOM! Newsletter (9 April 1997).

11. Cathleen Wild, *Corporate Volunteer Programs: Benefits to Business*, report 1029 (New York: The Conference Board, 1993), 35.

12. Charles S. Clark, "The New Volunteerism," *CQ Researcher* 6, no. 46 (1996): 1083.

13. Wild, *Corporate Volunteer Programs*, 35.

14. Ibid.

15. Ibid.

16. Gretchen Van Fossan, "Target: Benefits of Family Volunteering," *Service* 3, no. 3 (1996): 17.

17. Wild, *Corporate Volunteer Programs*, 36.

18. Ibid., 17.

19. Clark, "The New Volunteerism," 1083.

20. "UPS Trains Managers Through Volunteer Work," *The Community Relations Report* 15, no. 8 (1996): 10–11.

21. Michael Tuffrey, *Valuing Employee Community Involvement*, The Corporate Citizenship Company, London (1998).

22. Wild, *Corporate Volunteer Programs.*

23. Information provided by Special Olympics.

24. Harvey Meyer, "In Times of Change," *Service* 3, no. 3 (1996): 5–10.

25. Alice Korngold and Elizabeth Hosler Voudouris, "Corporate Volunteerism: Strategic Community Involvement," in *Corporate Philanthropy at the Crossroads,* ed. Dwight F. Burlingame and Dennis R. Young (Bloomington and Indianapolis: Indiana University Press, 1996), 23–40.

26. Points of Light Foundation and Gallup International Institute, "A Measure of Commitment: New Survey Gathers Data About Volunteering Aimed at Addressing Serious Social Problems," *Leadership* (1995): 13–16.

Chapter 4

1. Charrisse Jones, "Trying to Put the Inner City on the Internet," *New York Times: CyberTimes,* 3 August 1996 <http://www.nytimes.com/library/tech/reference/cynavi.html> (17 September 1998).

2. Molly Callender, *Libraries Online! Connections That Work.*

3. Tom McNichol, "Virtual Philanthropy," *Salon* [On-line], 27 January 1997, <http://www.salonmagazine.com/archives/#col> (16 September 1998).

4. Ibid.

5. Microsoft donated $73 million to charity that year, narrowly eclipsing Johnson & Johnson, IBM, Eli Lilly & Co., and Hewlett-Packard Co. on Corporate Giving Watch's top givers' list.

6. McNichol, "Virtual Philanthropy."

7. Barry D. Karl, "Corporate Philanthropy: Historic Background," in *Corporate Philanthropy: Philosophy, Management, Trends, Future* (Washington, D.C.: Council on Foundations, 1982), 134.

8. Joseph Frazier Wall, *Andrew Carnegie,* 2nd ed. (Pittsburgh: University of Pittsburgh Press, 1989), 829.

9. Karl, "Corporate Philanthropy," 133.

10. Karl, "Corporate Philanthropy," 134.

11. Craig Smith, "The New Corporate Philanthropy," *Harvard Business Review* 72, no. 3 (1994): 105–116.

12. Yankey, "Corporate Support of Nonprofit Organizations: Partnerships across the Sectors," in *Corporate Philanthropy at the Crossroads,* ed. Dwight F. Burlingame and Dennis R. Young (Bloomington and Indianapolis: Indiana University Press, 1996): 7–21.

13. Jerry D. Marx, "The Influence of Strategic Philanthropy on Corporate Contributions to United Way and Other Health and Human Services" (Ph.D. diss., Boston College, n.d.).

14. "'In the same way that Carnegie built buildings, Mr. Gates is providing the second wave that will continue the opportunities,' said Martin Gomez, executive

director of the Brooklyn Public Library." Kirk Johnson, *New York Times,* 9 October 1996. "Through Libraries Online, Microsoft aims to provide public libraries with funding, technology training and software to enable inner-city and rural communities to gain access to the internet." *Library Journal,* 15 October 1996. "Nearly 8,000 people in three and a half months signed up for half hour sessions on the computers. So many folks wait for the library doors to open each morning that the staff had to put down green tape on the floor to mark off a place to line up for a turn on one of the Pentium chip computers in the Jell-O blue reading room." Joshua Quittner, *Time,* 19 August 1996. Cited at <http://www.libraries online.org/press/breaking.html> (29 August 1997).

15. Callender, *Libraries Online! Connections That Work.*
16. Ibid.
17. Elizabeth Corcoran, "Microsoft's Gates Plans $200 Million Gift to Libraries," *The Washington Post,* 24 June 1997, A1.
18. K. Lynn Wheeler and Nancy Reger, "Redefining Reference Services: Transitioning the Public Library," Reference Service in a Digital Age Conference Proceedings, June 29–June 30, 1998, <http://www.lcweb.loc.gov/rr/digiref/ whereger.html> (30 December 1998).

Chapter 5

1. Faye Rice, "Denny's Changes Its Spots," *Fortune,* 13 May 1996.
2. Craig Smith, "The New Corporate Philanthropy," *Harvard Business Review* 72, no. 3 (1994), 112.
3. See *The Licensing Book* (April 1997) for more information on Save the Children's licensing program.
4. "Denny's Restaurants and Save the Children Announce Partnership," Press Release, Denny's, 6 October 1994.
5. "Best Practices," *Reputation Management* 3, no. 3 (1997): 66–67.
6. "Denny's Today," Newsletter 4, no. 1, Spring 1997.
7. Lisa Anderson, "Like It or Not, You May Be Donating to Save the Children," *Chicago Tribune,* 15 March 1998.
8. Matthew Sinclair, "Series of Stories Send Nonprofits into Spin Control: Fallout Expected After Investigations," *Nonprofit Times,* May 1998, <http://www.np times.com/May98/mayfro1.html> (15 September 1998).
9. Sharon M. Livesey, "McDonald's and the Environment (A)," Case 9-391-108 (Boston: Harvard Business School, 1993).
10. Smith, "The New Corporate Philanthropy," 108.
11. James Bernstein, "How to Handle, and Not to Handle, a Public Relations Crisis," *Newsday,* 13 August 1995, 5.
12. "Using CR to Make Friends, Avoid Problems and Influence Policy," *Corporate Community Relations Letter* 10, no. 6 (1996): 2.

13. Leyla Kokeman, "Odwalla Can Learn from Jack in the Box," *Seattle Times*, 1 November 1996.

14. Although the lack of preservative required the company to deliver the juice directly to stores, the company used natural gas in its delivery trucks to minimize environmental damage. Mary Scott, "For Outstanding Corporate Environmentalism: Odwalla Inc.," *Business Ethics* 9, no. 6 (1995): 35.

15. Martha Groves, "Juice Left in Odwalla; Company Posts Loss, But Sales and Cash Up Despite Recall," *Los Angeles Times*, 8 January 1997, home edition.

16. Cathleen Wild, *Corporate Volunteer Programs: Benefits to Business*, report 1029 (New York: The Conference Board, 1993), 22.

17. "The Diversity Elite," *Fortune*, 3 August 1998, 114–122.

Chapter 6

1. Roy Rivenburg, "Atlanta 1996/1 Day to the Games; In All Their Glory; With Corporate Sponsors, Space Age Materials and Splashy Graphics, One Thing Is Certain: U.S. Olympic Athletes Will Be Dressed," *Los Angeles Times*, 18 July 1996.

2. Douglas M. Bailey, "Wanted: Image Maker, Not Too Flashy, Bank of Boston Shops for Help with Its PR," *Boston Globe*, 23 February 1988, 45.

3. City Year, *Putting Idealism to Work: An Idealist's Handbook*, 5th ed. (Boston: City Year, 1997).

4. Steve Bailey, "Big Turnaround, Big Questions; Bank of Boston Is Sizzling, But Will It Be a Buyer or Seller as the Industry Consolidates?" *Boston Globe*, 9 July 1995, 43.

5. Ibid.

6. Lynda Gorov, "Profit to All as Bankers Lend Selves," *Boston Globe*, 18 June 1993, 1.

7. Michael Zuckoff, "Bank of Boston's Work with Poor 'Outstanding,'" *Boston Globe*, 8 April 1993.

8. Kate Zernike and Adrian Walker, "City Year Slips as It Rushes to Grow," *Boston Sunday Globe*, 18 August 1996, A1.

9. "City Year's Learning Experience," *Boston Globe*, 22 August 1996.

10. Lesa Ukman, *IEG's Complete Guide to Sponsorship: Everything You Need to Know about Sports, Arts, Event, Entertainment and Cause Marketing* (Chicago: IEG, Inc., 1996).

11. Ibid.

12. IEG Inc., *IEG Sponsorship Report* 17, no. 9 (1998).

13. IEG Inc., *IEG Sponsorship Report* 17, no. 8 (1998).

14. Patricia M. Martin, "Corporate Sponsorship: Building Revenues and Marketing Muscle," in *Marketing the Nonprofit: The Challenge of Fundraising in a Consumer Culture*, ed. Margaret M. Maxwell (San Francisco: Jossey-Bass, 1997), 27–37.

15. Ukman, *IEG's Complete Guide to Sponsorship*, 40.

16. Ibid.

17. Ibid.

18. A "qualified sponsorship payment" is defined as any payment made by any individual or entity engaged in a trade or business provided that there is no arrangement or expectation that the sponsor will receive any substantial return benefit other than the use or acknowledgement of the sponsor's name, logo and/or product lines in connection with the tax-exempt organization that receives the payment. Consequently, the following "acknowledgements" are permissible: (1) sponsor logos and slogans that do not contain comparative or qualitative descriptions of the sponsor's product, services, facilities or company; (2) sponsor locations/addresses and telephone numbers; (3) value-neutral descriptions, including displays or visual depictions, of a sponsor's product line or services; and (4) sponsor brand or trade names and product or service listings.

19. In 1997, the national corps was 24% African American, 5.5% Asian American, 43% Caucasian, 18% Hispanic, and 1% Native American. Eighteen percent had GEDs, 48% were high school graduates, 21% had some college, and 13% were college graduates. Forty-seven percent were male, and 53% female.

20. Information taken from City Year 1995–96 and 1996–97 annual reports.

Chapter 7

1. Debbie Shore and Catherine Townsend, eds., *Home Food: 44 Great American Chefs Cook 160 Recipes on Their Night Off* (New York: Clarkson N. Potter, 1995).

2. Bill Shore, *Revolution of the Heart* (New York: Riverhead Books, 1995), 51.

3. Ibid.

4. Ibid.

5. Seymour H. Fine, *Marketing the Public Sector: Promoting the Causes of Public and Nonprofit Agencies* (New Brunswick, N.J. and London: Transaction Publishers, 1990), 169.

6. Alan R. Andreasen, "Profits for Nonprofits: Find a Corporate Partner," *Harvard Business Review* 74, no. 6 (1996): 47–57.

7. Marge Salewic, "Charities in the Marketplace: A Look at Joint-Venture Marketing," *Insight* 2 (1987).

8. Maurice G. Gurin, "Phony Philanthropy?" *Foundation News,* May–June 1989, 32.

9. Betsy Hill Bush, "Cause Marketing Sparks Regulators Concerns," *The Nonprofit Times,* October 1991, 6, 13.

10. "Donor Survey on Charity-Business Marketing," *Insight* 3 (Council of Better Business Bureau's Philanthropic Advisory Board, 1991): 5.

11. Philip J. Webster, "The Case for Cause-Related Marketing," *Foundation News,* January–February 1989.

12. Don Oldenburg, "Big Companies Plug Big Causes for Big Gains," *Washington Post,* 1992.

13. "Donor Survey on Charity-Business Marketing," 5.

14. Ibid.

15. Cone/Roper Study, "Cause-Related Marketing Trends Report," study sponsored by Cone Communications Inc. and Roper Starch Worldwide Inc., Boston, Mass., 1997. See also "Cause/Citizenship/Marketing: A Competitive Branding Tool for the 1990's," study conducted by Roper Starch but sponsored by the Pearlman Group. The Pearlman Group affirms that corporate citizenship has entered the marketing mainstream: Nine in ten think it is very (68 percent) or somewhat (24 percent) important for companies to seek out ways to be good corporate citizens. The study says that Americans are putting the belief into practice: One in three say they frequently buy products because a company donates to a cause or issue they believe in. Another 37 percent do so occasionally. Similarly one in three choose investments based on whether or not they think a company is a good corporate citizen; another 31 percent do so occasionally.

16. Cone/Roper Study, "Executive Attitudes Toward Cause-Related Marketing," study sponsored by Cone Communications Inc. and Roper Starch Worldwide Inc., Boston, Mass., 1996.

17. Andreasen, "Profits for Nonprofits," 47–57.

18. John Davidson, "Cancer Sells," *Working Woman,* May 1997.

19. Phillip J. Longman, "Endorsements for Sale," *U.S. News and World Report,* 1 September 1997, 11. In 1998, Smith Kline settled with a dozen state attorneys general who were concerned that ads involving the American Cancer Society were misleading. In 1996, Johnson & Johnson and the Arthritis Foundation settled with nineteen attorneys general. Reed Abelson, "Marketing Tied to Charities Draws Scrutiny from States," *New York Times,* 3 May 1999, 1.

20. Associated Press, "AMA to Pay Sunbeam $9.9 Million," *Washington Post,* 2 August 1998.

21. "Summary of Report by Attorneys General on Charity-Business Marketing Deals," *Chronicle of Philanthropy* X, no. 13 (1999): 48.

22. "Marketing Deals May Reap $1-Billion," *Chronicle of Philanthropy* XI, no. 9 (1999): 40.

23. Cone/Roper Study, "Executive Attitudes Toward Cause-Related Marketing."

24. Using the retail sale as a trigger may be complicated if the actual "purchase" from the company is made by the retailer, not the consumer.

Chapter 8

1. Susan D. Otterbourg, *A Business Guide to Support Employee and Family Involvement in Education,* report no. 1200-97-RR (New York: The Conference Board, 1997), 7.

2. Child Care Action Campaign, *Child Care: The Bottom Line, an Economic and Child Care Policy Paper* (New York: Child Care Action Campaign, 1988).

3. Report of the Secretary of Labor's Task Force, *Childcare: A Workforce Issue* (Washington D.C.: U.S. Department of Labor, 1988), 4.

4. Nancy Rivera Brooks, "Employee-Sponsored Child Care Is Growing in Quantity and Quality," *Los Angeles Times,* 15 March 1998, 5.

5. The American Business Collaboration for Quality Dependent Care, Chief Executive Officers Statement (14 September 1995).

6. Diane Kunde, "Cooperative Effort by 21 Firms Easing Elder-Care Concerns," *Dallas Morning News,* 29 April 1998, 1D.

7. Patricia Braus, "When Mom Needs Help," *American Demographics Magazine,* March 1994, <http://www.demographics.com/publications/ad/> (16 September 1998).

8. "A Bridge to the Future," Speech given at Democratic National Convention, Chicago, Ill. (29 August 1996).

9. Lyn Hogan, *Blueprint For Business: Reaching the New Workforce* (Washington, D.C.: Welfare to Work Partnership, 1997), 23–29.

10. Ibid.

11. American Association of Community Colleges, <http://www.aacc.nche.edu> (13 October 1998).

12. Lyn Hogan and Marco Argentieri, *The Road to Retention* (Washington, D.C.: Welfare to Work Partnership, 1998).

13. Lynn Olson, *The School to Work Revolution: How Employers and Educators Are Joining Tomorrow's Skilled Workforce* (Reading, Mass.: Addison-Wesley, 1997), 8.

14. William T. Grant Foundation Commission on Work, Family and Citizenship, *The Forgotten Half: Pathways to Success for America's Youth and Young Families* (Washington, D.C.: William T. Grant Foundation, 1988).

15. *School to Work Opportunities Act of 1994,* Public Law 103-29, 133rd Congress (4 May 1994).

16. Brandon Copple and Louise Lee, "Formative Years: Labor Squeeze Forces Corporate America Back to High School," *Wall Street Journal,* 22 July 1998.

17. "Bringing School to Work to Scale: What Employers Report First Findings from the Administration of the National Employer Survey (NES II)" (Institute on Higher Education, Trustees of the University of Pennsylvania, 1997).

18. Ibid.

19. Irene Lynn and Joan Wills, *School Lessons, Work Lessons: Recruiting and Sustaining Employer Involvement in School-to-Work Programs* (Washington, D.C.: Institute for Educational Leadership, 1994), 28–29.

20. American Society for Training and Development, *Learning and Earning: An Employer's Look at School to Work Investments* (American Society for Training and Development, 1997).

21. Mary Ann Zehr, "Driven to Succeed," *Education Week,* 18 February 1998, <http://www.edweek.org/htbin/fastweb?search> (15 September 1998).

22. Ibid.

23. Associated Press, "Work-Family Policy Lacking at Many Firms," *Dallas Morning News,* 15 July 1998, 1D.

24. WFD Research, "Study Finds Corporate Work-Life Programs Fail to Meet Needs of Shiftworkers," Press Release, February 1996, <http://www.wfd.com/shift.htm> (16 September 1998).

25. Hogan and Argentieri, *The Road to Retention*, 5.

26. Families and Work Institute, *Employers, Families and Education* (Washington D.C.: Families and Work Institute, 1995).

Chapter 9

1. Dick Lilly, "Creating a Real Product: Self Esteem," *Seattle Times*, 6 December 1988, G3.

2. J. Gregory Dees, "Enterprising Nonprofits," *Harvard Business Review* 76, no. 1 (1998): 60.

3. Bill Shore, *Revolution of the Heart* (New York: Riverhead Books, 1995).

4. Dees, "Enterprising Nonprofits," 60.

5. Shore, *Revolution of the Heart*.

6. Ibid.

7. Richard Steckel, Robin Simons, and Peter Lengsfelder, *Filthy Rich and Other Nonprofit Fantasies* (Berkeley, Calif.: Ten Speed Press, 1989), 3.

8. Thomas Reis and Stephanie Clohesy, *Unleashing New Resources and Entrepreneurship for the Common Good* (Battle Creek, Mich.: Kellogg Foundation, 1999), 3.

9. Bennett Davis, "Pulling Their Weight," *TWA Ambassador Magazine*, January 1997, 34–36.

10. *Defining Aerospace Leadership*, The Boeing Company Annual Report (1997).

11. Jack Liberty, "Pioneer Trains Workers with Shop Floor Data Collection," *ID Systems*, November 1991.

12. "Pioneer Industries the First Washington Nonprofit to Earn International Quality Designation," *Business Wire*, 9 December 1996.

13. Linda Lang, "Human Services Thrive on Pioneer Spirit," *Puget Sound Business Journal*, 7–13 June 1996.

14. Ingrid Johnson and Dennis Baylor, "Hey Business Majors, Nonprofits Need You," *National Business Employment Weekly*, Spring/Summer 1993.

15. The Roberts Foundation, *New Social Entrepreneurs: The Success, Challenge and Lessons of Non-Profit Enterprise Creation* (San Francisco: Roberts Foundation, 1996), 314–315. Juma Ventures was formerly known as Larkin Business Ventures.

16. Bennett Davis, "Pulling Their Weight."

17. Ibid.

18. Cynthia W. Massarsky, "The Strategies of Enterprise," *The Nonprofit Times*, November 1993.

19. Community Wealth Ventures and Share Our Strength Case Studies Series, *Sacred Heart League Creates Gregory Productions—"The Spitfire Grill"* (draft).

20. Constance L. Hays, "Seeing Green in a Yellow Border," *New York Times*, 3 August 1997, 1.

21. Phat X. Chiem, "Chevron Gives Gas Station to NAACP," *San Francisco Chronicle*, 27 August 1997.

22. Jason L. Riley, "Black America Looks Homeward," *Wall Street Journal*, 3 May 1996.

23. Edward Skloot, ed., *The Nonprofit Entrepreneur: Creating Ventures to Earn Income* (New York: The Foundation Center, 1988).

24. Dees, "Enterprising Nonprofits," 55–67.

25. Vince Stehle, "A Charity That Earns Its Way," *The Chronicle of Philanthropy* VI, no. 14 (1994), 32–35.

26. Ibid.

27. Bennett Davis, "Pulling Their Weight," 34.

28. Reed Abelson, "At Minnesota Public Radio, a Deal Way Above Average," *New York Times*, 27 March 1998, C3.

29. U.S. Small Business Administration, *Unfair Competition by Non-Profit Organizations with Small Business: An Issue for the 1980s* (1984).

30. The Roberts Foundation, *New Social Entrepreneurs*, 46.

31. Ibid., 12.

32. Steckel et al., *Filthy Rich and Other Nonprofit Fantasies*, 56.

33. Ibid.

34. Community Wealth Ventures and Share Our Strength Case Studies Series, *Greater DC Cares Launching Cares at Law* (draft).

35. *Sacred Heart League Creates Gregory Productions—"The Spitfire Grill."*

36. The Roberts Foundation, *New Social Entrepreneurs*, 16.

37. Ibid., 13.

38. Rosabeth Moss Kanter, "Collaborative Advantage: The Art of Alliances," *Harvard Business Review* 72, no. 4 (1994): 34–46.

39. Neil Rackham, Lawrence Friedman, and Richard Ruff, *Getting Partnering Right: How Market Leaders Are Creating Long Term Competitive Advantage* (New York: McGraw-Hill, 1996), 3.

Chapter 10

1. Joel Bleeke and David Ernst, "Is Your Strategic Alliance Really a Sale?" *Harvard Business Review: Strategic Alliances* 73, no. 1 (1995): 26.

2. Council on Foundations, *Evaluation for Foundations* (San Francisco: Jossey-Bass, 1993), 84.

3. Cited in Andersen Consulting, "Beyond the Walls: Partnerships for a Better Future" (presentation materials at Drucker Foundation Management and Leadership Conference, Post Conference Roundtable, 2 November 1996).

4. Barbara Gray, *Collaborating: Finding Common Ground for Multiparty Problems* (San Francisco: Jossey-Bass, 1989).

5. We do not discuss in this chapter the process an organization should follow if it is not the initiator of the relationship. Nonetheless, an organization should be prepared to respond when contacted by a prospective partner. It will, ideally, begin by asking the questions laid out under "Self-assess" and "Identify." Planning will help a business to narrow its giving priorities strategically, which will make it easier to assess individual requests and provide guidance to potential partners as they prepare proposals. Large businesses, which may be contacted by thousands of nonprofits a year, need processes to respond to the many requests they cannot fulfill without alienating the public. Companies of all sizes need to know their own needs well enough to be able to respond positively when the right opportunity presents itself.

Social sector organizations are less likely than businesses to be deluged by prospective partners. They can, however, make themselves more attractive to business by building their assets, as discussed in this chapter. When approached by a business, a social sector organization should evaluate both its ability to help the company meet its needs and its own potential to benefit. Even when the dollars involved make the offer hard to turn down, it will not always be the case that the costs will outweigh the benefits. If partnering with the company means opening a new site, the nonprofit will need to consider whether the site is appropriate to its mission, whether other donors are likely, and whether it has the organizational capacity to expand, as City Year did when it turned down a potential million dollar sponsor who wanted to bring the program to an area of New Jersey where the program would have difficulty attracting local funding. If the partnership would require distributing products, the organization will need to consider whether the products are of use to its network, whether the products are worthy of such an implied endorsement, and whether the organization has a strong enough dissemination system to get the product into the hands of the people who will use it. If the company hopes to boost its image through the partnership, the organization will need to consider whether the business's past conduct will damage the nonprofit's reputation. Being prepared to make this assessment will help stop a social sector organization from making bad choices when confronted with seemingly good deals.

6. Minette E. Drumwright, "Company Advertising with a Social Dimension: The Role of Noneconomic Criteria," *Journal of Marketing* 60 (October 1996).

7. Seymour Sarason and Elizabeth Lorentz, *Crossing Boundaries: Collaboration, Coordination and the Redefinition of Resources* (San Francisco: Jossey-Bass, 1998), 95.

8. Drumwright, "Company Advertising with a Social Dimension," 18.

9. Ibid.

10. The companies we studied, as well as other business managers we spoke with, indicated they had some difficulty identifying nonprofit organizations as prospective partners. Several factors may contribute to this.

First, the worlds of the social sector and business rarely intersect. Second, social sector organizations have been slower to put up Web pages, although this is changing rapidly. Third, as we noted earlier, the mainstream media devotes a much more limited amount of coverage to social sector organizations than to businesses.

Specialized periodicals like the *Chronicle of Philanthropy* and *Who Cares* magazine address fundraising and management issues in the sector, and almost every organization from a local homeless shelter to a national association with a million members will have its own newsletter. There are also issue-oriented publications covering education (*Education Week* is particularly good), youth programs (*Youth Today*), and other topics.

Finally, unlike the relatively sophisticated systems that have been developed to help nonprofit organizations identify corporate donors (searchable CD-roms, whole libraries in major cities, and thick directories that are updated annually), we know of none that provides similar information about nonprofit organizations. One promising development in this regard is the commitment of IBM to provide the necessary hardware, software, and technical expertise to create an interactive database of the more than 2,500 service providers of the Welfare to Work Partnership. This database will be accessible to the 7,500 business partners through the partnership's Web site.

11. For example, *Advertising Age, Brandweek,* and *The Licensing Book* help organizations understand not just the baseline financial information and industry position of the companies they are targeting, but also their current marketing and other business strategies. Organizations such as Businesses for Social Responsibility and the Social Venture Network are also good resources.

12. Vickie Tassan, "Advice for Working with Banks" (keynote address at the AmeriCorps Renewal Conference in Baltimore, Maryland, 8 November 1995).

13. Neil Rackham, Lawrence Friedman, and Richard Ruff, *Getting Partnering Right: How Market Leaders Are Creating Long Term Competitive Advantage* (New York: McGraw-Hill, 1996), 101.

14. Ibid.

15. Rosabeth Moss Kanter, "Collaborative Advantage: The Art of Alliances," *Harvard Business Review: Strategic Alliances* 72, no. 4 (1995): 34–46.

16. Andersen Consulting, "Beyond the Walls."

17. Kanter, "Collaborative Advantage," 43.

18. Ibid., 38.

19. Daniel Kadlec, "The New World of Giving," *Time,* 5 May 1997.

20. Susan Sugawara, "Doing It Our Way," *Washington Post,* 14 June 1998, H1.

21. Conference Board, 1993, as cited in Andersen Consulting, "Beyond the Walls."

22. Kanter, "Collaborative Advantage," 38.

23. Rackham et al., *Getting Partnering Right,* 127.

24. William Berquist, Julie Betwee, and David Meuel, *Building Strategic Relation-*

ships: How to Extend Your Organization's Reach through Partnerships, Alliances, and Joint Ventures (San Francisco: Jossey-Bass, 1995), 80.

25. Kanter, "Collaborative Advantage," 41.

26. Writers from both the business and social sector fields support this point of view. See for example Larraine Segil, *Intelligent Business Alliances: How to Profit Using Today's Most Important Strategic Tool* (New York: Random House, 1996), 133; Henrietta S. Schwartz, "Introduction," in *Collaboration: Building Common Agendas,* ed. Henrietta S. Schwartz [Teacher Education Monograph No. 10] (Washington, D.C.: ERIC Clearinghouse on Teacher Education, 1990), 2.

27. Kanter, "Collaborative Advantage," 41.

28. Yves L. Doz and Gary Hamel, *Alliance Advantage* (Boston: Harvard Business School Press, 1998): 151–52.

29. Ibid., 42.

30. There is an entire industry devoted to strategic planning—there are many excellent consultants, books, and resources on the market to aid in this process. We don't attempt to elaborate here. Rather, once both parties have made the decision to make a long-term commitment, we simply encourage them to engage together in a planning process. We do not advise that the process be a seesaw, with one group floating a proposal and the other responding. Instead, we suggest the partners work together to seek consensus on several important elements. With their experience working together in mind, along with any results about their initial exchanges, they should reassess their vision for the relationship and redefine goals and objectives. They should identify measures of success, and commit resources to a continuous improvement process. Finally, they should adjust as appropriate the decisionmaking, staffing, and other structures of the arrangements.

Chapter 11

1. Neil Rackham, Lawrence Friedman, and Richard Ruff, *Getting Partnering Right: How Market Leaders Are Creating Long Term Competitive Advantage* (New York: McGraw-Hill, 1996), 72–73.

2. Ibid.

3. Rosabeth Moss Kanter, "Collaborative Advantage: The Art of Alliances," *Harvard Business Review: Strategic Alliances* 72, no. 4 (1995): 46.

4. Yves L. Doz and Gary Hamel, *Alliance Advantage* (Boston: Harvard Business School Press, 1998), 55.

5. Kenichi Ohmae, "The Global Logic of Strategic Alliances," *Harvard Business Review* 67, no. 2 (1989).

6. Bill Shore, *Revolution of the Heart* (New York: Riverhead Books, 1995), 77.

7. Rackham et al., *Getting Partnering Right,* 75.

8. Kanter, "Collaborative Advantage," 37.

9. Curt Weeden, *Corporate Social Investing* (San Francisco: Berrett-Koehler Publishers, 1998), 199.

10. Doz and Hamel, *Alliance Advantage*, 192.

11. Frederick F. Reichheld, *The Loyalty Effect* (Boston: Harvard Business School Press, 1996), 91–116.

12. Interagency Council on the Homeless, *The Story of Pioneer Human Services: A Case Study* (Washington, D.C.: Interagency Council of the Homeless, 1992), 10.

13. George R. Neumann, Roger C. Kormendi, Robert T. Tamura, and Cyrus J. Gardner, "The Benefits and Costs of National Service: Methods for Benefit Assessment with Application to the Three AmeriCorps Programs," June 1995.

Chapter 12

1. Jennifer Moore, "A Corporate Challenge for Charities," *Chronicle of Philanthropy* X, no. 20 (1998).

2. The business was shut down in February, 1998, because the organization was unable to raise necessary financing to expand the business to national markets. Ira Flatow, New York, "Earth Day: Problems, Talk of the Nation Science Friday," National Public Radio, 24 April 1998.

3. Moore, "A Corporate Challenge for Charities."

4. "Supporting local schools," "donating services and products," and "encouraging volunteerism by employees" were ranked 24th, 34th, and 39th out of forty-three criteria ranked. Study by Bozell Worldwide for the *Wall Street Journal* and Nihon Keizai Shimbun, cited in Curt Weeden, *Corporation Social Investing* (San Francisco: Berrett-Koehler Publishers, 1998), 30–33.

5. David Osbourne and Ted Gaebler, *Reinventing Government: How the Entrepreneurial Spirit Is Transforming the Public Sector* (New York: Plume, 1992).

6. Peter Drucker, "What Business Can Learn from Nonprofits," *Harvard Business Review* 67, no. 4 (1989).

7. Davis Billis, "What Can Nonprofits and Businesses Learn from Each Other?" in *Nonprofit Organizations in a Market Economy: Understanding New Roles, Issues and Trends,* ed. David C. Hammack and Dennis R. Young (San Francisco: Jossey-Bass, 1993).

8. Claudia H. Deutsch, "Corporations Adopt a Different Attitude: Show Us the Value," *New York Times,* 9 December 1997.

9. "Leading National Advertisers," *Advertising Age,* 29 September 1997, 36.

10. "New Law Clarifies Rules on Sponsorships," *Chronicle of Philanthropy* X, no. 5 (1997): 49.

11. Jennifer Moore and Grant Williams, "Corporate Giving, The Buffet Way," *Chronicle of Philanthropy* X, no. 3 (1997).

12. James C. Collins and Jerry I. Porras, *Built to Last: Successful Habits of Visionary Companies* (New York: HarperCollins, 1997).

13. Ibid., 31.

14. Ibid., 55.

15. Ibid., 73.

16. Robert W. Johnson, founder of Johnson & Johnson, as cited in Collins and Porras, *Built to Last,* 79.

17. Disney, as cited in Collins and Porras, *Built to Last,* 78.

18. David M. Browne, "The Role of Service in Times of Change," *Service* 3, no. 3 (1996): 4.

19. Christine W. Letts, William Ryan, and Allen Grossman, "Virtuous Capital: What Foundations Can Learn from Venture Capitalists," *Harvard Business Review* 70, no. 2 (1997).

20. Collins and Porras, *Built to Last,* xix.

21. Rosabeth Moss Kanter, "From Spare Change to Real Change: The Social Sector as Beta Site for Business Innovation," *Harvard Business Review* 77, no. 3 (1999): 122, 132.

22. Ibid., 130.

INDEX

About the Authors

Shirley Sagawa

Shirley Sagawa has played a leading role in the establishment of government agencies and nonprofit organizations alike. She served as Special Assistant to President Clinton for Domestic Policy and Policy Advisor to the First Lady during the Clintons' first year at the White House, and she was subsequently appointed Executive Director of the Corporation for National Service. In this position, she was an architect of Ameri-Corps, President Clinton's national service initiative, and other youth service programs. She had previously been appointed by President Bush as a founding Director of the Commission on National and Community Service.

Ms. Sagawa has served as Chief Counsel for Youth Policy to the Senate Labor and Human Resources Committee, where she played a major role in the development and passage of legislation concerned with education, child care, and national service. She has also served on numerous nonprofit boards, including My Sister's Place, the National Institute for Dispute Resolution, and Pan Asia. More recently, Ms. Sagawa served as the first Executive Director of the Learning First Alliance, a coalition of twelve leading education associations concerned with improving student learning in public schools.

Ms. Sagawa is currently Deputy Chief of Staff to First Lady Hillary Rodham Clinton.

Eli Segal

Eli Segal currently serves as President and CEO of the Welfare to Work Partnership. Located in Washington, D.C., the Partnership is a national, nonpartisan effort on the part of the business community to help move people on public assistance into private-sector jobs.

Mr. Segal served as Assistant to President Bill Clinton from January 1993 to February 1996. In this capacity, he was responsible for the design and enactment of the legislation that created AmeriCorps. In October 1993, Mr. Segal was confirmed by the U.S. Senate to the additional position of CEO of the Corporation for National Service, a post he held until October 1995.

Mr. Segal is a successful small business entrepreneur who applies his knowledge of the for-profit sector to his work with social sector organizations. Prior to 1992, he served as President of several consumer product companies, including the American Publishing Corporation and Bits & Pieces, Inc. Most recently, he was the Publisher of *Games* magazine.

Mr. Segal sits on several nonprofit and corporate boards of directors, including the Board of Overseers of the Heller School of Brandeis University. He is also Chair of the University of Michigan Center for Learning Through Community Service and Co-chair of the National Alliance to End Homelessness.